THE
LITTLE
DATABASE

Electronic Mediations

Series Editors: N. Katherine Hayles, Peter Krapp,
Rita Raley, and Samuel Weber
Founding Editor: Mark Poster

(continued on page 225)

The Little Database

A POETICS OF MEDIA FORMATS

DANIEL SCOTT SNELSON

University of Minnesota Press

Minneapolis / London

This book is freely available in an open access edition thanks to the generous support of Arcadia, a charitable fund of Lisbet Rausing and Peter Baldwin, and the UCLA Library.

 Available as a Manifold edition at manifold.umn.edu

Published by the University of Minnesota Press
111 Third Avenue South, Suite 290
Minneapolis, MN 55401–2520
http://www.upress.umn.edu

ISBN 978-1-5179-1881-1 (hc)
ISBN 978-1-5179-1882-8 (pb)
ISBN 978-1-4529-7345-6 (Manifold)

A Cataloging-in-Publication record for this book is available from the Library of Congress.

Printed in the United States of America on acid-free paper

The University of Minnesota is an equal-opportunity educator and employer.

For Sona Hakopian and Scott James Snelson

CONTENTS

INTRODUCTION

Reading the Little Database

Every day seems to open with another unfathomable invention of massive data. Today, I casually compute hundreds of millions of images to generate a single speculative scene with Midjourney. Yesterday, I adventured with friends through vast, fantastical realms owing to a large language model that makes use of trillions of texts in *AI Dungeon*. More darkly, my tomorrow is already written through fintech predictions regarding my credit, biometric data on my travels, and corporate adware tracking every click and eye saccade throughout the internet. For every shining genomic breakthrough made with expansive accumulations of data, we might also chart the looming shadows of mass dataveillance and predictive control. And yet, within the accelerating boom of what now feels quaint to call "big data," we all maintain smaller, more intimate, but still formidable accumulations of personal record.

In a day of access, I download compressed JPG images from Midjourney to an artistic inspirations folder, now mounting to the hundreds. I print/save the full transcript of my *AI Dungeon* playthrough as a PDF for future reference to a folder named TTRPG on my desktop that also stores hundreds of tabletop role-playing game rulebooks, campaign modules, and related academic texts.[1] On the same laptop that houses this document, now, as I type, I tally my own little database of financial records alongside adjacent folders that host more personal digital objects. These folders include hundreds of iPhone-captured images (mostly photos of photos) of my father, prepared for a memorial slideshow; digitized movies of my partner's youth, marked by the layered disintegrations of both VHS and DVD; untold notes and plans for the future in a thousand little TXT files occasionally interspersed with a JPG capture of a scrawl on paper or a calendar drawn on cardboard long since recycled.

At home in the hierarchy of these folders, I navigate their contents fluidly, often searching for this or that, but mostly letting them lie for some future point of access. Meanwhile, I continue to accumulate my own little collection: gathering new additions piecemeal among the computers I use, their occasional backup drives, and on "cloud" servers tasked with maintaining only the most important assets twice over. As an academic, my little database absorbs PDFs on a daily basis. Of course, I fall behind. Even my most urgent "To Read" folder currently tallies 408 documents, most of which remain firmly aspirational. This is to say nothing of the dozens of folders holding thousands of potentially useful texts for past and abandoned projects; or photos I'll never visually review; or the movies and sound files that now gather the digital equivalent of dust in long-forgotten sectors of my hard drive, vestiges from a time before ubiquitous streaming. It is all too much to read in any traditional sense. But it remains far too small and far too idiosyncratic for significant data analytics or statistical insight. Here, I'd like to introduce "the little database" as a usefully differential category of digital scale.

Large-scale information enterprises, including algorithms working for generative AI, the digital humanities, and sovereign states alike, stake their hopes for meaningful interpretation on the use of massive amounts of data.[2] I turn, instead, to the *little* database as an integral model for understanding the shifting terrain of our information environment. Like the little magazines of modernism and the historical avant-gardes, the little databases of the present offer a dynamic forum for investigating the global situation of politics, aesthetics, and meaning in a time of pervasive technological change. Bridging the private collections detailed above with public resources online, I examine a set of globally accessible little databases in an effort to inventory modes of interpretation aimed beyond the close reading of a single aesthetic object, while remaining below the threshold of big data analytics. With a focus on the transformative effects of networked digitization, this project explores mutually illuminating relations among encoding formats, online distribution circuits, and media-reflexive works in a series of platforms for experimental art and literature.

The little databases examined here include: *Textz* a plain text library of fiction, poetry, and critical writing; *Eclipse,* an image-based archive of small press poetry books and magazines; *PennSound,* a site distributing audio recordings of poetry readings; and *UbuWeb,* a sprawling collection that hosts a repository for experimental film and video art.[3] From Louis Zukofsky's poetry to Maya Deren's films, untold numbers of viewers encounter "old media" works online, increasingly to the exclusion of the analog iterations in which these works originally appeared. To be sure, the works we encounter online are thoroughly transformed by their digital situation. This book argues that the varieties of transformations that characterize digital objects more generally are most vividly evidenced in media-reflexive works of art and literature.[4] Bridging the materialist orientation of bibliographic study with the attention to infrastructure, platform, and format in recent media scholarship, I contend for a range of poetic practices for reading analog works situated within the windows, consoles, and networks of the present.

Caught in variable processes of digitization and resolutely embedded in intricate systems of media convergence, the digital objects that populate these little databases index a wide array of transformations.[5] Far from a simple act of remediation or media conversion, these transformations present an unpredictable set of radical alterations to historical works geared for reflexive forms of analog media. In 2001, Lev Manovich schematized these changes as a form of "transcoding," broadly defined as the processes of translation at play between analog material culture and attendant digital networks.[6] Building on the past twenty years of internet history and media scholarship, I contend for a layered methodology focused on four potential vectors of transcoding, each of which is sequentially examined in the chapters of this book. First, interfaces for computation; second, issues of preservation; third, conditions of transmission; and fourth, modes of contingent reading. Cumulatively, these chapters argue for reading specific digital objects within the variable effects of file formats, circuits of transmission, local database contexts, and a host of conditional sites of use. Tuning in to these effects enables us to understand the way in which our cultural past has come to inhabit the rapidly shifting terrain of what was once called the "world wide web."[7]

As cultural encounters have shifted from the relative stability of analog media to the unwieldy dispersion of digital formats, the continuous and indeterminate versioning of digital objects demands ongoing attention. The opening chapters work askance to interpreting the specific objects they discuss in order to prepare a frame for contingent reading by way of conclusion. In lockstep with each chapter, a series of interludes perform these readings through a range of experiments in media poetics that exceed the strictures of academic prose. Originating in my work for *PennSound* in 2008, these poetic experiments are presented with commentary as a means of opening critical and practical entry points for playing new meanings into any given little database. Beyond a supplement to the arguments made in this prose, the interludes make their own arguments, differently, rendering potential vectors that poetic engagements with the little database might afford. Working within and writing about the poetics of media formats, I aim to articulate the variable forms that a reading of the little database might take—and more importantly, to present inroads for others to play, discover, experiment, and rearticulate these collections otherwise.

The arguments in this book are made, like the online collections I study, toward speculative futures of use. Having worked as an editor for four of the sites I examine (*Eclipse, PennSound, UbuWeb,* and the *Electronic Poetry Center*) at various points over the past twenty years, my own understanding of the little database has been marked by personal experience, which warrants a quick summary.[8] In the summer of 2004, I began as a scanner for *Eclipse* while still a freshman in college. Then, in 2006, I started work as an "intern" at *UbuWeb,* producing an edited series of PDFs and contributing across the site toward a variety of digitization and acquisition projects. Two years later, while living abroad in Tokyo, I segmented MP3 files for *PennSound,* which eventually led to my graduate study at UPenn, where I also began work on the *EPC* some years later. When I began working for *Eclipse,* I knew nothing of these fields, and would never have imagined dedicating the following years to their production and study. In each instance, these websites also served as sites of my learning, ranging from the lessons found in the works themselves to the "back-end" features, community networks, and archival repertoires involved in building an online collection. Often, my personal hard drive and data practices came to mirror the workings of these public sites.⁹ They have also guided my poetic practice, often serving as both material and host to a range of creative interventions. These little databases have provided an education more valuable than coursework, delivering forms of hands-on knowledge as a by-product of the creation of new points of access for other users. With this book, I hope to continue the lines of preservation, distribution, and creative use that have driven this practice: to offer a poetics for creative play with the little databases that any user might encounter, or better, generate.

The Little Database

When asked for an example of the types of media-reflexive transformation I'm most interested in studying, I first turn to the *PennSound* MP3 file of William Carlos Williams's "The Defective Record," a poem that demands the concept of the gramophone even from the page.¹⁰ The final lines of the poem are printed: "Level it down / for him to build a house // on to build a / house on to build a house on / to build a house / on to build a house on to . . ." First recorded by Williams in 1942, these concluding lines call the skipping record into conversation with the destructive forces of mechanical reproduction. In his reading of the poem, Williams ignores the line breaks of the printed version and instead performs the metaphor of a defective record by mimicking his own vocal patterns in the repeated phrase, "to build a house on." Simulating the all-too-common scratched repetitions in analog records, Williams baits the listener into realizing the track itself is not, in fact, "defective," but rather presenting a material metaphor on the mechanisms of industrialization. Playfully amplifying the potential for a mechanical failure of the groove, Williams tricks his listeners in order to solicit a moment of productive confusion. This moment, this play with the meaning-making potentials of the material recording itself, is a hallmark feature of media-reflexive arts in the tradition of modernism and the historical avant-gardes. These playful encounters with media, I argue, sound out the otherwise inaudible effects of digitization.

For example, once "The Defective Record" is transcoded into an MP3 file, the poem's own reflexive gesture changes to accent instead

THE DEFECTIVE RECORD

Cut the bank for fill.
Dump sand
pumped out of the river
into the old swale

killing whatever was
there before—including
even the muskrats. Who did it?
There's the guy.

Him in the blue shirt and
turquoise skullcap.
Level it down
for him to build a house

on to build a
house on to build a house on
to build a house
on to build a house on to . . .

Figure I.1.
"The Defective
Record" by
William Carlos
Williams, from
*The Collected Poems:
Volume I, 1909–1939,*
copyright 1938 by
New Directions
Publishing.
Reprinted by
permission of
New Directions
Publishing and
Carcanet Press.

the work's *digital* formatting. Audio files on the internet, of course, don't regularly "skip" in the same way that a vinyl record might. The repetition of the line "to build a house on" finds a new foundation built on the MP3's compression algorithm, dramatically leveling the wave-like stream of the analog wax track and contradicting the originally plotted effects of the poem, with regard to the play of both politics and aesthetics. The material metaphor of the scratched record is itself rendered defective in the face of modular digital playback. If there are "no ideas but in things," as Williams first declared in a 1943 issue of *The Old Line* magazine, then what happens, we might ask, to the ideas when the things themselves rematerialize? Unlike the anticipatory readings performed by media archaeological studies that return to latent digital potentials found within historical works, *The Little Database* argues for ways of understanding the poem as a functioning new media object, operating within the parameters of its digital format and new media context.[11]

Beyond this point, there is much more at play in this file than a narrative of the formal and prosodic properties of the work, even if we track these changes from the page to the vinyl record to the MP3 and back. Reeling away from a close reading, to properly understand "The Defective Record" online, we must simultaneously consider the file playing alongside thousands of corresponding digital objects on sites like *PennSound* and *UbuWeb,* or indeed streaming to earbuds connected to my mobile device, or nested within the haphazard file folders that organize my laptop's hard drive. Inhabiting the vexed space between preservation and distribution, between memory and practice, little databases reconfigure the contemporary experience of historical artifacts, and thus transfigure interpretative methods for each work in turn. More than simply degrade or distort analog works of avant-garde art and literature, digital forms of archival collection and circulation dramatically rematerialize historical works for the use and reuse of untold numbers of contemporary users. The same could be said for how our mixed-media machines remediate analog culture at large. In this way, the failures, glitches, errors, slippages, and unlikely reversals of media-reflexive works enable the reader to glimpse, for a moment, the otherwise invisible structures that seek to conceal these transformations within the increasingly high-fidelity formats of cultural transcoding.

How then might we attune critical frequencies to channel the significance of "The Defective Record" playing today? I argue that a close reading of transcoded objects can occur only in cooperation with playful performances of interpretation that weave together relational databases, variable formats, and the contingent array of technical and cultural mechanisms that facilitate these files. In considering how these systems operate, I draw from recent scholarship on critical code studies, comparative media analysis, and data justice. Every display of a digital object is a unique performance.[12] Streaming bits are inscribed and reinscribed in hardware.[13] "Invisible" code is parsed into visual or aural display.[14] Interfaces and protocols control the expression of these streams.[15] Users and editors rip, post, and repost files in a variety of online contexts.[16] Updates render old formats inoperable.[17] Bias lurks in algorithms, data sets, and infrastructures alike.[18] Digital repertoires of care maintain, collect, and inflect each work in turn.[19] And so on it goes, in the continual flux of technological development and the ongoing versioning processes of the always-on, always-developing, internet. Even a scattered list of variables exhausts the interpretive equation. Each of these emergent properties plays into any reading of the instantiation of a digital object. I argue that such a scenario demands scholarship that is bound to exploratory methods of interpretive performance and contingent reading. *The Little Database* navigates these contingencies of meaning-making by exploring an array of digital formats and the features of online collections, occasionally to the pointed exclusion of reading the "content" of specific files. Scaling through methodological frameworks built to encapsulate interpretation at different orders of magnitude enables a poetic reading practice capable of traversing urgent concerns not accessible in seclusion.

In this way, it has proven useful to analogically cast online collections as "little databases" after the little magazines that served as a vehicle of modernism and the historical avant-gardes.[20] Periodical studies on the little magazine offer an array of methodological perspectives developed to address precisely the challenges of writing about heterogeneous websites that incrementally release new materials over time. That is to say, no magazine is defined by any single work included, but every work is inflected by its place within the social and material texts of the magazine. In addition, the sites I examine update the defining characteristics of the little magazines. *Eclipse,* for example, is driven by a set of arguments constructed by its founding editor, Craig Dworkin, whose archival interventions engage in contemporary aesthetic and literary practices through a provisional platform that develops in periodical increments over time.[21] Like the study of the full run of a magazine, these databases require a confluence of close, hyper, and machine reading practices.[22] These same reading practices could be extended not just to a range of public little databases online, but also to the private collections that inhabit user hard drives everywhere.[23]

The relation of the little magazine to the contemporary database is also indebted to trends in periodical studies that Robert Scholes and Cliff Wulfman have described as a transition "from genre to database."[24] In all these regards, the field of periodical studies presents an array of methodological and critical interventions that helpfully map onto the chaotic landscape of digital collections and online repositories. Despite the large number of objects hosted on these sites, it should also be noted that, from a computational standpoint, the data they contain, such as hundreds of issues of a little magazine, remain eminently computable. The question is why and how computational tactics might reveal, demystify, or disorient these collections. In each chapter, I explore the promises, pitfalls, and potentials of creative modes of computation—not only to better grasp these sites, but to extend an understanding into the personal collections and ordinary media practices that structure the experience of everyday network culture.

Resisting analytics, I contend that the little database instead courts varieties of creative research that might facilitate a poetics of computation, engaging with each idiosyncratic collection as a site-specific model for meaning-making activities. Following the logic of the little magazine for these experiments, I examine how these little databases have forged their own "periodical codes," inventing time-based tactics for circulating digital objects as patterns of use and standards of access continue to develop online.[25] When reading a little magazine, a combination of macro- and microscopic modes of analysis yields valuable insights not readily available to either method in isolation. Moreover, like pieces featured in a magazine, the transcoded work can be read only through its instantiation within the social and technical networks that deliver it, in a given moment of delivery. By the same token, in a kind of hermeneutic circle, to read the database we must enter through the individual works that are the collection's contents. In both directions, social networks, technical protocols, and cultures of use inscribe the limits of potential readings. In the second chapter, I pay particular attention to how the historical challenges faced by periodical studies might lend insight into the manifold difficulties of accounting for the little database on the internet.

On the other side of "little," this study of transcoded objects cannot proceed without acknowledging Manovich's now-historical account of the database as a cultural form in *The Language of New Media*. A database can be simply defined as any organized collection of data. From relational modeling in SQL (structured query language) to mundane tabulation in everyday spreadsheets, a wide variety of database models structure how data is organized, stored, indexed, displayed, and manipulated. When it comes to the indexical accumulation that undergirds the internet, Manovich argues that "every site is a type of database."[26] For technical purists, this statement might be something of an exaggeration, just as it's clear that the sites I examine extend far beyond the little magazine in accordance with its stricter definitions.[27] The play between these definitional boundaries serves as a guide to the grey area of the online collections I examine and how they relate back to ordinary hard drives everywhere. Online collections hover between periodical publications and structured databases. The tensions between site and database are most fully explored in the fourth chapter, which considers the database logic inherent even to the construction of a single digital compilation movie.

From the outset, however, my introduction of a "little" difference aims to disrupt some of the claims Manovich advanced in 2001. In particular, I depart from his assertions concerning the antagonism between database and narrative, the linguistic parallels between paradigm and syntagm, and the reading of the database as the dominant "symbolic form" through which contemporary culture reproduces itself.[28] Following the critique that N. Katherine Hayles levies in her book *How We Think*—to pick one among the many, which chart back to a forum at *PMLA* in 2007—my notion of the little database clusters instead around an unstable symbiosis between the narrative (and poetic) structures of the little magazine and the relational juxtapositions of the object-oriented database.[29] To distort a biological metaphor deployed by Hayles in this work, I explore the "technogenesis" inherent to the evolving relations between the life of an artwork and its digital afterlife. Further, I argue, the significance of this continuously evolving feedback loop can be accessed and addressed only at site-specific moments in time.

This practice of tracking the material instantiations alongside transcoded versions of works within the little database owes much to the bibliographic specificity of comparative media analysis developed by Hayles.[30] Following the bibliographic attention that media scholars like Lisa Gitelman, Johanna Drucker, Lori Emerson, and others pay to the history of the book within digital media contexts, I argue for a "material text" reading of these formats.[31] In this regard, the variable processes of online collections might be recoded in terms of circulating versions of format-based editions. Appending their digital versions to a long series of historical iterations of these works, I argue for a renewed attention to the technical specificity of formats and the contextual effects of little databases in use. Here, once more, the media-reflexivity of the works in the little database I study enables methods of what Hayles terms "media-specific analysis" that attend "both to the specificity of the form . . . and to citations and limitations of one medium in another. Attuned not so much to similarity and difference as to simulation and instantiation."[32]

This comparative practice requires a concept of interpretive change over time. In the title essay to *How We Think,* Hayles further develops a "theoretical framework in which objects are seen not as static entities that, once created, remain the same throughout time but rather are understood as constantly changing assemblages in which inequalities and inefficiencies in their operations drive them toward breakdown, disruption, innovation, and change."[33] Building on this frame, the little databases I examine have variously ceased operations *(Textz),* faced repeated dramatic interruptions *(Eclipse),* suffered the collapse of functionality *(Mutant Sounds),* supported a file format that has since been cancelled *(UbuWeb),* or faced innumerable breakdowns and disruptions *(EPC).* In these lapses, these glitches, the smoothly operating protocols that undergird little databases may be brought to comparative analysis and bibliographic scrutiny.[34] Just as "The Defective Record" reveals itself when it skips, the collection comes into view upon its breakdown. *The Little Database* lingers with these glitches to discover moments in which these "constantly changing assemblages" caught between old and new media formats might reveal themselves in the fissures.

Contingent Reading

The changing assemblages that constitute the little database hinge on a notion of contingency. Each chapter of *The Little Database* passes a series of "anecdotal" interpretive filters across the respective little database it queries; a tactical approach to what Alan Liu has termed, in plural, "contingent methods." Best encapsulated by Liu in the introduction to his collection of essays *Local Transcendence: Essays on Postmodern Historicism and the Database,* this contingency is rooted in the database format itself.[35] Liu traces the processes by which pervasive information management practices proceed to disengage form from content through database queries, which care little for either in a traditional sense. Contingency in this context demands a shifting tactical method, understood as the "methodical tangency of postmodern historicism" rooted in feedback modulations between the past, the present, and the future.[36] This tangency is marked by a "zigzag mode" of interpretive engagement wherein the posthermeneutical characteristics of contingency facilitate scholarship that unfolds across unanticipated, serpentine directions, in relation to the mediations at hand. In both the academic prose of these chapters and the expanded poetics described in the interludes, I follow Liu's recommendation to perform "the act of such mediation through actual media innovation or allusions to such innovations in its own form, thereby methodically bringing to view a sense of simultaneous sameness and otherness in our relation to history."[37] The contingency of the digital object is mirrored by the variability of methods and formats in the chapters and creative works described in this study.[38]

Just as the database introduces contingent relations to history, the cultural practices of the internet introduce transformations to how we might understand historical works subject to variable formats of digitized circulation. Hito Steyerl sketches the turbulence inherent to the variable lives of compressed files in the foundational essay "In Defense of the Poor Image."[39] For Steyerl, poor images exemplify the freedom of gift economies, on the one hand, while finding themselves caught up in the "vicious cycles of audiovisual capitalism," on the other.[40] The article summarizes popular discourses concerning the circulation of transcoded digital objects, offering an excellent précis of current discussions on the highly compressed formats that proliferate in the collections I examine:

> On the one hand, [the poor image] operates against the fetish value of high resolution. On the other hand, this is precisely why it also ends up being perfectly integrated into an information capitalism thriving on compressed attention spans, on impression rather than immersion, on intensity rather than contemplation, on previews rather than screenings. . . . It transforms quality into accessibility, exhibition value into cult value, films into clips, contemplation into distraction.[41]

Focusing on degraded forms of distribution, copyright politics, and pervasive qualities of cultural distraction, Steyerl presents a core paradox of file-sharing networks: the poor image is about "defiance and appropriation just as it is about conformism and exploitation."[42] By this account, the compressed file is a debased rendering of the original work, a "ghost of an image," interesting only in terms of its politicized accessibility or cultural indexing. Certainly, these forces are at play in the files I examine. However, alongside variables like speed and distraction, simulation and defacement, I argue for a radical revaluation of the meaning-making potentials inherent to compressed files. These "poor images," I contend, are significant aesthetic objects in their own right, with complicated (and fascinating!) stories well worth unraveling beyond concepts of copyright politics and degradation. A poorly captured JPG can inspire hours of longing just as a badly ripped MP3 of a poetry reading can warrant endless repetition.

The temporality of attention we might pay to any "poor" digital object might best be encapsulated by renewed critical attention to an economy of *care* in recent media scholarship. Increasingly, all our most meaningful encounters are mediated by the formats that populate our networked devices. Of course, we might also discover more affectively pressing forms of meaning inhering within the affordances of these same media formats. In league with Nanna Bonde Thylstrup's conclusion to *The Politics of Mass Digitization,* among others, I agree that we must move past "the predominant tropes of scale, access, and acceleration in favor of an infrapolitics of care—a politics that offers opportunities for mindful, slow, and focused encounters."[43] Especially now, as the era of always-on streaming media produced by mass digitization works to obscure the infrastructural formats of the digital objects we encounter, attending to the infrapolitics that shape those cultural encounters demands renewed attention and redoubled care. In other words, how might we see what we're seeing when we experience transcoded works online? At what points do the material specificities of these meaningful aesthetic experiences come into view?

Just as the operating systems and social networks of media platforms are subject to a continual state of development, the relatively stable conditions of protocols and standards present sturdy entry points for revealing layers of media formats in these experiences. Recent works on standards, infrastructures, and formats inform my approach to the localized transformations of digital objects.[44] Most directly, this project owes much to the "format theory" developed in Jonathan Sterne's *MP3: The Meaning of a Format.* Sterne urges media scholars to consider the cultural, social, and historical development of standard formats as a way to "modulate the scale of our analysis of media somewhat differently. . . . Studying formats highlights smaller registers like software, operating standards, and codes, as well as larger registers like infrastructures, international corporate consortia, and whole technical systems."[45] By attending to standard formats for text, image, sound, and movies on the internet, this study of digital objects works to ground the indeterminacy of medial formations and variable conditions of display. Sterne emphasizes the political urgency of this position in his conclusion: "Media remain on the scene, but they are diluted. . . . Future confrontations over democratic media systems and the right to communicate will be held over infrastructures, protocols, formats, portals, and platforms."[46] As Tung-Hui Hu, Safiya Umoja Noble, and Wendy Hui Kyong Chun have variously demonstrated, the political stakes of revealing the workings of digital infrastructures, algorithms, and formats have never been more urgent.[47] In each approach, an engagement with the political reality of networks requires modulating between what appears on the screen and the expansive, often invisible sociotechnical systems that code these appearances.

Working this network description down to the finer details of specificity, I turn to my coeditor at *Eclipse,* Craig Dworkin, whose practice of "radical formalism" has proven essential to each contingent engagement. Dworkin defines radical formalism in *Reading the Illegible* and applies the same reading tactics to *Eclipse* in his article "Hypermnesia," which I explore in chapter 2. Borrowing from Leon Roudiez's "paragrammatics" and Ihab Hassan's "misreading," Dworkin pursues "the closest of close readings in service of political questions," considering "what is signified by its form, enacted by its structures, implicit in its philosophy of language, how it positions its reader, and a range of questions relating to the poem as a material object—how it was produced, distributed, exchanged," wherein "form must always necessarily signify but any particular signification is historically contingent."[48] This radical formalism informs Dworkin's appraisal of the *Eclipse* archive, which is in turn augmented by a range of conceptual models for the dynamic procedures and material processes of digital objects. By way of its interludes, *The Little Database* seeks a radical formalism applicable to historical artifacts appearing as new media objects, within a set of historically contingent and contextually networked databases. The performance of interpretation is reductively sketched within the highly lossy compression format of an introduction: poetics find meaning in practice. In other words, this methodological blueprint relies on specific enactments of a media poetics.

A Poetics of Media Formats

Even while I focus on forces of dispersion in these pages, I aim to perform a great deal of synthetic activity. If the database as a form encourages contingent methods of scholarship, the samples from the scholarly database itself require variable, tactical uses geared toward specific medial situations. This book's methodological framework is indebted to a wide array of thinkers across fields including material text studies, the digital humanities, comparative media analysis, affect theory, critical code study, literary and art history, poetry and poetics, cinema studies, and cultural theory, among others.[49] As the title of the book indicates, my trajectory through this thicket can be provisionally categorized as "a" poetics of media formats. Following the foundational arguments laid out by Adalaide Morris in *New Media Poetics,* I consider this media poetics "an ongoing, elastic, and capacious process rather than a taxonomically precise product: as befits the processual or process-driven nature of computers, the emphasis . . . is on the act of making rather than the thing made, on forces rather than stable formations."[50] Locating each process of making as a singular path of discovery within an unstable field, the arguments of *The Little Database* explore the meaning-making activities of media formats and the possibilities for poetic thinking in media contexts new and old alike.

Indeed, I believe that a contemporary poetics practice can be articulated only through a rigorous consideration of coterminous writing technologies in all their complicating processes of mediation and remediation. As they say: "Our writing tools are also working on our thoughts."[51] This poses significant challenges to the intensive study of even the most mundane objects available to the contemporary poetics scholar. Not only is media built on the technoscience of programmers, mathematicians, and engineers, but the fields that plug into the cultural, political, and aesthetic aspects of media formats are so enmeshed in specialist discourses and disciplinary traditions as to muddle any comprehensive method. Given these conditional demands, my study necessarily surveys a widely interdisciplinary array of scholarly output in order to address the little database in variable configurations.

While methodologically indebted to the constellation of texts outlined above, *The Little Database* departs from these in its play through a focused exploration of an intertwined nexus of independent platforms for transcoded artifacts. The book is organized into four chapters, each addressing a primary little database and a correspondent methodological framework and file format. In an extreme of abstraction, these can be enumerated as follows:

1) computation,   text files,   and *Textz.com*;
2) preservation,   image files,   and *Eclipse*;
3) transmission,   sound files,   and *PennSound*;
4) dispersion,   movie files,   and *UbuWeb*.

This study proceeds from the macroscopic to the microscopic, and back again. It arrives at a close reading only in the final chapter. The first chapter attends to computation as the preeminent mode of critical data practices focused on parsing "big" data. The second turns to preservation, an issue at the core of archival questions within the digital humanities on a narrower band than computation at scale. The third examines the far-reaching circulation of sound files across multiple databases at the level of a small set of files rather than an archival collection. In the final chapter, I arrive at a close reading of three specific movies. From there, close readings expand into the broadest set of concerns, connecting back to standards and databases at scale. Operating kaleidoscopically, the closer we might get to a digital file, the more each pattern radiates outward.[52] More specifically, the act of radiating outward may lead to expanding networks of standardizing protocols, data infrastructures, conditions of display, algorithmic bias, patterns of circulation, and the technical and cultural issues that by necessity remain only partial captures bound to the modest scale of any little database.

The first chapter, "Textwarez: The Executable Files of *Textz.com*," examines computation through plain text standards and a series of playful visualizations and scripts deployed on a little database called *Textz,* edited by the German net artist Sebastian Lütgert from 2000 to 2004. I argue that the patterns of format analysis, container technologies, and computational performances that characterize the *Textz* project provide a basis for reading the increasingly complex formats examined in each following chapter. Ranging from experimental poetry and cyberpunk fiction to romantic literature and political tracts, the multilingual little database of *Textz* presents an idiosyncratic collection of text files that is at once too varied to compute and yet highly selective—not unlike a collection of files gathered over the years on any laptop. I contend that the text files hosted by the site shift into something more enigmatic once these texts are framed as a set of "textwarez," a neologism marking the files on the site as "executable software" that operates on their human readers. I explore the text file as a sophisticated reading interface for human and nonhuman operators that emphasizes searchability, portability, and transmutability. Expanding on the formal properties of the text file, the chapter concludes by reading a set of applications released by *Textz* that call the stability of digital file formats into question through a playful performance of encoding and decoding protocols among a variety of media formats. In addition to revealing new dimensions of the text file itself, these applications offer a provocative statement on the politics of distribution, the interchangeability of formats, and the performance of computational scholarship at large.

The second chapter, "Distributing Services: The Periodical Preservation of *Eclipse,*" explores preservation and periodicity in the image-based *Eclipse* collection founded by Dworkin in 2003. *Eclipse* produces facsimile editions of rare and out-of-print works of experimental poetry and poetics, primarily originating in the 1970s and 1980s. Evaluating trends in periodical studies, this chapter considers *Eclipse* as a metaperiodical, with occasional releases of full magazines built into its archival database. To materialize this juncture, I offer a close reading of the formats that preserve *L=A=N=G=U=A=G=E* magazine in an extended comparison of a database of images, a set of reading copies, and the print run of the magazine. The highly compressed images hosted by *Eclipse* are seen to reveal unexpected layers of transcoding at play in the republication of this influential poetics magazine. From Xerox printing in the late seventies, to the GIF images presented on *Eclipse,* to the ongoing development of

Adobe PDF capabilities, this decidedly low-fidelity magazine finds revised signification in its shifting formal and bibliographic codes. The distributing services of the website, I contend, paradoxically amplify the republication practices of the print magazine, while the site itself illustrates a resistance to the preservation systems of the internet. These resistances are demonstrated in an extended discussion of the archival captures compiled by the "Wayback Machine" web crawler developed by Alexa Internet for the Internet Archive. In contrast to the stripped-down text files of *Textz.com,* which emphasize algorithmic use, *Eclipse* presents transcoded images for human reading. Similarly, unlike Google Books, *Eclipse* remains mostly unsearchable, asking: what is lost and what remains of the book beyond the algorithm? Caught with losses alongside gains, this chapter concludes with a discussion of the stakes of compression, which carry throughout the book.

The third chapter, "Live Vinyl MP3: Echo Chambers Among the Little Databases," opens by returning to "The Defective Record" by William Carlos Williams. Following the movement from gramophone to MP3 as detailed above, I turn to the same procedure's reversal, tracking how a single glitched audio file produces a network of poetic practices centered on the vocal performance of Tracie Morris. These transmissions, often happenstance, capture the contingent forces that generate the meaningful interactions and poetic productions driven by a poetics of media formats. Amplifying the transformative properties of transmission, the chapter traces an autobiographical narrative of a small set of MP3 files recorded by queer Canadian poet, painter, and musician bill bissett in 1968. I track the passage of these files as they move through several little databases online, with a special emphasis on the *PennSound* collection. Founded by Charles Bernstein and Al Filreis in 2005, *PennSound* has digitized and hosted tens of thousands of poetry recordings, which have been freely downloaded by hundreds of millions of users. The narrative of this chapter tracks the dispersion of bissett's album with Th Mandan Massacre, *Awake in th Red Desert,* through its initial release on *Mutant Sounds,* to its subsequent uploads to *PennSound* and *UbuWeb.* By following the thread of a particular poet's output, in an attempt to tease out a description of each online collection, this chapter investigates how little databases inflect the works they host, and how we might begin to understand contemporary iterations of audio formats through this network. I argue that, while *Mutant Sounds* and *PennSound* host precisely the same MP3 files, the textual conditions—and thus the significance—of these two iterations could not be more radically different. By way of conclusion to this narrative, I examine a remixing tool entitled MUPS, developed by David (Jhave) Johnston, which introduces a new interface to a select set of files hosted by the *PennSound* archive.

A final chapter, "Dropping the Frame: From Film to Database," examines the dispersion necessitated by close readings of media-specific films streaming in the *UbuWeb* collection. The *UbuWeb* platform, founded in 1996 by Kenneth Goldsmith and supported by a team of mostly student volunteers, hosts an extensive collection of text, image, sound, and "Film & Video" art. The proprietary nature, cultural dominance, and technical affordances of Adobe Flash once characterized the works hosted in this section of the site, and their traces remain long after the standard was discontinued in contemporary browsers. Reflecting on internet history and changing protocols for even the most pervasive file formats, this chapter reads through the ways in which media-specific film and video works amplify the effects of digitization. A close reading of Nam June Paik's *Zen For Film* connects to the various remixes that artists have performed on the work to reveal the unpredictable layers of transcoding that Paik's film releases online—all in stark contrast to the celluloid reflexivity of the original filmic performance. Similarly, once situated within the browser, Vito Acconci's *Theme Song* shifts from the impersonal context of the art gallery to the intimate seduction of a confessional video blog. In the opposite direction, I also explore contemporary movies made specifically for internet release, honing in on a database movie by People Like Us (Vicki Bennett) entitled *We Edit Life*. By blending colorful pixels with aged frames drawn from found footage films, Bennett zooms in on the unwieldy distortions of digitization. On *UbuWeb*, these videos stream alongside the text, image, and sound formats examined in previous chapters. I conclude this reading with an extension to the little databases hosted on every computer, from iTunes music libraries to folders full of PDF files to increasingly uncommon hard drives packed with downloaded movies. These examples build on previous chapters to present an argument for a renewed attention to the poetics of the little database, attuned to the media formats that continue to shape user experience of art and literature online.

Finally, in a short conclusion, I discuss the relation of downloaded content to streaming media. Rather than displace downloads, the always-on streaming internet allows us to interrogate what it means to gather a collection. Indeed, a history of digital practice throws into relief the everyday repertoires we continue to employ. Today's social media driven internet is built alongside the "web 1.0," which persists in its shadow. I point to the *Electronic Poetry Center (EPC)* as a particularly interesting example of happenstance longevity. Founded by Loss Peqeño Glazier with Charles Bernstein at the Poetics Program of the State University of New York at Buffalo in 1995, for a very brief window, the *EPC* was the largest site on the public internet. Now archived and maintained by the University of Pennsylvania, the site is full of holes, anachronisms, and broken links. Within these glitches, an alternate vision of the network continues to subsist alongside mainstream practices. Here, the little database presents an opportunity to reimagine the internet a little more strangely, where future developments might rediscover older forms of invention made long before the establishment of the generic conventions that undergird the 2020s internet as of this writing.

The media poetics of these chapters carry over into a series of interludes that outline practical methods to perform the arguments of *The Little Database* in variable formats of creative scholarship. Presenting reflexive performances of each chapter's argument, these interludes articulate the project in their own terms, through medial formations that the written document cannot address. My approach to these interventions is inspired by a practice of creative remaking articulated in the essay "Deformance and Interpretation" by Jerome McGann and Lisa Samuels. Calling for "a practice of everyday imaginative life," they offer a set of tactics for creative scholarship as a way to open up the conventions of academic prose to experimental discovery.[53] Following this line of inquiry, each of the four interludes in this book seeks a reading of the little database from beyond what McGann and Samuels call "the textual looking glass."[54] It should be noted that these interludes do not function simply as supplements; nor are they merely additional creative works that accompany discrete chapters. Just as Bernstein's definition of poetics includes the "continuation of poetry by other means," this project performs the media poetics described here as the continuation of *scholarship* by other means.[55]

In this respect, the creative work discussed in each interlude could effectively stand in for corresponding chapters of the book. That is to say, this project does not simply address the little database, or inscribe the ways in which works of art and literature are transformed by digital formats—it also demonstrates how scholarly performances of variable formats might occur through creative methods of media poetics. Of course, depending on how the reader might find these words, this practice is variously determined by the affordances of the black-and-white print codex, the full-color ebook, the open-access digital interface, or hopefully, the rogue PDF file nested within a shadow library. In print-based editions, the reader will find typographic links to expanded digital materials for all creative interludes via the project's open source Manifold Scholarship page (https://manifold.umn.edu/projects/the-little-database).[56] The materials I present offer another way to reveal the source code behind the arguments I make while also amplifying the play of meaning within the transformative media formats I discuss throughout. These mediatic performances, once more, are presented in every instance as a model for yet unimagined interventions that the reader might make.

This book is an invitation to play with the little database as one might piece together a slideshow for loved ones, produce a mix-tape for a significant other, or even capture citations for an essay. It aims to open up personal collections to the same methods that might unpack an institutional archive. To offer a range of tactics to read cultural history through playful engagements with the contingent networks of the present. It hopes to open new windows for the reader to explore undiscovered networks of meaningful experience among experimental arts, internet cultures, ordinary collections, and the play of variable media formats.

CHAPTER 1

Textwarez

The Executable Files of *Textz.com*

> we are not the dot in dot-com, neither are we the minus in
> e-book. the future of online publishing sits right next to your
> computer: it's a $50 scanner and a $50 printer, both connected
> to the internet. we are the & in copy & paste, and plain ascii is
> still the format of our choice.
>
> —A. S. Ambulanzen (Sebastian Lütgert et al.),
> "napster was only the beginning," 2001

Textz.com hosted 831 plain text files at the time the site was abandoned in early 2004.[1] Released periodically on the influential <nettime> listserv, *Textz* grew at a rate of roughly 250 files per year. Ranging from experimental poetry and cyberpunk fiction to media theory and political tracts, the *Textz* database presents a diverse, yet highly curated, selection of text files gathered by a collective and edited by German artist-activist-programmer Sebastian Lütgert from 2000 to 2004. Its fiercely copyleft position garnered the site international attention following a lawsuit and arrest warrant filed by the copyright holder to a substantial portion of Theodor Adorno's works. Freely distributing these works, *Textz* combated the economic structures of the about-to-burst dot-com bubble, while rallying against the tightening of intellectual property debates.

Ambulanzen, the anonymous collective speaking for *Textz* cited above, offers a précis of the logic governing the site's operating procedures. They declare that digital texts are *not* electronic books, but rather executable binary files dispersed as free software or cracked programs. Not only do ASCII characters write executable files, *Textz* argues, but text files can be considered executable programs in their own right. In this way, the pirated "textwarez" of *Textz* presents a radical reevaluation of the ubiquitous ASCII text file. Reconceiving the *.txt* format as executable code running in the brain of its reader, *Textz* calls into question the limits of a file type while presenting an unlikely metaphor for computational processes.

From a critical digital humanities perspective, the site offers a compelling portal into online collections and the forms of poetic computation enabled by texts on the internet. The fact that *Textz* kept obsessive and inventive user logs is fortuitous. This chapter offers the example of *Textz* as an outlier counterpoint to a range of debates concerning the computational study of digital objects and techniques of literary interpretation formulated within the field.[2] Marked by a playful skepticism toward statistical analysis and the neoliberal politics of copyright, the site challenges the field's defining formulations in league with a range of global debates toward a critical digital humanities on the horizon of the present.[3] Without lingering on the terms of these debates, which remain beyond the scope of my study, this chapter instead presents *a* little database demonstrably resistant to programmatic systems for computational interpretation. As Nan Z. Da reminds us, it is often the reality that the literary corpora subject to computation are, in fact, "usually not so large."[4] Indeed, the little database is eminently computable, even from a smartphone, which alone merits some exploration of the modes of reading that this capacity might enable or limit. Putting scale to the side for a moment, I contend that *Textz* and the contingent demands of the collections I study throughout necessitate an approach that departs from the prevailing methodologies of computational literary studies, and in particular the statistical analysis of texts.

I make this argument by playing a reading of what Ian Bogost has termed the "system operation" of *Textz* against a range of "unit operations" functioning in the site itself.[5] Unit operations privilege discrete, contingent, interpretive components over the static structures of systematic operations—systems that we might properly align with the processes of standardized encoding protocols writ large. In so doing, unit operations tactically deemphasize totalizing, analytical structures and interpretive closures. Put into practice, my approach follows the feminist media practices initiated by Laine Nooney, a kind of media-archival "speleology" more common in studies of games and interactive fiction, following the twisty little passages of the collection as one might traverse a colossal cave system.[6] Aubrey Anable further develops this method of spelunking, "to explore a potentially vast space that can be apprehended only a small section at a time."[7] Traversing the networked components of the *Textz* collection and related provocations, I conclude the chapter by exploring a series of "textwarez" code-works by Lütgert. Such code-works reimagine the *Textz* collection through a range of playful conceptual games with file formats, oriented toward a poetics and politics of distribution. These explorations lead toward an expanded conception of media format poetics, presenting an opportunity to consider how a little database long-since erased from the internet might yet yield new potentials for scholarship in today's networked milieu.

Collections and Contents

To begin, a site like *Textz* is remarkably difficult to situate in relation to analog forms. Is it a collection, a library, an archive, an anthology? In colloquial terms, this kind of site is often referred to as an "online archive" or "digital library."[8] Neither classification quite works: "online archive" would be technically inaccurate given the absence of prepublication materials; and "digital library" doesn't quite map onto the distribution mechanics or location characteristics of the database. *Publisher,* with its root in the act of *making public,* nearly fits, despite the absence of the imprimatur of a press. What's clear, however, is that each of these tags imports a specific set of historical, contextual, and operational frames into our understanding of the site.

In 2009, when the question of naming was still somewhat fresh, Kenneth M. Price outlined the stakes of nomenclature in an article on *The Walt Whitman Archive* entitled, "Edition, Project, Database, Archive, Thematic Research Collection: What's in a name?" For Price, each of these classifications, as well as Peter Shillingsburg's proposed "knowledge site," inevitably fails to account for the specificity and variety of scholarly projects online.[9] Instead, Price offers the term *arsenal* for its "emphasis on [the] workshop since these projects are so often simultaneously products and in process."[10]

Moreover, for Price, *arsenal* holds appeal for its etymological connection to the magazine. However, *arsenal,* too, is jettisoned in a
final footnote to the article. Price writes, "I am less concerned that
arsenal catches on than I am that we recognize the fresh features of
new work underway and that we are self-conscious about what we
want any new term to convey."[11] Indeed, Price's dilemma usefully
demonstrates the pitfalls of developing a classificatory matrix for
works trafficking online. Nevertheless, a tentative typology of such
projects is necessary to reflect on the way we understand diverse
outputs of online collections, from renegade art repositories like
Textz to scholarly websites like *The Walt Whitman Archive.*

Jeremy Braddock treads similar terrain in his introduction to
Collecting as Modernist Practice. Braddock emphasizes a public model
of the collection that mediates relationships between audience and
artwork under the rubric of a "provisional institution."[12] These provisional institutions are privately assembled but publicly exhibited.
Retaining the terminological specificity of museums and antholo-
gies, Braddock foregrounds a "collecting aesthetic" tied to the asser-
tion that "a material collection is itself an aesthetic object, even, more
pointedly, an *authored work.*"[13] What Braddock insists upon here is
that a kind of authorial sensibility guides the assembling of a given
collection. Or, as he puts it, "the anthology and the art collection
exist not simply for the sake of their individual works; they are also
systems with meaning in themselves."[14] Braddock's conceptualiza-
tion of the collection might helpfully be ported into a unit for understanding *Textz* as a provisional institution operating under Lütgert's
stewardship. Following Braddock, this chapter could sketch the collecting aesthetic of *Textz* while remaining attentive to the particularities of naming a digital collection of texts offered on the internet.[15]

Or, we might look at the more recent work of Abigail De Kosnik,
who approaches these same questions from a decidedly vernacular
vantage. Primarily tracking the growth of the fic hub *Archive of Our
Own (AO3),* De Kosnik proposes the concept of a "rogue archive"
maintained by the "archival repertoires" that modify the traditional
categories of bibliographic terms.[16] Just as the roguish repertoires
of amateur archivists seek to preserve content the academe might
never begin to register, these same "archontic productions" counter staid conceptions of otherwise dynamic processes of digital creation, collection, and preservation.[17] In this regard, we might con-

sider the little database to be a rogue archive: built and maintained by archival repertoires as a labor of love and subject to the vicissitudes of both academic and popular sea changes in the archival arts. Writing on the long "archival turn," Kate Eichorn notes how these practices are bound to ordinary digital use, speculating that "the timing of the archival turn is primarily related to the digital turn (a technological and epistemological shift that brought the concept and experience of archives into our everyday lives)."[18]

In anticipation of the repertoires of rogue archiving, Craig Saper outlines the "sociopoetics" that structured the mail art and magazine assemblages of the last century. Saper describes sociopoetics as the "inherently social process of constructing texts . . . expanded to the point that individual pages or poems mean less than the distribution and compilation machinery or social apparatuses."[19] Like the poetics of repertoire, sociopoetics designates a field wherein the networked circulation of aesthetic products assumes a privileged status that exceeds the works themselves. In dialogue with the "net.art" practices of the late 1990s, *Textz* explores new modes of publication and dispersion as a sociopoetic practice. Not unlike the "libraries" that populate user hard drives, the *Textz* collection also presents a case study for reading heterogeneous sets of user-curated digital files, though published for wider audiences online.

Between archival repertoires, sociopoetics, and collecting aesthetics, we might begin to chart the instrumental agency of *Textz* as a collection, a rogue archive, and a provisional institution. Or, as Braddock puts it, paraphrasing Walter Benjamin, "as a mode of *practice* as well as an aesthetic (or historical) form."[20] Importantly, *Textz* represents a provisional institution developed in lockstep with the emergence of an internet activist community. It indexes a fascination with situationist politics alongside speculative narratives, media theory, and a wide range of titles in vogue around the turn of the millennium. Gathering these constituent parts together under the term "little database" is an attempt to retain a sociopoetic emphasis on network distribution and periodicity in the lineage of the little magazine while refreshing the technical apparatus to match the provisional repertoires of internet collections.

Updating the preceding media historical analogies, we might just as easily classify the site as a "pirate network" or "shadow library." Indeed, as a profusion of recent studies of internet piracy have shown, "napster was only the beginning."[21] Though they feature prominently in the site's legacy, an extended discussion of intellectual property and online piracy lies beyond the scope of this chapter. My intent is not to negate the importance of this line of inquiry. The literature on copyright is extensive and reveals many of the most pressing issues related to cultural objects trafficking online, including their very right to exist.[22] Readers interested in this subject might most usefully turn to the excellent collection assembled by Joe Karaganis, *Shadow Libraries: Access to Knowledge in Global Higher Education,* which again and again highlights the asymmetrical and deleterious effects of IP policing on global knowledge communities.[23]

Rather than pursue well-trafficked avenues on intellectual property and fair use, I have elected to attend to qualities of the site that remain underrepresented in studies of little databases, whatever one might call them: the formats that undergird this communications circuit; the transformations that the online collection introduces into the works it hosts; and the processes of meaning-making that emerge among these manifold relations. While issues of copyright necessarily arise in any discussion of a site like *Textz,* the specific properties of the database's objects and the interpretive possibilities of the literary works it hosts are rarely explored. From the outset, it should be clearly stated that *Textz* is nothing if not wanton in its disregard of copyright law. Distilled to its core conceptual premise, the site is predicated on the illegal transmission of intellectual property. The mere fact of illegality, however, often obscures the opportunity to investigate the significations produced by these influential, if shadowy, endeavors. Given that "napster was only the beginning," *Textz* presciently anticipates the growth of cultural piracy on the internet, seen from the present as a missed opportunity in light of streaming ubiquity and platform hegemony. Nevertheless, it marks an anticipatory aesthetic of distribution that endures through the file lockers, peer-to-peer networks, bit-torrent platforms, and emerging "Web 3.0" decentralized internet currents that define file-sharing today.

Textz is not Project Gutenberg

Textz formed the theoretical core of Lütgert's expansive web-ring of digital works known as *Project GNUtenberg.* Of course, the GNU in the name plays on the free software GNU Project, itself a recursive acronym for "GNU's Not Unix." The "GNU" in the title ciphers an approach to historical texts that is at once computational, critical, and communitarian, set forth at a moment of transformative technological change on par with the introduction of the printing press. At the same time, the *GNUtenberg* tag codes *Textz* as the shadowy double to Michael Hart's public-domain collection, *Project Gutenberg,* the first text collection of its kind.[24] By contrast, the site defines itself through a rejection of these digital publishing norms in its founding manifesto, contending that "this is not project gutenberg. it is neither about constituting a canonical body of historical texts, . . . nor is it about htmlifying freely available books into unreadable sub-chapterized hyper-chunks. texts relate to texts by other means than a href. just go to your local bookstore and find out yourself. the net is not a rhizome, and a digital library should not be an interactive nirvana."[25] With some historical distance, however, the projects might be seen to share more in common with each other than the paywalled digital libraries and "interactive nirvanas" of today's internet.

Like Hart's enterprise, *Textz* offers "plain vanilla texts," ready for computational processing and easily reformatted for any variety of reading systems. Unicode text remains the functional backbone of digital text and all functional code, registered beneath the page of searchable PDFs, books, subtitles, search algorithms, large language models, and other text-based components of the media landscape. Beyond a shared format, *Textz*'s copyleft politics intensify Hart's ideology of accessibility. In its similarity to *Gutenberg, GNUtenberg* is best able to articulate its politics as a differential gap. Where Hart's historic first e-Text encoded "The Declaration of Independence" in 1971, the first file *Textz* distributes is Gilles Deleuze's short article "Postscript on the Societies of Control." The political valences of the two foundational releases could not be more disparate, situating these projects at radically opposed ends of the spectrum of online distribution practices.

Pitting *Textz* against *Project Gutenberg,* Lütgert against Hart, and Deleuze against the "Declaration of Independence" is precisely in line with the kind of playful statistics that *Textz* gathered in a series of "statz" pages. Keeping detailed logs of users and patterns of use was once a core component of internet publishing practices. The excitement of immediate publication was paired with the power to document a global network of IP addresses and access points.

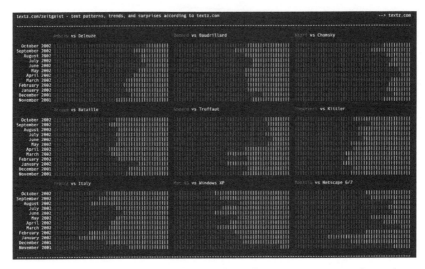

 Figure 1.1. ASCII data visualization tracking "text patterns, trends, and surprises according to textz.com" between November 2001 and October 2002. Captured via Internet Archive.

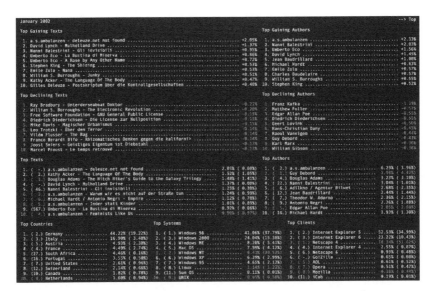

Figure 1.2. A data visualization tracking top gaining authors and texts; declining authors and texts; and top countries, systems, and clients for textz.com in January 2002. Captured via Internet Archive.

In Figure 1.1, "text patterns, trends, and surprises according to textz .com" are mapped as a series of ongoing serial contests between writers, countries, operating systems, and internet browsers. Similarly, Figure 1.2 presents an example of monthly updates published on the site that track these same categories as though they were stocks, rising and falling through gains and declines in public use.

As though anticipating contemporary trends in statistical analysis within the digital humanities, these "statz" seem to offer much of the content that a digital humanist might hope to see. And, indeed, these charts do offer insight beyond their respective numerical data sets. The selections made in Figure 1.1 map the attention of the site's editors and users. Of course, among a net art milieu in 2001, Negri is besting Chomsky, Godard overwhelms Truffaut, and Mozilla is winning out over Netscape. More surprising on an intellectual history note, perhaps, is that Adorno continues to gain more readers than Deleuze over this period. In retrospect, we might speculate that *Textz* always had a particular fascination and draw toward Adorno on intellectual-property grounds. Ironically, media attention surrounding this copyright battle may have worked to drive up user downloads of the contested Adornian files. In this light, the "gaining" use of Adorno can be seen as a harbinger of the site's demise in a few years' time. Despite the conjecture we might make here, it remains difficult to imagine how these charts present questions that studying the site wouldn't already reveal.

In Figure 1.2, the reader might track the range of texts that appealed to a specific audience at a particular historical moment (many long-since out of fashion). While it's notable that Franz Kafka was down and David Lynch was up in January of 2002, there is little to offer by way of comment on these changes beyond the raw data of these surface-level statistics. For example, Douglas Adams seems a strange mainstay among Kathy Acker, Michael Hardt, and Guy Debord. One might also note that the editorial collective running the site—writing as A. S. Ambulanzen—tops the charts in both author and text categories. More interesting insights can be drawn from the demographic and interface statistics in Figure 1.2. German users commanded 44.22 percent of the site's usage, while the United States trailed at seventh place with a mere 2.61 percent. Older versions of Windows and Internet Explorer topped their newer counterparts. Meanwhile, Mac OS and Mozilla captured small percentages of the user base in 2002. Comparing these numbers to stats collected by similar sites over time might lead to a productive historical conclusion concerning international use patterns and interface preferences. Nevertheless, from this vantage, the facts remain merely interesting: nearly trivia, given verifiable historical outcomes. Each figure and every comparative data set is incidental to the collection itself, and to the internet at the time.

Eschewing the efficacy of data analysis, we might instead consider the sociopoetics of these statistical displays. Just as "gains" in the digital humanities have delivered a newly invigorated critical perspective on quantification and the aesthetics of data-mapping, the early internet's affordances for user tracking and graphical display created a vernacular fascination with visualizing the statistics of use. It was common for early sites to proudly display visitor counts, guest books, and other "widgets" for the quantification of usage, a once-pervasive (and still-available) aesthetic feature of the early internet that has long since fallen out of fashion, excepting nostalgic trends in postinternet art circles. On the one hand, *Textz* critiques this gesture by offering unlikely comparisons and an excess of information, suggesting a sly mirroring of stock exchange trackers and updated RSS (really simple syndication) news feeds. On the other, it presents these statistics with an ASCII art aesthetic more common to Usenet and BBS (bulletin board system) forums of the late 1970s and early 1980s, which predated the graphical display that has defined the internet since 1993.[26] Instead of shaping recognizable figures with the stylistic flair for monospace glyphs in ASCII art, *Textz* uses a plain text approach to the representation of data. This historical gesture interfaces the *Textz* collection with an aesthetics of piracy featured in the warez scene (or "The Scene") of the BBSes, which often featured ASCII art as a tag for the hacker or group that offered cracked software.[27] Much more than summarizing the user logs of the site, these visualizations perform a pointed poetic intervention that connects the millennial internet with the secret histories of network aesthetics best left unmentioned and only discovered by interested parties.

With this in mind, we can turn to the definitive visualization of the site. Continuing the approach seen in statz, it is presented as an elaborate work of ASCII art. This multifaceted graph (Figure 1.3) was produced by Lütgert and released on the site in the spring of 2004. In one extraordinary data visualization, simply titled "textz.com/logs,"

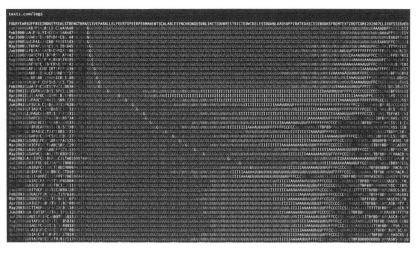

textz.com/logs

Figure 1.3. A multicolor data visualization representing four years of logs for visitors to textz.com, from January 2000 until December 2003, organized by month. For print readers, see the e-book or Manifold edition for full-color images throughout. Captured via Internet Archive.

the user can explore the extensive tracking logs that *Textz* collected over four years. Condensing the massive volumes of data presented in Figures 1.1 and 1.2 into individual color-coded glyphs, this single page offers an incredible quantity of information about the global use of *Textz* from January 2000 until December 2003. Every character, color, and position in this grid transmits significant data. Additional data points are encoded within each letterform using embedded links and tooltips, which are revealed by hovering over any character with a cursor.

A brief excursus to parse this graph yields many fruitful insights. Rendering white text in all caps against a black background, the graph opens with the following text on a single line (with spaces added for ease of reading):

FOUR YEARS OF FREE INDUSTRIAL STRENGTH MASSIVE PARALLEL PEER TO PEER PERMANENT SCALABLE SYNCHRONOUS UNLIMITED UNRESTRICTED WIRELESS DOWNLOADS OF PIRATED ASCII EBOOKS FROM TEXTZ DOT COM 1292907 CLIENTS SERVED

The rest of the graph outlines the temporal and geographic dimensions of the 1.29 million "clients served." In the first section, each

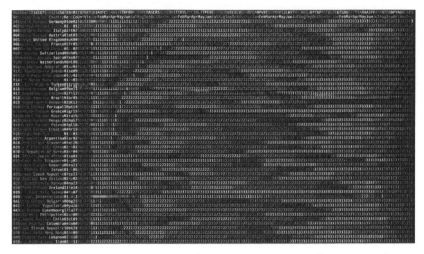

Figure 1.4. A multicolor data visualization representing four years of logs for visitors to textz.com from January 2000 until December 2003, organized by country. Captured via Internet Archive.

line prints a new month of logs from 2000 to 2004. These lines can be parsed as follows: first, the month and year of the line; second, single characters standing in for each of the top twenty countries in assorted colors ordered by ranking; third, the rank that month had in users over the four-year period displayed in white; fourth, the number of users that month represented on a grayscale spectrum, with lighter values for greater numbers. Finally, the remaining 144 characters display proportional values of the month's use log, distributed by color-coded characters representing the top twenty countries for each month. Additionally, a single white character is plotted once per line in the final 144 characters to chart overall volume across the four-year span. The overwhelming density of the graph continues in the following section, which indexes proportional use volumes for each of the 199 countries that accessed the site (Figure 1.4). Even after repeated viewing, it is difficult to comprehend the rationale guiding this chromatic excess: its maximalist approach to data aesthetics yields informatic wonder.

Scrolling through this dizzying array of statistics, the user finds the grayscale conclusion to the graph before a final line that repeats the phrase "NO COPYRIGHT 2004 TEXTZ DOT COM NO RIGHTS RESERVED." In this concluding set, fifty-three countries appear with

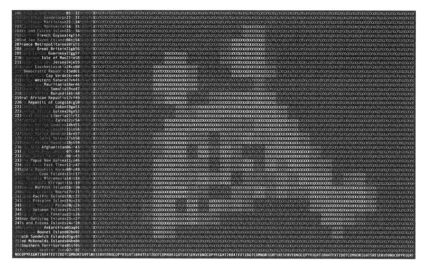

Figure 1.5. A multicolor data visualization representing four years of logs for visitors to textz.com from January 2000 until December 2003, organized by country, ending in an upturned shopping cart icon. Captured via Internet Archive.

zero use, including, for example, both Antarctica and Afghanistan. Each of these countries' lines is accompanied by grayscale *X*'s that together form the emblematic *Textz* icon: an upturned shopping cart (Figure 1.5). No rights are reserved and none of these countries are "served." Dissolved nations (Czechoslovakia), military territories (Indian Ocean Territory), and in the final position, ambiguous non-places ("Neutral Zone") highlight the absurdity and excess of the entire metric exercise. The data aesthetics of tracking and logging are themselves overturned in the gesture. The form of the chart is retained in the service of an extended display of nonuse, which is in turn aestheticized as an elaborate work of conceptual ASCII art. The display of these statistics not only indexes the site's visitor data itself, but also points back to a moment when such data was habitually rendered visible online. By amplifying these tracking systems, the site speaks back to these surveillance systems in a kind of "dark sousveillance."[28] That is to say, there are manifold political stakes inherent to *Textz*'s playful statistics, which bring to the surface the conditions of an internet not yet subsumed by the forms of infrastructural opacity, proprietary algorithmic logic, and systemic obfuscation common online today. Just as *Textz*'s charts offer up numerical data for statistical analysis, they also foreground the limitations and absurdities of such an analytical exercise. If this is the definitive statement that *Textz* makes on the statistical uses of its own collection, how might we compute the little database otherwise?

One approach is to turn from use to content: where *Textz* quantified the way its collection was used, a scholarly approach might attempt to chart the contents of the collection itself. This, at least, was a driving question when I began my research on *Textz*. A plain text archive with a full collection ready to process seemed a generative entry point into computational modes of literary scholarship. However, a number of problems with this approach immediately suggested themselves. A quick scroll through the names of authors reveals a critical failure so obvious it doesn't require statistical confirmation: the collection is overwhelmingly white and male.[29] Aside from the obviousness of this core fact, the collection is remarkably heterogeneous in terms of genre and language. As a whole, it remains *strange*. The contents are too generically diverse to provide insight through topic modeling tools. Network analysis and other "cultural analytics" techniques similarly fail to furnish a new lens through which to view the collection. The greatest challenge to computation is the multilingual nature of the texts. Just over half of the works are presented in English, nearly a third are in German, and the remaining portions are split among Italian, French, and Spanish texts. Even if, to consider it, the texts were translated (causing a range of new problems), the most comprehensive analytic tools would prove incapable of producing meaningful patterns in the strange assortment that comprises the *Textz* corpus. Frequency charts, topic models, and network diagrams of collections like *Textz* manage to be both obvious and obfuscatory. An attempt to import the collection into machine learning NLP (natural language processing) models would effectively erase and flatten the most distinctive features of the corpus, regardless of the context window.

These challenges are not unique to *Textz*. Scholars working with diverse datasets collected from multilingual or transdisciplinary contexts are routinely advised to focus their research on more readily computable collections, in size or self-similarity. Preparing multilingual parallel corpora for *Textz* would be as futile as modeling the topics or affects of literary documents ranging from poems to speculative fiction to political tracts. Attempting to decipher se-

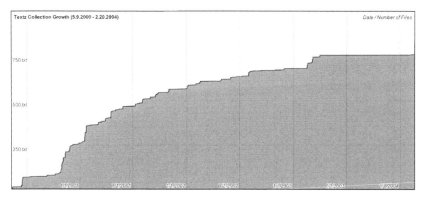

Figure 1.6. A chart tracking the growth of the *Textz* collection by number of files between the dates of May 9, 2000, and February 20, 2004.

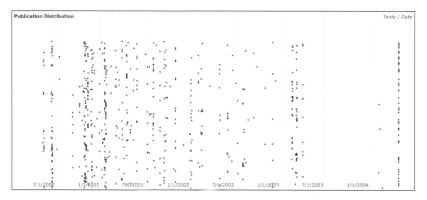

Figure 1.7. A plot tracking the publication distribution of files released by *Textz* between the dates of May 9, 2000, and February 20, 2004.

mantic patterns through Text Encoding Initiative (TEI) markup for this type of collection approaches a 'pataphysical level of absurdity. Beyond certain statements about the collector's preferences or the circulating availability of specific genres of texts, there is little to be done with the contents of files hosted by the site. The little database, like my own collection of haphazard files housed within the device receiving these letter-strokes, remains resolutely idiosyncratic.

Given these challenges, one potential solution involved tracking the release patterns of all files featured on the site. Figures 1.6 and 1.7 respectively chart the growth and periodicity of *Textz* releases. In Figure 1.7, each scattered dot represents the digital publication of a text file. As this figure demonstrates, the files are released in bursts around certain dates, with scattered releases occurring in between. Activity skews toward the founding of the site, with the highest concentration of releases in the winter of 2000–2001. Before the site goes on hiatus, there is a large release of files in early 2003. Finally, the remaining texts are released in May of 2004. This narrative is enriched by the parallel chart of the site's growth in Figure 1.6 as steep cliffs of productivity surrounded by plateaus of inactivity. Anyone who has worked on a blog, captured citations to Zotero, or attempted to clear an email inbox might quickly recognize these bursts in productivity as the familiar temporality of working amidst endless data streams.

But these aggregate numbers fail to account for the most important dates in the *Textz* timeline. Pairing these graphs with textz.com/logs, one wonders why June and October of 2002 boast such exceptional user numbers. Reviewing the contents of the site, it's clear that the release of Max Horkheimer and Theodor Adorno's *Dialektik der Aufklärung* (published in English as *Dialectic of Enlightenment*) on April 30, 2002, resulted in critical user mass following widespread media coverage—leading to a lawsuit in June and an official response by *Textz* in October. In a similar vein, there are plausibly hundreds of reasons for each spike in use. A broad spectrum of speculative interpretations might address how the periodicity of the collection interfaces with social contexts, external publications, intellectual trends, and so forth. However, these speculative metrics would surely fail *Textz* as squarely as the user logs. Following Lütgert's suggestion, I propose that the statistical cart ought, in this instance, be overturned. Central to the site's aesthetics, a rejection of computational analysis serves as both an invitation to examine its contents more closely and a method to evaluate the upturned cart in its own right. In what follows, we'll move from the computation of content to the technical effects of the container. In this way, I consider how a contingent media poetics might articulate the *Textz* collection otherwise.

Content to Container

From the webmaster motto "content is king" (as relevant now as it was in 2001), *Textz* presents the dis-contents of the dethroned, cracked, and stolen text file.[30] They write: "They say there was a time when content was king, but we have seen his head rolling. our week beats their year. ever since we have been moving from content to discontent, collecting scripts and viruses, writing programs and bots, dealing with textz as warez, as executables—something that is able to change your life."[31] As an exaggerated plural derivative of software, "warez" emerged on BBSes as slang for a pirated or "cracked" commercial program distributed across illicit file-sharing channels. The act of distribution itself seems to "beat" the content as such, assuming a privileged status that eclipses the digital artifact being distributed. While this analogy certainly plays out in the guerilla scanning and dispersion activity of *Textz,* the re-rendering of its contents as executable software programs is a still more radical gesture. Beyond the politics of copyright, *Textz* presents a novel interface between digital formats and the written word. Alongside viruses, we find "scripts." Programs and bots are, of course, "written." And the "contents" of each text are transformed into pirated software: "textwarez." To understand the implications of these claims, we might start at the feudal roots of content: "From medieval Latin *contentum* (plural *contenta* 'things contained')."[32] As Jonathan Sterne might put it, following Lewis Mumford, *Textz* transforms through the introduction of a significantly different "container technology."[33] What *Textz* introduces to these historical texts is not only an illicit new venue and distribution system, but also a markedly new format. Not just an ASCII file, but a text-based software program that operates on and executes within a human operating system.

This bold claim set forth in the *Textz* manifesto raises a series of questions. Is it possible to take its provocation seriously? What does it mean to present works by Kathy Acker, Guy Debord, William Gibson, or Theodor Adorno as "executable" code? What changes to interpretation does this framing mechanism introduce? More importantly, what modifications might we chart in the transcoding from print codex to plain text file? To offer a response to these queries, we'll begin by examining the protocological structure of ASCII itself. From there, we can consider possible computational actions enabled by a notion of textwarez. These actions will be discussed in relation to both the *Textz* collection and a series of works that Lütgert performs as textwarez. Finally, these inquiries will lead us to reconsider the relation of container technologies and operational software to the work of literary criticism after the digital turn. Beyond the computational metrics of textual analysis, *Textz* suggests a transformation that is more far-reaching in its recoding of each digital text file. Put differently, the question of how we might use computational tools to understand literature is less urgent here than understanding how textwarez might transform literary sources in the computation of each user.

"Changing meaning with each new medium, *text* is a truly chameleonic word," writes Adriaan van der Weel in *Changing Our Textual Minds*.[34] As medial formations continue to shift, our concept of the text must be resituated within the operations of each new media system. Extending from the practical and theoretical ambiguity that Stanley Fish once questioned, digital media have injected a complex of new queries into the task of defining text as a conceptual category.[35] Dennis Tenen signals these new challenges to the task of definition: "Digital texts form a live lattice, a multi-dimensional grid, that connects a letter's tactile response at one's fingertips to its optic and electromagnetic traces. . . . It is impossible to give the entire structure over."[36] More directly: "Ideas about form, content, style, letter, and word—change profoundly as texts shift their confines from paper to pixel."[37] Attending to the poetics of such changes remains an open query throughout this chapter: tracking how the *ideas* change alongside revised material situations.

Working from the other end of the spectrum, it may be useful to begin instead by sketching the definitional boundaries of media. Van der Weel's model provides a succinct entry point, summarizing "medium" as "a structure consisting of a technological tool with its (explicit) technical protocols and any implicit social protocols with the function to communicate information."[38] Lisa Gitelman provides a slightly more expansive definition—and, as Craig Dworkin notes, an important pluralized formulation—in *Always Already New: Media, History, and the Data of Culture*. Gitelman writes: "Media are socially realized structures of communication, where structures include both technological forms and their associated protocols, and where communication is a cultural practice, a ritualized collocation of different people on the same mental map, sharing or engaged with popular ontologies of representation."[39] Both of these formulations are inflected by the constant flux of ever-shifting medial forms.

Reinvented as technological and social protocols within ritualized cultural practices, media are reshaped along the contours of a constantly transforming terrain. Naturally, this problem is exacerbated by the acceleration of digital media forms: as new computational platforms and distinct internet cultures emerge along the same exponential rates that continue to amass dead media and defunct sites, any study of digital media's role in communication technologies is marked by an incredibly short life expectancy. Wendy Hui Kyong Chun theorizes "the material transience of discrete information and the internet" in a foundational essay that surfaces the complications of "digital media's archival promise."[40] As Chun writes, degeneration "belies the promise of digital computers as permanent memory machines" at the same time that digital media "depends on a degeneration actively denied and repressed."[41] Along those same lines, *Textz* and the little database broadly construed are subject to the fluctuations and inconstancies of digital objects' *enduring ephemerality*.

While technical and social protocols continue to coevolve with new media releases, the infrastructural layer of standards defining the file format remains relatively stable. The infrastructural history of binary text formats, for example, reaches into the development of telegraphy and the five-bit system devised by engineer Émile Baudot in 1874.[42] This prominent standard (International Telegraph Alphabet No. 1), along with a few variants like the six-bit IBM BCD punched-card code, determined the protocol for teletype and related technologies for nearly a hundred years. Close to a century later, an updated version of this same protocol, known as the American Standard Character International Interchange (ASCII) format, was proposed in 1963 and approved as a standard in 1968. This same ASCII format has remained the relatively stable core of textual transmission in media systems, from the military origins of ARPANET to the ubiquitous presence of digital text today. ASCII character-encoding protocols still undergird the text file, despite the incessant waves of new media technologies that deploy the format and the various expansions that have been introduced by the larger character sets of Unicode. As the *Textz* manifesto has it: "electronic gadgets [are] dead media on their very release day. forget about your new kafka dvd. i already got it via sms."[43] Short Message Service (SMS), of course, is also supported by the protocol built upon backward compliance with ASCII. To this day, the textual practices of SMS, or in the gerund, *texting*, still return us to the 7-bit ASCII character set standardized in 1968.

In the purest form of ASCII, the character set is anything but neutral. The text is rigorously constrained by its letterforms: 95 printable characters in strict 7-bit ASCII; 191 in Extended ASCII, or the various ISO-8859 standards. In terms of literary stylistics, the problems brought about by the limitations of this set are legion, as even a quick perusal of *Project Gutenberg* will indicate. All passages previously formatted for italics, underline, or boldface are presented in ALL CAPS, a feature quickly disappearing amidst formats more adaptable to nuanced stylistic markup. Footnotes, pages, and other basic properties of textual formatting are either rendered impossible or creatively sidestepped. The attendant difficulties of negotiating these formatting dilemmas are demonstrated in the *Textz* database. For example, a multilingual database like *Textz* falls prey to what Daniel Pargman and Jacob Palme have termed "ASCII Imperialism."[44] This includes everything from the dollar sign encoded in the original 7-bit ASCII, whose use is obviously restricted to the United States despite its pervasive presence in code, to the absence of innumerable multilingual glyphs from a wide range of language systems beyond the United States. Because *Textz* predates the Unicode standard widely adopted in 2007, myriad glitches occur as my U.S. browser or text editor tries to parse ISO 8859–1 into ASCII or Unicode base binaries, which are fundamentally structured around ASCII. Vast swaths of French and German texts are thus rendered all but unreadable without the aid of systematic re-encoding.

Tenen amplifies the politics of encoding in his definitive study of the format, *Plain Text: A Poetics of Computation,* by "exposing the technological bias" of text within the poetics of "plain" text's technical and literary formulations.[45] Most mistakes we find in these works are not rooted in material limitations, but are rather the products of standards shaping our use, beyond the geopolitical and linguistic limitations of encoding in their moment of distribution. In this way, Tenen argues, plain text is both "a file format and a frame of mind" that requires a "computational poetics [that] breaks textuality down into its minute constituent components."[46] In league with breaking, Sterne writes, "infrastructures tend to disappear for observers, except when they break down."[47] Working with the *Textz* collection today, the infrastructural politics of encoding systems from the early internet most clearly reveal themselves not through analytics, but rather through their most minute components: the poetics of every glitch and error.[48]

Text to Textwarez

In the strictest sense, the neologism "textwarez" is purely a metaphorical invention. The .txt file format is explicitly used to demarcate unparsed textual data from the executable file, defined generally as an operable program that causes a computer to perform tasks according to encoded instructions. Put differently, the standards and protocols built into an executable software program are needed to parse the data encoded in the text file. Despite the fact that, from an operational standpoint, the same glyphs make up both *.exe* and *.txt* files, the difference could not be more important with respect to use. Incorporating human readers into the technical schematic begins to blur these sharp delineations. Jerome McGann offers a series of provocative arguments for the executable nature of text in *Radiant Textuality: Literature After the World Wide Web*. He contends that both "grapheme and phoneme are forms of thought and not facts—not character data but parsed character data, or 'data' that already function within an instructional field."[49] This line of thinking is intended to counter a blind spot that the digital humanities often have regarding the "algorithmic character of traditional text."[50] Of course, as Gitelman reminds us, "raw data" is an oxymoron.[51] Data is always shaped and constructed by the systems of classification and interpretation that determine what constitutes "data" in the first place. All parsed data becomes information.

In McGann's view, all texts contain both protocols of figuration (a graphic representation) and instructional options (for readers navigating the text). If we are to draw computational metaphors between readers and texts, we must admit that the instructional field is parsing its reader, not the other way around. In line with *Textz*'s emphasis on the transformative potential of textwarez, McGann argues that "readers do this as a matter of course as they move through a text and make *themselves* the measure of a process of transformation."[52] Poet and scholar Tan Lin presents a more radical variant of this position across a series of works that deploy his theorizations of "Disco as Operating System." Lin relates disco to a wide range of cultural forms, including the text, writing that "such a programming language was once called literature."[53] It is this operating system that writes its reader in a play of affect programmatically exercised by the text file itself. "Disco is not, as is mistakenly thought, an explosion of sound onto the dance floor but an implosion of preprogrammed dance moves into a head."[54] Lin's alignment of disco with an operating system finds its corollary in *Textz*'s approach to text files as pirated software, as textwarez. In both, the metaphor of executability is built into the user, rather than the text itself.

This, it seems, is the core of the *Textz* project. To quote again from the manifesto: "we have been moving from content to discontent, collecting scripts and viruses, writing programs and bots, dealing with textz as warez, as executables." Lütgert proposes a more technically precise sense of the executable text file in a series of works that radiate out from the *Textz* archive. The first of these was generated in response to a cease-and-desist letter received by *Textz* from a lawyer representing the press Suhrkamp in the summer of 2002. At the time, a scandal was brewing in Germany over conservative writer Martin Walser's book *Tod Eines Kritikers* (Death of a critic), a work of "deep incompetence" that was widely critiqued for its anti-Semitic caricatures.[55] Anticipating further rebuke for publishing the book, Suhrkamp made the mistake of sending out PDF review copies of a file titled "walser.pdf" to various news organizations who they hoped would issue favorable appraisals of the project before the book went to press. In what was a novel development at the time, these files leaked online, prompting Suhrkamp to scramble to remove them from distribution. In an activist gesture of resistance to the press's attempt to sanitize the book's anti-Semitic content and its attempt at crisis management, *Textz* put up a file entitled "walser.pdf" on its site. In actuality, the file in question contained a PDF of Bruce Sterling's *The Hacker Crackdown,* a nonfiction work on the history of phreaking (that is to say, illegally accessing the telephone system) and cracking: a tongue-in-cheek intertextual riposte to Suhrkamp's ham-fisted attempts at crackdown. In spite of this, Surhkamp's legal threats were issued, suggesting that the claimants had not bothered to open the file. In response to this series of events, Lütgert crafted a file entitled "walser.php.txt." It contained a simple

PHP script (a general-purpose scripting language geared toward web development) that had the sole purpose of reconstructing Walser's *Tod Eines Kritikers* in full plain text (and "plaintext") ASCII format under the title "walser.txt."[56]

Here, finally, the textwarez metaphor meets the realization of the executable text file. Lütgert's cryptographic project would be the start of a series of *Textz* initiatives exploring encoding formats under the guise of copyleft politics. This ambitious program—operating somewhere between text and warez, from "walser.pdf" to "walser.php.txt" to "walser.php" to "walser.txt"—remains far more compelling than the now-familiar genre of dispute over copyright of an errant file online. The PHP script might be considered a legally protected piece of software released under a General Public License. Its string of glyphs in no way resembles Walser's text and presents, in a sense, an entirely original piece of writing:

```
$z.="64000a20212728292c2d2e2f30313233343536373
8393a3b3f414243444546474849 4a4b4c4d4e4f";
$z.="505152535455565758595a616263646566676869 6a
6b6c6d6e6f707172737475767778797 a849293";
$z.="9697a9b4c4d6dcdfe0e1e4e7e8e9edf1f3f4f6fbfc
0c022635474a40460a373c48504351103b5147";
[. . .]
```

Textz dubiously maintains in the script's release notes that hosting and distributing the PHP file would be well within the confines of the law. Only the execution of the script, producing *Tod Eines Kritikers* as walser.txt, would result in a breach of intellectual property. By enciphering the text within an executable code, the work calls both TXT and PHP formats into question. At the hexadecimal level, both files would be unreadable to an unaided human agent. Accessing the content thus requires that these formats be displayed, transmitted, and processed by a range of platforms and operating systems. By introducing an auxiliary step for rendering the text legible to human readers, "walser.php" concretizes the process of encoding and decoding that enables textual transmission on information networks while eluding easy classifications of text and executable. Beyond this, the decision to encode the text as a .php file of illegible glyphs can be understood as a political intervention insisting that this particular book's content should not be made readable, bringing us back to the human reader at the *Textz* interface, whom we might now add back into this circuit of format poetics.

Information Does Not Want to Be Free

Working against nascent formulations of "The Californian Ideology," *Textz* refused the heroics of digital piracy from its inception, contending that "information does not want to be free. in fact it is absolutely free of will, a constant flow of signs of lives which are permanently being turned into commodities and transformed into commercial content. http://textz.com is not part of the information business."[57] By negation, *Textz* grounds Stewart Brand's famous slogan "information wants to be free" in the particularities of information theory and digital communication. The "walser.php" script provides a clear demonstration of information as functional parsed data—text put to computational use. Every text can also traffic as machine-readable code, and vice versa. If the "information business" is built on the demand for knowledge in a neoliberal economy, *Textz* is an artwork that explicitly counters the "free trade" of transparent information. Instead, the collection is mobilized as warez to perform the interplay of compression, data formats, and the poetics of digital communication at large. In both form and content, the collection refuses neoliberal currents that direct the constant flow of data toward profit. Instead, *Textz* actively devalues the corpus with difficult texts that demand reflexive reading.

Following on the inaugural publication of "walser.php," *Textz* would release a series of more complex conceptual games that drew together formats of encryption and decryption under the sign of textwarez. To begin with, in the footer to "walser.php.txt," the project also includes a short script called "makewalser.php." The PHP script's function was to easily generate a similarly executable PHP script for any text file. That is to say, any writing stored in a plaintext file format could be re-encoded as an executable file. This addition, in just eighty-one lines of code, reconfigures the entire *Textz* collection as potentially executable PHP script. The plaintext file contains the same input alphabet used by HTTP protocols and software programs. This infrathin play (to use Marcel Duchamp's term for the most minute shade of difference) between text file and executable script highlights the interoperability of glyphs in fluid text formats.

The segment of "makewalser.php" that generates a new header for any file makes the interchangeability of the *Textz* collection clear:

```
header("content-type: text/plain");
[. . .]

echo " $self v1.01 (includes make$self)\n";
echo " this script generates the plain ascii
version\n";
echo " of \"$title\" by $author.\n";
echo " it can be redistributed and/or modified
under\n";
echo " the terms of the gnu general public
license\n";
echo " as published by the free software
foundation,\n";
echo " but may not be run without written
permission\n";
echo " by $owner.\n";
```

The "echo"-language construct outputs each of these lines into the header of a newly minted "makewalser.php.txt" file. Using the double extension ".php.txt" is another winking nod to the executable character of textwarez. The file is both script and text. If you remove the ".txt" extension, the PHP script can execute. By constellating variables for the PHP script ($self) alongside the author, title, and owner, the program accommodates bibliographic data within its translation scheme. Any text in the collection, from Gibson's "Agrippa" to Deleuze's "Postscript," can be thrown into this scheme, with radically altered results for literary interpretation. This is the fundamental challenge that software poses to literary study: all potential instances of transformation overcome the actualized use of the script on any given text. Reading is contingent on how the text materializes. In one of the few published articles on *Textz,* Inke Arns writes that "the poetry of codeworks lies not only in their textual form, but rather in the knowledge that they have the potential to be executed."[58] Returning us to Saper's claims for sociopoetics, these codeworks prioritize networked methods of database transmission beyond "their textual form." Following the development of Lütgert's *Textz* codeworks offers possible points of departure for addressing a poetics of media formats. Olga Goriunova notes:

The decision of considering walser.php, walser.pl or any other text generated with makewalser.php something that can be run through a Perl or PHP interpreter is entirely up to the reader's viewpoint and imagination. The text may just as well be considered literary works of their own, resembling concrete poetry and conceptual art. As a matter of fact, nobody can rule out the possibility that a text file of, say, the fairytale "Cinderella" executes as algorithmic sourcecode on some programming language interpreter or compiler and generates de Sade's "120 Days of Sodom" as its output.[59]

Later in 2002, Lütgert released a work entitled "pngreader," a project that extends beyond the "walser.php.txt" release to apply the same operational concept to a variety of potential formats. Navigating an intuitive interface, the user of "pngreader" may encrypt any standard file format into a multicolored PNG image (see Figure 1.8). Or rather, as the program's readme.txt explains, the script includes a "pngwriter()" function that may "restore" a lost PNG image from any given file format:

> pngreader is a free, open source php script that reads png images, parses the input according to a defined set of rules, and displays the results. . . . the output format will normally be plain text, even though the program can return a variety of content types, including archives, images, music, video, and more. png images can be created with most graphic editors (a sample gallery can be found at http://pngreader.gnutenberg .net/gallery). pngreader also includes a currently unused function named pngwriter() which is able to recover lost images. given the output of pngreader(), it will restore the original png.[60]

These "lost images" reverse the direction by which information is usually encoded into an encrypted image: the image is a visual cipher for its hidden text rather than a conduit for text to hide within. In this way, "pngreader" brings into fruition Jorge Luis Borges's imagining of the infinite-monkey theorem in the universal archives of the library of Babel, given sufficient time and input to a typewriter.[61] Its readme.txt file asks: "to paraphrase a famous question: how long will an ape have to play around with photoshop until he

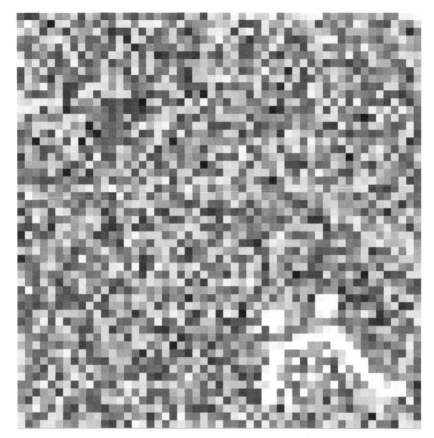

Figure 1.8. An encrypted image of Jorge Luis Borges's short story "The Library of Babel," produced using Sebastian Lütgert's "pngreader," which can encrypt any standard file format into a multi-colored PNG image.

draws a png that returns borges' library of babel? the answer is: it has already been done (http://pngreader.gnutenberg.net/gallery /babel.png)." Encoded texts and artworks include Borges's "The Library of Babel," Adorno's *Minima Moralia,* Public Enemy's "Burn Hollywood Burn," and the PDF of Michael Hardt and Antonio Negri's *Empire,* among other "recovered" PNG images.

These carefully plotted media-format poetics, playfully operating on the interface between file types and the transcoding of culture on the internet, question our relationship to data displayed in the browser. As Florian Cramer has written, "pngreader thus allows artists to create images which, accidentally of course, might also be read as certain pieces of literature."[62] Conceiving images as works of literature—or executable PHP scripts as concrete poetry or conceptual art—brings us to the crux of the enigma that *Textz* presents. Where might we draw the line between text and textwarez? Or, following on recent studies of generative image platforms like Stable Diffusion and Dall-E, perhaps, within the pngreader project we might glimpse a way in which these lines might be erased altogether, anticipating what Hannes Bajohr has termed "operative ekphrasis": the collapse of inherited models of text–image distinction in the multidimensional space of neural network architectures.[63] In this way, the lost images of pngreader gesture toward weird futures of media transmutability that are only now coming to light.

The Conceptual Crisis of Private Property as a Crisis in Practice

Completing this cycle of cryptographic projects, consider a final work: "The Conceptual Crisis of Private Property as a Crisis in Practice" by Robert Luxemburg (a pseudonym for Lütgert).[64] Its lengthy title is drawn from Hardt and Negri's *Empire* in an allusion to the site's success at cracking the encrypted file before Harvard University Press was able to publish the first printing of the book. Like the response *Textz* produced for *Death of a Critic,* this work comes in three parts: "crisis.php" (a decoding script), "crisis.txt" (an explanatory readme file), and "crisis.png" (a desktop screenshot that contains encrypted data). Plugging "crisis.png" into "crisis.php" according to the instructions given in "crisis.txt," the user is able to reconstruct the entirety of cyberpunk author Neal Stephenson's novel *Cryptonomicon*. A clue to guide the user is concealed within the screen capture, which spells out the novel's title in icons along the bottom of the image (Figure 1.9). Stephenson's novel represents a deliberate act of editorial selection. Its narrative fictionalizes an alternate history of the very cryptography at play in "The Conceptual Crisis," while the book itself was also subjected to U.S. export restrictions due to trade secrets embedded within a cryptographic algorithm featured in the text. "The Conceptual Crisis" merges these layers into a conceptual game that incorporates speculative fiction, real-world circulation politics, encoding formats, and an elaborate ruse of steganographic play.

Whereas previous works like "walser.php" and "pngreader" vis-

Figure 1.9. Robert Luxemburg's "The Conceptual Crisis of Private Property as a Crisis in Practice" (2003). This screen capture enables the user to reconstruct the entirety of Neal Stephenson's novel *Cryptonomicon.*

ibly displayed their cryptographic function, this work presents a new steganographic impulse: the text is hidden in plain sight. "The Conceptual Crisis" calls up these contexts in its play between quotidian image, illicit data transfer, and secretive encoding hiding plaintext. To accompany the artwork, a grandiose "law" is proposed that undergirds each of the previously described projects: "Any digital piece of intellectual property can be transformed into any other digital piece of intellectual property with a relatively short and simple shell script."[65] Issued alongside this law, a very low-resolution image of Walter Benjamin (begging to be unpacked) is proven to harbor the data for a cracked version of Final Cut Pro 4, a highly sought after video-editing suite at the time, which is itself presented as a *.mov* file. The layers of masking constellate software with text, and formats with poetics: an image of a famous writer is simultaneously a cracked software program masquerading as a movie. Steganography can be thought of as another form of compression or encoding, it is a container technology that transmits a given input into a desired output for use. Decompressing these files calls the entire collection

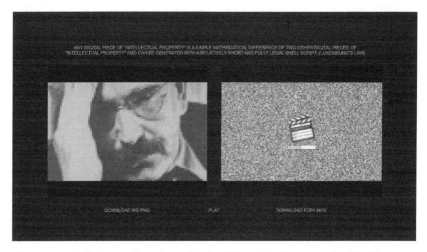

ANY DIGITAL PIECE OF "INTELLECTUAL PROPERTY" IS A SIMPLE MATHEMATICAL DIFFERENCE OF TWO OTHER DIGITAL PIECES OF
"INTELLECTUAL PROPERTY" AND CAN BE GENERATED WITH A RELATIVELY SHORT AND FULLY LEGAL SHELL SCRIPT (LUXEMBURG'S LAW)

DOWNLOAD W8.PNG   PLAY   DOWNLOAD FCP4.MOV

Figure 1.10. A link to a free download of Final Cut Pro 4 embedded in a representation of "Luxemburg's Law," which claims that "any digital piece of intellectual property can be transformed into any other digital piece of intellectual property with a relatively short and simple shell script." After downloading both files, the Walter Benjamin image decrypts pirated software. Captured via Internet Archive.

into view as interchangeable, mutable code, a collection parsing its reader. Or, following Benjamin's most famous notes on decompression: for the collector of digital files, it is "not that they come alive in him; it is he who lives in them."[66]

The conclusion to this steganographic work, as it interfaces with the *Textz* collection, remains unpublished. Following extended litigation with Suhrkamp, which included a warrant for Lütgert's arrest, the site went static in early 2004. In 2005, an ASCII rendering of the date "5/23/06" appeared on the *Textz* front page, promising updates that never arrived. More recently, Lütgert has written about future plans for the site: "For amateur cryptographers or Internet art historians, the most interesting find may be DePNG, short for 'DePNG Probably Nothing Generator,' developed between 2005 and 2008. The corresponding re-implementation of textz.com would have no longer hosted books, but only a gallery of cover images. A highly obfuscated script to transform the covers into full books would have been offered on the DePNG companion site."[67] Lütgert illustrates how this process would have operated. Each plaintext file in the *Textz* collection was to be embedded in a PNG "cover" for the text, which could be activated (and decrypted) by a code stored in the "spine" through the use of DePNG. Simulating a library or the remediated virtual bookshelf featured in a range of commercial e-books platforms, this unrealized *Textz* project points its user back to the codex even while it reveals pervasive mechanisms of digital encoding. Through a complex set of procedures, the final transformation of *Textz* would render every plaintext file as an executable steganographic PNG image. To read any of the works in the collection, the user would first be called on to recognize the historical, legal, and technical protocols that structure textual transmission on the internet. They would then have to participate in a playful enactment of format poetics to access the text.

Lütgert's approach to textwarez thus sets forth a conceptual poetics for digital objects as a *mise en abyme* of encoding protocols and file formats. Sterne reminds us: "All formats presuppose particular formations of infrastructure with their own codes, protocols, limits, and affordances."[68] By revealing, distorting, and reconfiguring the limits of these protocols, *Textz* furnishes a compelling direction for the poetics of digital scholarship. These poetics emerge from interpenetrating actions of framing, constellating, contextualizing, and transmitting. There is a famous, if reductive, diagram from the annals of 1990s net.art history:

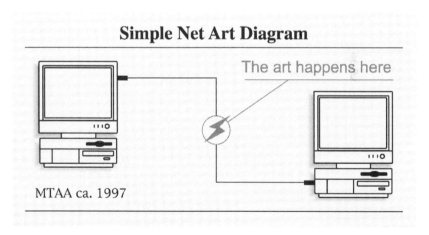

Simple Net Art Diagram

The art happens here

MTAA ca. 1997

Figure 1.11. MTAA (M. River & T. Whid Art Associates), *Simple Net Art Diagram* (1997). Keeping lines of transmission open, in 2011 the collective announced: "Using a Creative Commons Attribution 2.5 Generic (CC BY 2.5) license and general lazy disregard, MTAA give our 1997 artwork *The Simple Net Art Diagram (SNAD)* over to academics, artists and the general public for re-purposing. We hand it over carte blanche. Have at it."

Transmission is everything. It should be noted that this diagram condenses a fantastically intricate communications circuit into two nodes and a single line of connection. Derived from the rigorous network conceptualism of the 1990s, this aesthetic of relationality reconfigures Saper's sociopoetics toward digital access and sharing—or, for that matter, piracy and open-source movements—periodizing the work both technically and aesthetically. Indeed, Lütgert writes, "the nineties of the net are over."

Given contemporary trends toward a more decentralized web in the 2020s, the possibility remains that we might yet reimagine digital practices through dreams and failures nested within the 1990s of the net. Simultaneously deploying a radical politics of distribution, new software for old media genres, and a visualization of "invisible" compression and transcoding processes, *Textz* directs us to a new horizon for media poetics. In so doing, it necessitates a corresponding model for scholarship on the internet: one that attends to the limits of collection and distribution, questioning the file itself alongside its use. Presenting a little database within elaborate models to highlight the demographics, politics, and technics of its dispersion, *Textz* is the lost digital humanities project that continues to anticipate endeavors to follow and new futures for poetic computation. In an interlude following this chapter, I propose a scholarly textual mechanism that follows *Textz* in ways that the essay cannot attempt to pursue. In a generous reading, the chapter may serve as a prelude to this gesture.

Interlude 1
EXE TXT

If texts are rendered executable in encounters with readers, how might readers hack into their code? Lisa Samuels and Jerome McGann designate the type of expanded scholarly poetics presented in these interludes as a mode of "deformance," a practice-based approach that moves "beyond conceptual analysis into the kinds of knowledge involved in performative operations."[1] In their foundational essay "Deformance and Interpretation," they begin with a consideration of Emily Dickinson's proposal to read poems backwards, line by line, as a tactic for releasing hidden vectors of meaning within a work. By reworking the material of the poem, they contend, new knowledge might emerge from its tactical rearrangement. If this simple operation contains the potential for "rethinking our resources of interpretation," then *Textz* and the little databases I examine all offer substantial inventories prepared for modes of interpretive poetics.[2] Other practitioners have used more expansive terms for this kind of activity: "creative scholarship," "critical making," "applied poetry," "qualitative digital humanities," and, most simply, "remix," (among others).[3] Trained in the creative forms of critical knowledge building in the expanded lineage of *L=A=N=G=U=A=G=E,* discussed in the following chapter, I prefer to group my creative scholarly interventions in this book under the heading of "media poetics."

This "continuation of poetry by other means," in Charles Bernstein's formulation, is emphatically prepared for questions of meaning-making in experimental forms and formats that appear online.[4] The collection subordinates the "content" of text and theory to the poetics of transmission, encryption, and format. In alignment with Bernstein, media archeologist Lori Emerson emphasizes the illuminative capacities of media poetics within the play of reading and writing alongside networks and algorithms that also read and write their users.[5] Given the contingent specificities of format and context in the play of "readingwriting" the criticism of digital objects, this project invokes strands in the digital humanities that turn not only to data visualization and information design for interpretative inroads, but also to experimental art and poetry. Further, the project contends that these modes can work in cooperation, given the right conditions. *Textz* navigates a path between code and concept, collection and dispersion, text and software—all within a coherent set of aesthetic and political aims. In the following interlude, I explore a scholarly mode that might deploy one vector of *Textz*'s poetics of the variable format.

When I began conceptualizing the preceding chapter, one outrageous idea occurred to me. What if I were to exclusively deploy texts within the *Textz* collection to theorize the site? With its transhistorical assemblage of media theory, internet criticism, and related readings, this seemed a productive gesture. How might a collection theorize itself? Or, how could I develop an approach that would allow *Textz* to "speak for itself," as it were? This idea was abandoned for a number of reasons: institutional, representational, and critical alike. The gains afforded by studying the site's operations from the present seemed to outweigh the benefit of inhabiting the discourse of the collection itself. At least this seemed to be the case for the chapter proper, which by necessity focuses more on the contexts and techniques of the site than on the works that it contained. This decision also closed off opportunities for close and sustained reading of specific texts within the collection (tactics to which I'll return in chapter 4). Given these limitations, I began to consider a scholarly poetics project that might accomplish the same task beyond the book you're reading.

This work, entitled *EXE TXT*, endeavors to perform the collection's self-theorization in both format and process. It includes a final document (as both a plain text file and print-on-demand book), a python script, and an archival record of the complete set of *Textz* textwarez. My intervention includes a text that was constructed with a relatively simple python script that extracts sentences containing variants of the strings "text" and "software" from the complete set of textwarez (including multilingual strings like *texte, testo,* and *texto*).

In this way, it queries how *text* might meet *software* within the works that *Textz* hosts. The complete python script is as follows:

```python
import re
import sys
import random

def write_lines(filename, data_lines):
  with open(filename, 'w') as f:
    f.write(' '.join(data_lines))
    f.write('\n')

def match_word(text, word):
  return re.search(r'\b{0}\b'.format(word), text)

def split_sentences(filename):
  with open(filename, 'r') as f:
    data = f.read()
  data = data.replace('\n', ' ')
  parsed = re.split(r'([.!?])', data)

  text = parsed[0::2]
  ending = parsed[1::2]

  return [t+e for t, e in zip(text, ending)]

if __name__ == '__main__':
  if len(sys.argv) < 3:
    print('usage: {0} input_file word'.
    format(sys.argv[0]))
    sys.exit()
  filename = sys.argv[1]
  word = sys.argv[2]
  basename, ext = filename.rsplit('.', 1)
  outfile = "{0}_{1}.{2}".format(basename, word,
  ext)

  lines = split_sentences(filename)
  target_lines = [line.strip() for line in lines
  if match_word(line, word)]
  random.shuffle(target_lines)
  write_lines(outfile, target_lines)
```

Figure 1i.1. *EXE TXT* perfect bound paperback book (6 in. × 9 in.; 242 pp.); image captured by "Library of Artistic Print on Demand" (apod.li/exe-txt).

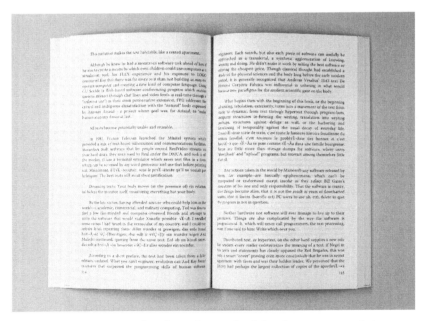

Figure 1i.2. *EXE TXT* perfect bound paperback book, open spread; image captured by "Library of Artistic Print on Demand" (apod.li/exe-txt).

The output of this script was then edited for coherence and consistency within the generic conventions of the academic monograph. The line breaks are mine, as well as certain minor typographical adjustments. Nevertheless, the aim is to have the collection speak for itself as clearly as possible—to offer a poetic intervention via code that surfaces otherwise unseen connections in the little database. It is presented in plaintext ASCII format as another work of textwarez, which I first published with the internet publisher Gauss PDF in 2015, adding its critical form into conversation with the experimental poetry projects published there. Like all linear textual formats, it presents one narrative trajectory among the limitless potential routes a user might follow through the database.

However, it is also a little database, or inventory of effects, in its own right. The reader/user is invited to repeat this operation on the *Textz* corpus using the enclosed python script, both of which are included in the publication *EXE TXT*. Simple terminal instructions for executing the python script on the corpus are contained in a "readme.exe.txt" file. More than a statement of authorial invitation, it is a prepared command that initiates a program called textwarez for any user of the book. The final two lines of the python script read "random.shuffle(target_lines) / write_lines(outfile, target_lines)." With these two lines of code, the extracted sentences are randomized and written in succession to a new text file. You may select your own terms for generating your own random-access *Textz* study. Or you may rewrite the program or throw it out altogether to generate something new from the corpus. Offered as both a media poetics of *Textz* and a tool for future play, *EXE TXT* hopes to render itself variable, encompassing any subsequent texts derived from its mechanism.

See: *EXT TXT* (2015).

CHAPTER 2
Distributing Services
Periodical Preservation and *Eclipse*

From the first issue, *L=A=N=G=U=A=G=E* magazine (1978–1981) was figured as a project in recovering "out-of-print books and unpublished manuscripts."[1] This description should strike a note of dissonance in the chorus of common knowledge concerning the influential little magazine edited by Charles Bernstein and Bruce Andrews, which is best known for shaping the emergent poetics of the Language writing community. Indeed, among the dozens of frameworks that Bernstein presents in his essay "The Expanded Field of L=A=N=G=U=A=G=E" for the *Routledge Companion to Experimental Literature,* there is no mention of archival or bibliographic practices in even an expansive view of the poetics within and beyond the magazine.[2] However, just by skimming along the surface of the issues today, the reader is struck by the density of bibliographic notes on access and availability. Among the position pieces, poetic reviews, and short experimental essays that characterize the bulk of the magazine, one finds offers from the "L=A=N=G=U=A=G=E Distributing Service," a kind of door-to-door photocopy delivery mechanism for out-of-print works. A catalog of books and magazines could be ordered for fifty cents from the home address of editor Charles Bernstein, who ran this (re)print-on-demand service through a neighborhood Xerox machine. Beyond the formal inventions of the poetics articulated within *L=A=N=G=U=A=G=E,* we might consider this archival distribution system as the most forward-looking gesture of the magazine, anticipating the digital modes of circulation that would come to define editorial practices in poetics nearly fifty years later.[3] In this chapter, I consider how the distributing practices of this little magazine model the forms of access and preservation that drive the little database, all with a focus on making out-of-print poetic materials available from the jump.

In the first issue of *LANGUAGE* (February 1978, see the previous endnote on the tactical deletion of the equal sign for a more inclusive text), the reader notes that David Melnick's *Pcoet,* first published by G.A.W.K. press just three years prior, could be photocopied by the Distributing Service for $3.[4] Similarly out-of-print titles by Barbara Baracks, Johanna Drucker, Lyn Hejinian, Bernadette Mayer, and Hannah Weiner, among others, were on offer in Xerox format from the distributing service. The full run of Ron Silliman's foundational *Tottel's* poetry newsletter was announced in both issue 4 of *LANGUAGE* and issue 17 of *Tottel's.* A slim catalogue for these republished works opens with a statement by Bernstein, Silliman, and Andrews highlighting the ephemerality of titles within experimental writing circuits of the late 1970s:

> Even when published, writing we wish to read often goes out of print with dismaying rapidity—closing off a dialogue. Out-of-print and unpublished works may still circulate among a limited circle of friends. Here, we hope to sustain that dialogue, and expand that circle.[5]

While one node in the "expanded field" of *LANGUAGE* may have re-formatted the intensive qualities of this "dialogue," the project of the magazine extended into a network of issues related to preservation, distribution, and accessibility. Copies of magazines like *Big Sky, Hundred Posters,* and *Toothpick* were also listed in the inventory. The catalog included scores of such entries, most of which have never been "properly" republished. For those who follow the distributing services of Craig Dworkin, however, these titles should sound familiar. In fact, all of the above-mentioned works can be found on *Eclipse,* Dworkin's roving little database of facsimile images of rare small-press publications. Not only does the site "sustain the dialogue" begun under the sign of *LANGUAGE,* but it also works to "expand the circle" of readers and users into the present.

The connection of *Eclipse* to *LANGUAGE* is indicated early in the history of the *Eclipse* site. On the front page, the site is currently described as "a free on-line archive focusing on digital facsimiles of the most radical small-press writing from the last quarter century."[6] This quarter century is marked with astrological precision. An Internet Archive capture of the site dated February 19, 2003, notes that *Eclipse* "will launch in February, marking the 25th anniversary of *LANGUAGE* magazine." For a site named after the alignment of the sun and moon, the launch date is anything but incidental.[7] In point of fact, the site had been in operation for nearly a year preceding the promised launch in February of 2003.

The fluidity of websites affords this kind of ludic play with the moment of publication: in this instance, the temporal emendation intensifies the historical engagements that guide the collection. Of course, "the complete run of the journal *LANGUAGE*" was also included in the earliest iterations of the site. Since then, in private correspondence, Dworkin has noted that the *LANGUAGE* magazine files have accounted for roughly half of the site's usage from the site's inception. This little magazine is both the most accessed object in the collection and the evident cause of the emergence of *Eclipse* on a quarter century delay.

In many ways, this convergence was scripted into the foundation of *Eclipse*. The site has been described as a corrective to the trend that Dworkin notes in the opening line of his "Language Poetry" entry for *The Greenwood Encyclopedia of American Poetry*: "The discrepancy between the number of people who hold an opinion about Language Poetry and those who have actually read Language Poetry is perhaps greater than for any other literary phenomenon of the later twentieth century."[8] This paradoxical situation is likely the result of two difficulties: not only the discursive difficulty inherent in the debates surrounding Language Poetry and poetics, but also the difficulty involved in accessing primary documents in experimental poetry before sites like *Eclipse* made them readily available to anyone with an internet connection.[9] Reasoning through this dilemma for scholarship on Language Writing, Dworkin notes: "'Language poetry,' in short, became simply whatever was published by a handful of specific presses and journals. . . . For anyone who wanted to pursue these talismanic publications, the situation was frustrating; the 'little magazines' of modernism—a century old—were easier to find in libraries than any of these journals which had been published only a few years earlier."[10] Correcting this frustration, *Eclipse* is comprised of the "tantalizing—and seemingly *de rigueur*—catalogs of fugitive titles" that came to define Language Poetry in its most common formulations.[11] Continuing the accessibility platform of the *LANGUAGE* Distributing Service, *Eclipse* affords the sustenance of this dialog using contemporary digital formats. It performs this distribution from a scholarly perspective that looks back over the last quarter century while looking forward to a media poetics of the present. Dworkin describes this process as the "Janus-faced logic" of avant-garde archives, "which look in two directions as they realize their own position: they conservatively index the past, and they index the future with a wagered risk."[12]

As of this writing, the complete title index to *Eclipse* links to 301 entries in the collection. Of these titles, twenty-eight direct the user to a little magazine. The published artifacts for these entries range from a single issue (or nonissue, in the case of the index to *This* magazine, edited by Robert Grenier and Barrett Watten) to fifty issues (in the case of Lyn Hejinian's *Tuumba* chapbooks, which are pointedly listed as a periodical on *Eclipse*). When I began work on this chapter, there were less than half as many works in the collection. In 2009, the year that Dworkin wrote his site-defining article, there were even fewer. Shifting away from the stable collections marking defunct sites like *Textz.com,* the chapters that follow all examine little databases in a state of flux. *Eclipse* is ongoing, some twenty years later. As an associate editor of the site, I can attest to at least a dozen digitization projects that are forthcoming as of this writing. Each of these additions would dramatically alter any stable reading of the collection. Additionally, the site has already been hosted by two universities and one independent server. Future changes remain unpredictable. Just as the scarcity of primary documents defining Language Poetry and poetics continues to pose a challenge to scholarship, the ephemerality and flux of *Eclipse* produces its own set of complications to scholarly readings of this type of archival cultural production online. To write about the little database is to make do with materials that may well have altered dramatically by the time these words make it to press; it is a process of contingent reading, given a set of conditions at the moment of inscription.

Dworkin's own critical reflections on *Eclipse,* published in a paper titled "Hypermnesia" (a medical term for exactingly precise memory), characterize the destruction necessitated by archival digitization: "Once again, the twin impulses of the digital archive—to preserve and to present, to reproduce and to distribute—are at fundamental odds with one another."[13] These impulses are caught between the compression inherent to digital formats scalable to online distribution, on the one side, and accurate facsimile reproduction, on the other. Despite higher-resolution images or more perfect digital facsimiles, the archival paradox outlined by Jacques Derrida in *Archive Fever* remains acute: these digital objects are yet fetishes for the material memories that rely on the creative destruction of archival holdings.[14] In Dworkin's formulation, the tension between preservation and distribution in digital formats can be summarized as follows:

> Part of what the archive seeks to conserve with its insistence on representing the pagination and typography of the originals is precisely what a digital archive necessarily loses: the facture and material specificity of the book or printed document as an object.[15]

However, he reminds the reader:

> In the context of "new media," this focus on the "old(-fashioned) media" of the page and the book may seem quaint or retrograde, but those attachments are not, in fact, romantically nostalgic. They are coldly semiotic.[16]

The "coldly semiotic" register that Dworkin invokes is his own brand of "radical formalism" that attends to the bibliographic and material significations of the social text as published document.[17] In this methodological vein, Dworkin pursues "the closest of close readings," where "form must always necessarily signify but any particular signification is historically contingent."[18] While these contingencies already flourish on the page, they multiply exponentially through the variable mechanisms of archival digitization and networked dispersion. As new layers of mediation emerge, the rematerialized object requires renewed attention to the interplay of analog and digital counterparts.

For example, Dworkin highlights the "pointed role" that fanged staples play in Lorenzo Thomas' *Dracula* or the fruitful vestigial flaps of Bernstein's *Disfrutes* in the edition done by Potes and Poets Press.[19] Both haunt the digital images, despite requiring recourse to bind each digital capture to the work's material substrate. Even as Dworkin focuses on the persistence of bibliographic codes and material texts in the online archive, *Eclipse* continues to build its own system of codes in its unique processes of digitization and dispersion. This chapter concludes at the opposite end of the spectrum, working from these same sorts of digital files to enter into what Alessandro Ludovico, Florian Cramer, Silvio Lorusso, and others have termed a "post-digital" publication.[20] In this reversal, the image files and the website itself work as a new bibliographic system to generate print artifacts of the page and of the book, given the generative capabilities of stylistic transfer with large language models. In this respect, it serves as a preparatory argument for the contingent interchange of digital objects, little databases, and material artifacts generated in the present.

In this chapter, I prepare a reading of *Eclipse* by outlining the resistances that the site poses to computational analysis and systematic criticism while pointing to meaningful futures of digital remix and correspondent opportunities for historical play in material republication. To maintain the specificity of these questions, the explorations of this chapter cluster around the *Eclipse* edition of *LANGUAGE* magazine. First, and most germane to *LANGUAGE*, I explore the relations and disconnections between periodical studies and the study of online collections. Given that this little database is centered on collecting a range of little magazines, these relations are most clearly rendered in the context of *Eclipse*. The site offers a singular glimpse into the various ways in which an archival internet publication might overlap with the bibliographic registers tracked by periodical studies. For instance, print magazines present a clear delineation between published issues. In sharp relief, we might ask how a periodical scholar would describe the variable release patterns of a little database. Further, we might complicate concerns around notions of periodical preservation. If *Eclipse* is designated as an "online archive" to preserve certain print artifacts of radical small-press writing from the last quarter century, what might it mean to preserve *Eclipse*? Put differently, what (or who) maintains the ephemeral archive of a little database, and by what repertoires? How might we read *LANGUAGE* as a variable artifact carried along by each new capture within these ongoing patterns of transformation and transformative modes of preservation?

Finally, this chapter explores the resistance presented by graphic-image formats for text on the internet. Unlike Google Books, *Eclipse* primarily offers facsimile images for human readers. How might these file formats speak to the collection? From the GIF (graphics interchange format) files that encode *LANGUAGE* to the PDF (portable document format) files that present reading copies, each format enacts a new set of bibliographic questions and localized transformations. Following questions of archival periodicity, a reading of *LANGUAGE* on *Eclipse* might begin with the digitization itself: opening with low-resolution GIF captures, moving to its intermittent external preservation by the Internet Archive, and concluding with the periodicity of these captures. From the outset, this chapter maintains that the opposite direction would be just as valid. Again, there is a kind of hermeneutic circle to reading digital objects. One might begin at scale by reading the universal standard of a file format down into the localized transformation on any given file. Or, in the opposite direction, we might just as well start with the local context of an individual work to scale up to the broadest context of networked collections. All directions are valid, while each exploration is contingent upon a moment of access and the illuminative capacities that any given scholarly narrative might afford. Articulating what happens at these decisive narratological junctures holds a key to navigating literary history inscribed on an ever-changing digital landscape.

Periodical Poetics

In *Modernism in the Magazines: An Introduction,* Robert Scholes and Clifford Wulfman track changes in the history of periodical studies across the twentieth century. Unsurprisingly, this study begins and ends with Ezra Pound. From Pound's characterization of "the free magazine or the impractical or fugitive magazine" in the article "Small Magazines" to a series of articles published in *The New Age* under the unrealized title "Studies in Contemporary Mentality," Scholes and Wulfman outline how Pound inaugurates "the serious study of periodicals as a way into modern culture."[21] Tackling problems of classification in the periodical, Pound characterizes his approach as that of a "simple-hearted anthropologist" sorting periodical specimens into different generic boxes.[22] In contrast to the methods of ideological critique and genre studies that remain central to Pound's periodical criticism, Scholes and Wulfman chart the movement of the field "from genres to database."[23] Their account highlights "a different approach, made feasible by the digital resources becoming available to scholars, . . . a move from ideological or cultural constructions to the collection of data."[24]

Drawn from a chapter titled "Rethinking Modernist Magazines: From Genres to Database," the argument is nevertheless concluded by an appendix comprised of a hundred-page reconstruction of Pound's "Studies in Contemporary Mentality," republishing a complete series of his column in *The New Age*. Indeed, through Pound, the critical voice reigns, even as the database attempts distributed scholarship. Not unlike the archival impulses that drive *Eclipse,* Scholes and Wulfman collect and republish Pound even while arguing for new modes of digital humanities scholarship in periodical studies. This tension among issues of archival scholarship, the categorical imperatives of analytical data, and the long-standing genre classifications of cultural criticism arise, they argue, from the "enormously intertextual affair" of reading a magazine.[25] While pointing to an enormously intertextual affair is one thing, enacting intertextual formats as scholarship is another entirely. The focus on critique, inaugurated by Pound and carried out in their pages, distills reading little magazines to one mode of understanding, built on the negation of all other forms. Here, as elsewhere in *The Little Database,* my hope is to point toward an expanded practice of contingent reading that enables critical engagement while also making space to afford adjacent tactics of describing, mapping, performing, and making, all of which occur in embodied and contingent moments of articulation. In other words, in contrast to this model, I aim to introduce a poetics for creative engagement with historical materials through digital tools, which are subject to the same continuous technological developments that transform the works themselves.

For Scholes and Wulfman, the performance of periodical study calls for an unwieldy compilation of bibliographic information, circulation figures, reader demographics, content tags, subject analysis, advertisement catalogs, generic classification, and any number of imagined quantitative and qualitative data for large-scale textual computation.[26] Ambitious in scope and supported by ongoing trends in digital humanities and critical data practices, this method of scholarship offers certain notable possibilities for the little database working in the present. Outlining the project of a digital periodical studies might begin with exhaustive bibliographic volumes such as Frank Mott's *A History of American Magazines, 1741–1930*; rigorous cultural inventories like Jed Rasula's *American Poetry Wax Museum*; focused periodical studies such as Eric Gardner's *Black Print Unbound: The Christian Recorder, African American Literature, and Periodical Culture*; extensive archival reconstructions such as Alan Filreis' *Counter-Revolution of the Word*; or the exploratory catalogs included in works like Gwen Allen's *Artists' Magazines,* Beatriz Columina and Craig Buckley's *Clip/Stamp/Fold: The Radical Architecture of Little Magazines, 196X to 197X,* or Steve Clay and Rodney Phillip's *A Secret Location on the Lower East Side.*[27] Through each, and any number of other titles, a variable set of periodical metrics might be tracked. Taken as data, then, these books could be seen as corpora prepared for immediate computational applications. A wealth of analytic, archival, and interpretive supplements are *already* harbored in their contents. Of course, these studies are also models that could generate discrete digital approaches given any range of interests in periodicals: alternate databases could be compiled elsewhere. In either case, they argue, a digital humanist could then attempt to open new possibilities of undiscovered patterns and unimagined connections in these archival collections of periodical publications, moving from genre to database with any potentially meaningful bibliographic or semiotic components in the periodicals under examination.

By digitizing, standardizing, and networking periodical print artifacts, in other words, we might reveal patterns within the (quite large) datasets of the little magazine. Currently, for example, it's possible to imagine the implementation of increased precision and wider scope within Rasula's economic study of poetry publications, or a more exhaustive catalog of works forming the mimeograph revolution gathered by Clay and Phillips. However, patterns in content, form, and genre in little poetry magazines or data visualizations of groups of writers enmeshed in publication networks (to name only two potential outputs) remain subject to ongoing experiment. By deploying analytics at scale, Scholes and Wulfman suggest, "we can move beyond the methodology of Pound's 'simple-hearted anthropologist' and dispense with boxes, large and small, altogether," even while working within the same matrix of critical concerns.[28] At first glance, this seems apt for sites like *Eclipse,* which presents a substantial portion of works catalogued in *A Secret Location on the Lower East Side,* for example. Indeed, even with just 301 current entries, *Eclipse* has outgrown a comprehensive accounting in any given study. With it rendered instead as a database, a scholar might attempt to locate the most compelling entry points by tracking the most useful or critically insightful datapoints to graph or map their statistical significance to a logical conclusion.

It is interesting, though perhaps not surprising, that precisely the type of information called for by Scholes and Wulfman in *Modernism in the Magazines* is absent from contemporary databases of experimental writing like *Eclipse, PennSound,* and *UbuWeb.* These, and others like them, are notably focused on accessibility rather than computationality. It's worth noting that projects like *Blue Mountain* (Princeton University) and the *Modernist Journals Project* (Brown and Tulsa University) bridge these gaps in their attempt at a fuller accounting, primarily geared toward the production of scholarship, rather than focus on the more prosaic features of public use. I will discuss the implications of the dynamics of access further in chapter 3, but for now we might recall Jerome McGann's observation in *Radiant Textuality*: "Modern computational tools are extremely apt to execute one of the two permanent functions of scholarly criticism—the editorial and archival function, the remembrance of things past."[29] The little databases I examine perform this archival liaison beautifully and provide a rich network of access for students, writers, and scholars in the field. The other function, which we might summarize as critical reflection—or in McGann's terms, the capacity to "imagine what we don't know in a disciplined and deliberated fashion"—remains an ongoing challenge to critical data practices, now navigating machine learning alongside developments in network mapping and visualization. Notably, such practices rely on essayistic articulations to a broader scholarly audience that rarely make their way into a more general readership. McGann's own solution can be found in the conclusion to *Radiant Textuality,* outlining the "quantum poetics" he developed with Johanna Drucker that emerged through playful performances of the speculative programming enacted by "IVANHOE: A Game of Interpretation."[30] His explorations in how computation might aid us in the endeavor to "imagine what we don't know" by presenting new modes of play serve as one notable response to the analytical impulse of networked scholarship.

We might surmise that these early queries on the imaginative potentials of the digital humanities point more toward a problem of scholarly mores than to any inherent structural deficiencies in a computational approach. Listing successful endeavors is beyond the scope of this chapter: as the field continues to develop, new projects emerge regularly. Potential directions are emblematized by a wide range of online platforms like Ben Fry's mesmerizing visualization of variant texts in *On the Origin of Species: The Preservation of Favoured Traces,* the Traditional Knowledge Labels and cultural protocols of the Indigenous hosting platform Mukurtu CMS, or the comprehensive multimedia database and hugely collaborative digital initiative *SlaveVoyages.*[31] Critical data practices remain an open field for experimentation in digital scholarship that continues on the path to discover unseen patterns and provide new modes of engagement with digitized materials, while enabling the play of interpretation of future readers. Speculative analysis and critical scholarship still rely on digital archival practices to prepare data for any given engagement. While the database is an apt aid to memory, the poetics of scholarship yet demands a human actor to prepare a corpus capable of imagining critical activity "past Z," as Filreis writes in *Counterrevolution of the Word,* and into the "miscellaneous, unidentified, anonymous, uncataloged, misindexed."[32]

For periodical objects awaiting identification, cataloging, and indexing, we might return at this juncture to McGann's canonical exploration of "the text as a laced network of linguistic and bibliographical codes."[33] Within this laced network, "textuality is a social condition of various times, places, and persons."[34] Whether the answer is presented through geographic mapping, community network analysis, topic modeling, cultural protocols, or periodicity charts, this "laced network" continues to offer some resistance to most computational analyses. Even the most minute levels of textual analysis, as seen in the mechanistic reading of variant texts performed by Randall McLeod, call for a human to interface with an analog collator to decipher the output.[35] Unexpectedly, under this aegis, McGann argues that "poets understand texts better than most information technologists," as the noise of materialist hermeneutics and autopoietic mechanisms escape the strictures of informational structures.[36] Given the immense challenge of digital scholarship presented by periodicals and collections, a turn away from analytics and toward contingent modes of data poetics may serve to illuminate some possibilities for moving "past Z" in the study of a site like *Eclipse.*

Some of the most compelling contemporary poetic scholarship can be traced to an innovative use of even the most prosaic off-the-shelf tools for writing through digital platforms. Given the potential inherent to a wide range of computational aids, we might ask what tools are already in common use, and what poetic forms might transform our understanding of those tools. For example, on the most basic level, consider cut-and-paste. In a post to the Tumblr page hosting Troll Thread, a press for print-on-demand and digital publications, Holly Melgard published a remarkable work of poetry—or poetic scholarship—called *The Making of The Americans.* This work was simply composed. Melgard sequentially processes the entirety of Gertrude Stein's *The Making of Americans* by removing all but the first instance of every word in the book. Using Stein's own poetics statements as a premise, Melgard describes the process in a foreword: "NOW 'there is no such thing as repetition' in *The Making of Americans,* because I deleted it. Herein, every word and punctuation mark is retained according to its first (and hence last) appearance in Gertrude Stein's 925-page edition of the book."[37] The results are strikingly revealing. Though we may have long thought of Stein as a master of linguistic simplicity, after the first paragraph of Melgard's poem, it becomes clear that Stein deploys an extensive vocabulary with a delirious lexicological register in this work. From the canonical first line to the final page, adverbial constructions begin to overcome the poem. Over a hundred pages are summarized by novel words in a single passage of Melgard's editorial intervention: "drearily joyously boisterously despondingly fragmentarily roughly energetically repeatedly funnily hesitatingly dreamily doubtingly tilling boastingly delightfully touchingly quaintly."[38] Through this process, Melgard reveals hidden layers within the work in ways that would prove difficult to recapitulate otherwise. The poem produces a pleasurable poetic encounter while simultaneously performing a serious work of scholarship by the same formal gesture. Not only does the poem transform our sense of Stein's book; it revises our understanding of what the ordinary process of "search, cut, copy, and delete" might accomplish, given the right conceit applied to a contingent set of objects and queries. In this sense, it is not the complexity of the tools that might be used to understand the little database, but rather the poetics that guide the use of any given tool to yield new knowledge. In other words, it is not necessarily more advanced tools that are needed for textual analysis, but the tactical and contingent use of poetic methods that may present novel discoveries.

If one contemporary strand of experimental poetics comprises diverse projects utilizing found and recontextualized text, the long-standing practices of editorial theory, social text, and material textuality present a robust and underused apparatus for understanding the fluid dynamics of semantic modulation in transcoding processes online.[39] For example, consider a rearticulation of what John Bryant has termed the "fluid text," given the radical transformations to editions in digital networks.[40] Borrowing a term from editorial theory opens a productive array of historical discussions around editing textual objects and charting the changes in ongoing compositional processes. Slightly transforming Bryant's study of versions and revisions in Melville's *Typee* to suit contemporary media poetics, we may cite a resonant passage to define the editorial interventions that define the poetics of a fluid text:

> To come to the point, the cultural meaning of a fluid text is in the pressure that results in changes made in one text to create another and the degree of difference, or the distance, between two texts. Thus, a poetics of the fluid text is a poetics of revision. . . . When we read a fluid text, we are comparing the versions of a text, which is to say we are reading the differences between the versions, which is to say we are reading distance traveled, difference, and change.[41]

This "poetics of revision" is an invitation to reimagine historical texts through inventive filters that illuminate what was once unseen to a contemporary readership. It is precisely what Melgard achieves with *The Making of The Americans*. To this dynamic, we might add algorithms, file formats, contextual shifts, large language models, and other bibliographic operators. The poetics of revision remain pertinent to the republication of historical materials as unique editions under dramatically altered textual conditions. Bryant notes: "A revision occupies space and reflects the passage of time; it reveals options and choices; it has direction. It is a chord of dissonances and harmonies, and not a single note."[42] As Drucker, McGann, Bryant, and others within the tradition of editorial theory have often argued, to edit is to transform. Importing this lesson to the digital collection bears all the difficulty of the source materials (say, *LANGUAGE* magazine) alongside the challenges of scholarship operating within the shifting terrain of networked databases.

In this regard, the study of the little database could find no better vantage for tracing revisions to social texts than by retracing the challenges presented by the little magazines. Peter Brooker and Andrew Thacker adapt McGann to construct a useful inventory of possibilities for "the *periodical codes* at play in any magazine," worth citing here at length:

> . . . a whole range of features including page layout, typeface, price, size of volume (not all 'little' magazines are little in size), periodicity of publication (weekly, monthly, quarterly, irregular), use of illustrations (colour or monochrome, the forms of reproductive technology employed), use and placement of advertisements, quality of paper and binding, networks of distribution and sales, modes of financial support, payment practices towards contributors, editorial arrangements, or the type of material published (poetry, reviews, manifestos, editorials, illustrations, social and political comments, etc.). We can also distinguish between periodical codes internal to the design of a magazine (paper, typeface, layout, etc.) and those that constitute its external relations (distribution in a bookshop, support from patrons). However, it is often the *relationship* between internal and external periodical codes that is most significant.[43]

Tracking these codes, each facet of the little magazine can generate works of scholarship in its own right. Radiating out from the material text, each magazine offers a wealth of interpretive possibilities built on the relationship between internal and external periodical codes, among textual actors, media formats, and social contexts as layers for interpretation. A thick description of these various relations—in concert with a close reading of the semiotic codes of the digital object itself—may construct a more nuanced understanding of digitized works circulating within a larger network or social text. A poetic response that deploys these vectors of signification as a means to "imagine what we don't know" offers a similarly rich potential for understanding.

This networked poetic analysis is precisely Craig Saper's approach to reading the "intimate bureaucracies" formed among experimental writers engaged in periodical exchange.[44] Following French literary theorist Roland Barthes, Saper presents a socio-poetic mode of reading the various assemblings of "receivable" art and poetry, which find meaning in various schemes of distribution and reception. Sociopoetics are characterized by a scenario wherein the "inherently social process of constructing texts is expanded to the point that individual pages or poems mean less than the distribution and compilation machinery or social apparatus."[45] Adding to McGann's expanded field of material hermeneutics, Saper considers the periodical in relation to Barthes' concept of the *receivable,* differentiated from both the *readerly* texts of narrative realism and the *writerly* texts of modernism.[46] Highlighting this third category of intimate distribution, Saper presents a mode of reading periodical-based experimental writing from the 1960s and 1970s that sidesteps the dominant art-historical discourses of pastiche within the neo-avant-gardes. Intensely intimate, collectively constructed, and decidedly off-market, Saper frames fugitive publications through the perspective that this "sociopoetic practice was the production, distribution, and use of periodicals *as* artworks and poetry."[47] We might hear this sociopoetic practice echoing Bernstein's "Conspiracy of 'Us'" from a periodical perspective:

> We see through the structures which we have made ourselves & cannot do even for a moment without them, yet they are not fixed but provisional . . . that poetry gets shaped—informed and transformed—by the social relations of publication, readership, correspondence, readings, &c (or, historically seen, the 'tradition'), and, indeed, that the poetry community(ies) are not a secondary phenomenon to writing but a primary one.[48]

Perhaps the most remarked upon aspect of periodical studies from the avant-garde through to contemporary digital iterations is the construction of groups and the constellation of traditions or politics within group formations. The magazine provides one material basis for unraveling these knotty issues. Beyond reading exceptional objects or symptomatic inscriptions, the magazine provides literary history with networks of association to chart and vast bodies of interrelated documents to map. Within a single issue of *LANGUAGE* magazine alone, a robust network map of contributors might draw out community dynamics in ways that an essay might find difficult to approximate. This approach, for example, has been deployed insightfully in the network graph of linked data presented by the *Black Bibliography Project*: mapping titles, publishers, and personal names listed in William Andrews's "Annotated Bibliography of Afro-American Autobiography 1760–1865."[49] Similarly successful network mapping projects have been deployed at the *Modernist Journals Project* and elsewhere. For our purposes here, it should suffice to note that much has already been written on the networks of association and sociality through which the Language Writing movement coheres.

Beyond group formation, Saper recovers threads in his alternate history that enable us to observe that, "from the perspective of the twenty-first century, assemblings [periodicals] may look like experiments in networked productions in general and serve as a model for electronic media networks."[50] As forms of experimental archiving continue to evolve across the dominant social media platforms of the present, the study of periodicals presents both a robust frame for a distributed sociopoetics and a wide array of alternate futures for networked digitization. Immediate analogies are abundant. Scholes and Wulfman figure Pound's periodical series "Studies in Contemporary Mentality" as an exercise in blogging ("something like contemporary bloggers, discussing what comes to hand, taking up a new project each week").[51] Similarly, extended engagement across issues of magazines and sociopoetic publications were intensified by the development of forms like the poetry listserv or personal blog. Independent publishing throughout the mimeograph revolution anticipates instant digital "publication" ("in a very real sense, almost anyone could become a publisher"), and the list goes on from here.[52] In this way, digital initiatives like *Eclipse* both expand and continue the dialogue initiated by the formal and material codes of little magazines.

It has become commonplace since Marshall McLuhan's *Understanding Media* that previous forms of media make up all "new" media. In *Remediation,* David Bolter and Richard Grusin characterize this process of remediation as the double logic of hypermediacy and transparency: "Our culture wants both to multiply its media and to erase all traces of mediation: ideally, it wants to erase its media in the very act of multiplying them."[53] For precisely this reason, attention to historical formats of time-based networked distribution (the periodical publication) has much to offer the study of contemporary digital collections. If "all mediation is remediation," as Bolter and Grusin argue, and "older media can also remediate newer ones," there is no aspect of media communication that escapes the forces of remediation, including archival digitization and transcoding.[54] The importance of this approach is a recurrent aspect of digital media studies. Take, for example, the way in which Lev Manovich has demonstrated the computer's cultural operations according to the history of cinema, or Lisa Gitelman's imaginative explorations of the character of digital markup languages via "the editors' barbed wire" in the six-volume transcription of Emerson's journal.[55]

Experimental writing magazines have always offered this kind of protracted catalog of effects, given the relative freedom from normative economic pressures as a consequence of their playful poetics. The array of bibliographic codes, experimental arrangements, distribution mechanisms, and formal inventions on full display in the archive of little magazines provide various passages that highlight the complexities of digital platforms operating today. It's difficult to conclude this media-historical line of reasoning without recourse to a soft citation of Friedrich Kittler's maxim: "Media determine our situation, which (nevertheless or for that reason) merits a description. . . . Operating at their limits, even antiquated media become sensitive enough to register the signs and indices of a situation."[56] In this way, the "antiquated media" of Xerox and mimeograph textual reproduction might register the signs and markers of a digital situation indexed by *Eclipse.* In the other direction, the periodical positioning of *Eclipse* may offer a momentary glimpse back into the medial situation of the objects it remediates. Taken together, *Eclipse* and the little magazines like *LANGUAGE* that it hosts, work to mutually illuminate the conjunction of material-print histories alongside contingent digital networks.

Periodical Preservation

Like the solar event invoked in the site's title, *Eclipse* flickered out of sight in December of 2012. Due to an oversight in the restructuring of university servers—as much a surprise to the editors as the site's users—one day the collection simply vanished. When I began this chapter, the site was functioning regularly at an ".edu" URL hosted by the University of Utah. Over the decade since, it has run smoothly at a new address, eclipsearchive.org, on a server hosted by XMission, a company based in Salt Lake City with a particular devotion to hosting sites for local businesses and nonprofits. Before either of these iterations, from early 2002 until the spring of 2006, *Eclipse* ran on Princeton University servers. After a summer offline, the site returned in the fall of 2006 through the University of Utah's English subdomain.

Charting the rhythms of academic semesters, university technical restructurings, and Dworkin's passage from one university position to another, the archive bears witness to a personal history alongside its material contents. The current iteration's reliance on XMission, instead of any number of global providers, emphasizes the collection's link to a geographic locality within global media networks. Further, the spatial coordinates of each new edition of *Eclipse* signal the full republication of its materials. In much the same way, each time a user loads an image, its representation is reassembled anew from its underlying code. The play of presence and absence in digital preservations, Wendy Chun reminds us, works to "create, rather than solve, archival nightmares. They proliferate nonsimultaneous enduring ephemerals."[57] Written and rewritten in each refresh of a page online, the periodical poetics of *Eclipse* demand new ways of registering the social text of digital files in the moment of their use. All of these relations became most clear in a moment of occultation.

In the shadow of this 2012 syzygy, sketching the contours of the site's disappearance, we might pause for a moment to consider the *de*-publication of *Eclipse* from the internet. While offline, the files once physically inscribed to subdirectories within university servers could be found only amid the petabytes gathered by the Internet

Archive in San Francisco. As anyone who has lost a domain server or looked for a defunct site might tell you, there is little need to turn to the Internet Archive unless one requires access to a site no longer available online.[58] However, upon browsing the haphazard collection of captures, date by date, a whole network of automated and variable processes can be traced over time. From a bibliographic perspective, the reader may thus contend with the trickier aspects of digital publication: continually updated (or disappearing) content, changing forms and formats, and a host of contextual and intertextual modulations. Each of these features dramatically impacts our understanding of the material conditions of a little database like *Eclipse*. Looking at the site note, aside from the occasional missing links to scanned pages or slips in HTML and CSS (cascading style sheets) markup, the site functions perfectly in its newest iteration, as though it had never returned a 404 error or lost a server. Turning instead to the partial preservation of *Eclipse* through the Internet Archive, the slow development of the site over time can be charted and a social text can be reconstructed from the fragments of what has been lost or gained over time.

Through this mechanism, the careful reader might explore the variantology presented through a range of captures of the site from the Internet Archive "Wayback Machine." That is, this *would* be possible if the Internet Archive crawler had uniformly captured the high-resolution facsimile images of the *Eclipse* collection in each instance. Unfortunately, that was never the case. As Dworkin has described the "negative ontology" of the library, wherein "libraries are defined not by what they have on their shelves, but by what they exclude from them," the Internet Archive records of *Eclipse* might best be understood by what they lack.[59] Through lapses and shadows, the remnants of *Eclipse* in the Internet Archive alert us to how the site was used. Only the most popular pages and most accessed works are captured. A web crawler called Alexa (a reflexive counterhomage to the burning library of Alexandria) determines what is shown and how often sites are preserved based on usage statistics. For example, in 2012, there was not enough time for the images of Gil Ott's *Paper Air* magazine to yet be paged through by the site's users, nor enough exposure for Clark Coolidge's *Polaroid* to be fully captured. Other facets of the archival interface are not captured at all: javascript navigational tools and unrecorded images

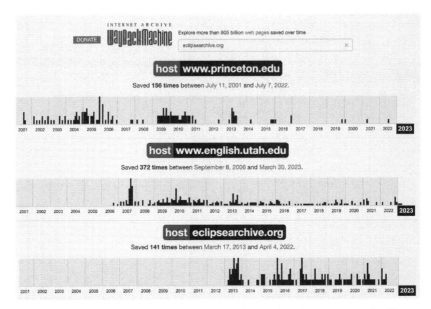

Figure 2.1. A representation of the Wayback Machine's captures of *Eclipse* across three servers in the Internet Archive, dating from July 2001 to March 2023.

mar the page with "Error" notifications, red X's, and broken symbols.[60] Within this glitch-ridden record, the persistent presence of *LANGUAGE* marks the magazine's continued use. Popular interest and course syllabi are sure to maintain the magazine's Alexa ranking and hence its preservation. The Internet Archive records of *Eclipse* remind us that, unlike paper books whose sustained use promises disintegration, frequently accessed digital objects are only *more* likely to endure.

An attentive user of the Internet Archive might also gain some insight from the periodicity of *Eclipse*. From the twenty-three titles featured in the site's first capture (February 15, 2002) to the most recent snapshot, a series of discrete archival release dates can be broken down for examination. The various captures of the site's index, as presented by the Internet Archive, can be seen in the figure above. Of particular note is Alexa's continued querying of the defunct URLs long after the site moved to a new host. Like a subscriber who was never notified about the end of a periodical, it continues to submit inquiries into a void. Collating the data contained on captures of *Eclipse* pages that feature a full site inventory—first titled "facture.html" and later changed to "titles.html"—we could reconstruct the release patterns of *Eclipse* as published by an external entity. From this vantage, it is as though Dworkin continually edits a magazine that is only periodically distributed by an unpredictable algorithmic publisher. Insofar as the previous iterations of *Eclipse* have ceased to exist on their original university servers, the Internet Archive has subsumed them into a massive archival publication. As the calendar view of the Internet Archive captures of *Eclipse* notes, "this calendar view maps the number of times http://www.princeton.edu/eclipse/facture.html was crawled by the Wayback Machine, not how many times the site was actually updated." The authorship of these pages is maintained by an automated crawler rather than the editor of the site. With lapses of months between captures, it is not possible to recreate the precise movements of *Eclipse*'s construction, although a general arc can be calculated between the data points. Of course, this system of preservation discourages such computation. Like *Eclipse,* the Internet Archive is a platform built toward the use function of preservation. Unlike *Eclipse,* the periodicity of the automated capture process is its most significant feature: these are not just sites to be read in general, as stable texts, but sites *at a given moment in time* to be read through the variantology of the fluid text. In this way, it also diverges from digital humanities collections geared toward analytics beyond questions of periodicity and variance. Rather than discourage these types of readings, they are precisely what the site demands. Variant and periodical codes are made valuable not just because they demonstrate the ongoing preservations of the collection but also as a metric to index how the collection itself changes over time, like any little magazine online or offline.

Focusing on the periodicity of use, these intermittent site captures encourage retroactive engagements with the most stable elements of the site's infrastructure. Based on the arbitrarily periodic nature of the Internet Archive, *Eclipse,* already diverging from the special collection or perverse library, now inches toward the formal properties of the periodical, the generic conventions of which anticipate so much of the time-stamped internet. If lacking in discrete paper-based "issues" of the site, the Internet Archive reveals an arbitrary periodicity that may nevertheless be tracked. In every regard, the little database, like the little magazine, is subject to the circulation of content over time. Updating the periodical codes that constitute the online collection's material text, we might expand the "range of features" enumerated by Brooker and Thacker above. This expansion may include changes in CSS and HTML, organizational features and outward links, bibliographic records (and what they exclude), embedded content on external sites and social media, usage statistics, institutional server configurations, regional prices of hosting and internet services, available screen resolution and browser affordances, software workflows for web development and document scanning, file hierarchies, hidden folders, database configuration, and file formats, among other manifold technical and social artifacts of its moment of access. Each of these may be read into "the *relationship* between internal and external periodical codes"[61] Enfolding the magazine within the mechanism of the format, the material conditions of both may come to light only in a moment when preservation is overshadowed by accessibility, when the archivist is eclipsed by the algorithm.

This could be the strongest argument against the categorization of *Eclipse* as "archive." Turning instead to the re-publication of materials within the transformative contexts of periodical release patterns in a little database, we retain the active forms of transformation at play in the performance of publication. In his writing on the collection, Dworkin rightly considers the conservative paradox of an "avant-garde archive." This phrase, he suggests, "highlights the Janus-faced logic of all archives, which look in two direction as they realize their own position: they conservatively index the past, and they index the future with a wagered risk (or revolutionary delusion), anticipating some user and some use, some moment for which the archived material is being saved."[62] While Dworkin makes a compelling case for the feverish archival logic of preservation and presentation at play on *Eclipse,* one wonders whether the editorial model of the little magazine might not be a more appropriate print-based tradition for understanding a site like *Eclipse.* Little magazines redistribute text under significantly revised bibliographic codes; they publish new contexts and yet-unrealized conversations among various textual materials that often circulate elsewhere. The editorial selection and digital transformation that *Eclipse* introduces is at least as radical as these transformative elements. The site grows periodically, with "releases" not unlike the issues of a magazine. Unlike archival acquisitions, which rarely go viral online, new issues of online magazines reliably draw visitor counts, and the latter characterizes new archival drops in the *Eclipse* collection. In this way, the collection is never a passive recipient of materials, but an active force in redistributing text into circulation across the socio-poetic networks of the present.

Here, the orbit of our hermeneutic circle returns to *LANGUAGE* magazine, featured in each capture of the site, dating back to the origin of *Eclipse*. I contend that *LANGUAGE* can be seen as a metonymic conceptual arsenal within the little database of *Eclipse*. It emerges as such through excerpts and reviews, lost documents of the avant-garde and new provocations within historical traditions, bibliographic details, and distribution services. As Dworkin notes, by "archiving books, the archive itself adds to their bibliographic information, and the digital archive produces entirely new editions."[63] By digitizing magazines, *Eclipse* folds new periodical codes into each release within the ongoing shifts in its own role as a little database. There are Princeton University editions, University of Utah iterations, and independent XMission versions, each with a new bundle of contextual registers appended to the periodical codes of the magazine. Alongside this continual republication, we might consider that the *LANGUAGE* Distributing Service photocopied as many issues of its own magazine as were ever printed in the first place. With this reminder, we may turn to the magazine hosted by *Eclipse* as a scattered set of HTML documents, GIF images, and PDF files, each with a unique set of formal properties to examine.

Variable Formats

In shades of gray, the full run of *LANGUAGE* is hosted in both GIF facsimile images and slightly higher quality PDF reading copies. Like these images of *LANGUAGE,* the site itself is styled in gray tones. More precisely, the background of *Eclipse* can be coded as #303030. It is perhaps no accident that newer versions of Firefox present a slightly darker gray (#222222) as the most neutral background for image viewing. At any rate, the emphasis on grayness in *Eclipse* is of particular note in relation to the PDF format, which Gitelman argues is a kind of formal equivalent to "gray literature" in *Paper Knowledge:* ". . . gray in the field of library and information science because they are typically produced and circulate outside more formal publishing

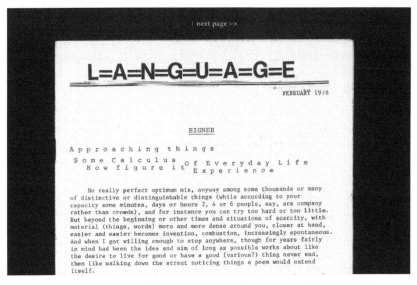

Figure 2.2. A screenshot of the cover of the first issue of *LANGUAGE,* as captured in the *Eclipse* archive.

channels, often in small editions that can be hard to locate, prove problematic for cataloguers, and quickly become obsolete. . . . Because of the vagaries of online publication, the digital medium may itself turn communications variously gray, in other words, in ways that compound gray subgenres of the document."[64]

The PDF of *LANGUAGE* magazine was made in February 2003, while *Eclipse* was still hosted by Princeton University. This is validated by the Adobe Acrobat creation data, which points to version 5.0, released in 2001, long before the OCR (optical character recognition) feature was implemented that currently affords embedded layers of searchable text in line with the facsimile images. The browsing GIF files were generated in August of 2006, when the full run of the magazine was coded into the new servers hosted by the University of Utah, and again in February of 2013 when the files were rewritten to XMission servers. When I began research on this chapter, I wrote the phrase "the page itself hosting the magazine is last modified on September 30, 2010 at 1:44:59 PM, the precise date and time that the first index to *LANGUAGE* was published, hypermediating the full contents and creating a new interface to the magazine as a whole." The information was true at that writing. The exact point in time was particularly compelling in that instance, since it seemed to suggest how the publication of an index could radically alter the publication date of a release. But the time of this page's publication has now changed, and should be revised to "05/10/2017 09:34:40," as the current last modified HTTP date indicates. It is only the most recently refreshed edition that the user can speak of without further remediation by services like archive.org. With this metadata written into both the web page and the digital facsimile, the string of constantly disappearing dates trace the history of the archive along with its objects.

If the Internet Archive charts the temporal patterns and maps the spatial conditions of the database, the variable formats of *Eclipse*'s facsimile images present the most telling narratives. For the first four years of operation, the images were all presented as GIFs, encoded in a highly compressed grey scale. Despite the promise that full-resolution TIFF (tag image file format) images were being archived elsewhere, in practice the site presented only GIF files encoded for grayscale presentation. Starting in 2006, these GIF files were gradually replaced by higher resolution JPEG files (joint photographic experts group; also as JPG) in full color, and the site has variously suggested that this process is underway for all files. At the moment, however, few works in the collection retain their GIF encoding, with *LANGUAGE* magazine notable among them. The "lossless" pixelation of the GIF format perfectly reflects the earliest stages of the periodical's publication patterns. Poorly transcoded images of the magazine transport the reader to a medial environment of Xerox and photocopy, of distributing services and mail networks. This is the bibliographic paradox of compression. Beneath the accelerating arc toward greater "fidelity" to analogue formats, there is a strange magic in the lo-fi defiance of the GIF image. Put differently, through a more radical transformation of the historical document, these processes of transcoding can better surface the questions of materiality in all iterations.[65] As Bolter and Grusin might articulate this effect, the loss of immediacy draws attention to a range of remediating factors. Dispelling the illusion of immediacy, the "poor image" reveals deep layers of technical remediation while pointing to the historical specificity of both original and facsimile.

The GIF transcoding of *LANGUAGE* magazine seems to offer a prime example of the aesthetics and politics of the "poor image" theorized by Hito Steyerl: "It transforms quality into accessibility,

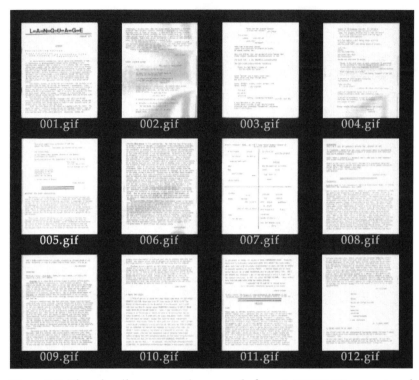

Figure 2.3. Thumbnails representing spreads from *LANGUAGE,* as captured in the *Eclipse* archive.

exhibition value into cult value, . . . contemplation into distraction."[66] It is "thrust into digital uncertainty, at the expense of its own substance. . . . It is passed on as a lure, a decoy, an index, or as a reminder of its former visual self."[67] We might recall here that Dworkin notes how images on *Eclipse* operate according to a "continual dynamic between fidelity and degradation, accurate facsimile and serviceable impersonation," wherein "the twin impulses of the digital archive—to preserve and to present, to reproduce and to distribute—are at fundamental odds with one another."[68] Even Cory Arcangel, an artist best known for working with highly compressed image formats, maintains that, with JPG compression, the user creates "an image which is only a shadow of its former self."[69] The alignment of these values attributed to the poor image produces a misguided appreciation of low-resolution archival objects on an internet increasingly marked by high fidelity forms of replication. Not incidentally, the same rhetoric pervades discussions of "degraded" print technologies. In a response to Steyerl entitled "The Defense of Poor Media," Silvio Lorusso argues that "the whole history of the book, not just since the advent of digital networks, can be understood as the sacrifice of a certain idea of material quality in favor of a faster duplication or a broader reach."[70] The Gutenberg Bible was, of course, a heavily compressed form of the hand-painted medieval manuscript. By the same token, the duplicators of the "mimeograph revolution," from which *LANGUAGE* stems, were a cheap and unruly offshoot of office-based exigencies.

And yet, when reading *LANGUAGE* magazine online, are the only qualities of note those of accessibility, cult value, distraction, and degradation? These are, of course, qualities of the image rather than the text of *LANGUAGE,* which remains clearly legible. Is the admittedly compressed GIF nothing but a decoy, an index, "a reminder of its former visual self" from a material text perspective? If the focus is on an absent "original"—a pristine filmic artifact, in Steyerl's case, or the remarkably precise material substantiation of a codex, as Dworkin has articulated—these readings of the digital object bear the truth of archival duplicity. However, might it be possible to imagine these objects beyond their analog iterations, as new editions with revised material codes that are as significant, complex, and layered as the substrates from which they derive? More readers have encountered *LANGUAGE* magazine online than have ever handled print copies: what if we began by evaluating this reading experience in its own right? Indeed, in the case of *LANGUAGE,* this approach gains heightened urgency under the sign of "the resonating of the wordness of language."[71] In an expanded field of poetics concerned with material, form, and structure, it is hard to overlook the experience of the page in the process of reading, especially if that page is on a screen. The surrounding fields of bibliographic notes, suggested magazines, and residual print artifacts all amplify the specificity of the reading experience, as mediated by the digital image. As the gap between contemporary writing technologies and the paper-based networks of the mimeograph revolution continues to widen, these mediating layers only lend greater visibility to the temporal distance of the reader and present the depth of significance across medial formations subject to ongoing processes of transformation.

Despite the fact that digital objects lose "the facture and material specificity of the book or printed document as an object," Dworkin contends for an intensive reading of precisely these bibliographic qualities in his account of *Eclipse*.[72] As though peering through the distortions introduced by digitization, Dworkin demonstrates the ways in which even facsimile images direct the attentive reader to the semiotic codes through which the paper-based material texts continue to signify. "Hypermnesia" is built around a series of "instance[s] of the bibliographic information recorded by the archival scanning protocols for Eclipse."[73] Variously, this bibliographic data reads Dracula into the fangs of rusted staples in Lorenzo Thomas's *Dracula*; typographic resistance in Tina Darragh's Avant-Garde typeface in *on the corner to off the corner*; periodicity and binding techniques in Lyn Hejinian's *Gesualdo*; and the significance of self-flaps in a 1981 edition of Bernstein's *Disfrutes*. Each example is persuasive. Indeed, these facsimile images record a deep array of textual codes that we may project into interpretations of the small press publications digitized by *Eclipse*. However, reversing the direction of this analysis, we might focus not on the preservation of bibliographic traces etched by the original works, but rather on the bibliographical specificities that the digital files introduce. In so doing, a reading of *LANGUAGE* as a new edition within a little database that yields its own periodical and bibliographic codes may yet emerge.

In the powerful conclusion to "In Defense of the Poor Image," Steyerl sharpens this point: "The poor image is no longer about the real thing—the originary original. Instead, it is about its own real conditions of existence: about swarm circulation, digital dispersion, fractured and flexible temporalities."[74] This is not to deny a reading of the "facture and material specificity of the book or printed document as an object," but to call for the expansion of these specificities to include the real conditions of the objects radiating out from *Eclipse,* in the flexible networks of digital dispersion that facilitate their use.[75] That expansion is not without its difficulties. Textual scholars must still contend for the very significance of material substrates in the literary arts, despite decades of editorial theory and material text study. Once this "facture" is fractured by new and unpredictable temporal and medial layers, each contingent on a host of technical protocols and viewing environments, the case is yet more difficult to make.

Boris Groys articulates this challenge in his article "From Image to Image File—And Back," which examines the nonidentity of image files, oscillating between "invisible" code and visible image. Reading along with Groys we might say: "The digital image is a copy—but the event of its visualization is an original event, because the digital copy is a copy that has no visible original. That further means: A digital image, to be seen, should not be merely exhibited but staged, performed. . . . But to perform something is to interpret it, to betray it, to distort it."[76] This is perhaps the best case for a contingent or performance-based method of digital scholarship, and is written into the ethos of the creative scholarly arts theorized by McGann, Drucker, Liu, and others. To take Groys's argument out of context, we might agree with the sentiment: "There is no such thing as a copy. In the world of digitalized images, we are dealing only with originals."[77]

Reading Copy

Where *Textz* demonstrates the mutability between file formats, based on the textual equivalence of numerical representation, *Eclipse* highlights a renewed specificity to each file format in the republication of historical artifacts. In contrast to the stripped-down text files of *Textz,* which emphasize algorithmic use, *Eclipse* almost exclusively presents transcoded objects for human reading. A great irony in the site's organization concerns the presentation of digitally re-set documents in PDF presented by links that read "Download Reading Copy." Many of these carefully retyped documents sacrifice all traces of the material specificity of the books they transcribe in order to present "clean" reading copies to supplement the facsimile editions that define the site. However, these files are also some of the only machine-readable texts in the collection, the only artifact files that Google can easily index for its algorithms or that scholars might repurpose for in-document searches. For whom is the PDF reading copy presented? On *Eclipse,* each "reading copy" is an offering to potential algorithmic or human readers uninterested in the texture of the page in the digitized works. Or, in an important note of access, these two readers meet for the vision-impaired, for whom a "reading copy" requires text-to-speech functionality. Unlike the text-utility of Google Books, the GIFs and JPGs of *Eclipse* remain largely unsearchable relics entirely dependent on visual parsing by human readers. In particular, "poor" GIF images like those that constitute

LANGUAGE online resist even the most advanced OCR software that might convert the image into a machine-readable text. This resistance mirrors the various resistances that were articulated in the poetics of *LANGUAGE* magazine, such as to the "accessibility" of the lyric voice or to the easy parsing of clear meaning from a text.

And yet, alongside the "read" links to issues of *LANGUAGE* magazine in GIF format, the user finds corresponding links to "download" full issues of the magazine for external use in PDF format.[78] These PDFs present the comforting stability of a text that can be printed on paper that is 8.5 inches by 11 inches and can be read online or stored in a local folder as "documents" rather than images. The PDF is an unusual format in that it was always planned as a postscript device for printing, and became popular as an archival format for digital media only through a confluence of preferences for print-based reading habits within enterprise solutions for business documents. The ubiquity of the PDF reinforces its invisibility as a mediating format. It is remarkable that despite the fact that JSTOR (short for "journal storage") is built entirely upon its delivery of searchable PDFs to academe, there are practically no critical studies of the PDFs on its server—Gitelman's *Paper Knowledge* provides the exception that proves the rule. In contrast to the GIF images of the early *Eclipse,* these reading copies offer what Gitelman has isolated as a primary feature of the PDF format, "a measure of fixity because of the ways they simultaneously compare to printed documents and contrast with other kinds of digital documents that seem less fixed—less print-like—as they are used."[79] Unlike TXT, HTML, or PDF, it is exceptionally unusual to "read" images on the internet, aside from the bold face captions of the image macros that facilitate memes, article headline images, and social media clickbait. Hosting archival copies of radical press books in GIF and JPG images is an increasingly perverse endeavor, especially as the PDF expands its pervasive role as the standard for all scanned documents that circulate online. In this way, the image files of *Eclipse* combat the illusion of immediacy, reminding the reader that every page is a newly transcoded file.

When John Warnock developed Postscript and the PDF for Adobe Systems in 1991, the format was imagined as a solution to the transmissibility of the specifically bibliographic qualities of the page: type, layout, and size. A history of Adobe Systems, developer of the PDF, could be written through the bibliographic proclivities of its inventor.[80] Aside from being part of the original team out of Xerox, Warnock is an accomplished collector of Shakespearean texts (from early quartos down through a range of ephemeral textual artifacts). His development of the PDF standard was scripted to serve both as a vehicle for the "paperless office" of the early nineties and as a way to deliver facsimile images of Shakespeare to the computer through his short-lived CD-ROM company "Octavo."

Unlike the codex, which is bound by certain material limitations, the open-standard PDF continues to develop beyond its proprietary origins with Adobe Systems.[81] Despite the fact that the format's freely available specifications are unprofitable by necessity, Adobe may yet capitalize on more sophisticated articulations and expanded features of the PDF, the TIFF file, and the Creative Suite of applications that make these publications possible, including advanced editorial options in newer editions of Adobe Acrobat, as featured in the following interlude. Over time and responding to use patterns, the PDF has increasingly skewed toward machine reading in both bureaucratic and archival systems. With embedded text, the PDF can present facsimile images simultaneous to searchable text through automated processes that put no significant demands on a human editor. This capability facilitates everything from the JSTOR database to Google Books. Such massive data operations throw a little database premised on image files like *Eclipse* into sharp relief. The entire site could be indexed for full searchability, rendered machine-readable through OCR, offering a concomitant range of network graphs and semantic analyses. However, the obscurity of the image file presents a markedly different reading protocol for nonalgorithmic users who might linger between the bibliographic codes of digital formats under the influence of paper artifacts under the influence of digital formats.

Interlude 2
L≠A≠N≠G≠U≠A≠G≠E

As with *Textz,* while lingering with larger issues of preservation in *Eclipse,* I felt simultaneously inclined toward a scaled-down study of *L=A=N=G=U=A=G=E* magazine.[1] Not just to perform readings of the document that has taught me so much of what I know about poetry and poetics, but to work within its forms and formats, to engage the content of its pages with the same generative critical-poetic mimesis that has come to define its cluster of writers. My introduction to digital file formats, the little database, and indeed the entire field of contemporary poetry was delivered by scanning Language Poetry periodicals over a flatbed scanner while employed as a work-study student for *Eclipse* in the spring of 2004.[2] Intertwining little magazines with an archival poetics of the scanner, reading in this way requires oscillating among print artifacts and digital objects transitioning through unstable states. Their transcoding processes track diverse modes of reading: checking for errors in the scan, dawdling with compelling poems, trying to keep the spine intact, following inter-issue debates, straying into search engines, attending to bibliographic data, and posting online for future use. My understanding of Language Writing emerged in the gaps between slow-form captures of magazine spreads on a glass platen, as though the digitization of the page might stand in for the mental images these sessions produced.

In retrospect, it should come as no surprise that the forms of critical making or media poetics that guide the interludes assembled here can be traced to these generative practices. "Wreading" unfolds as performative knowledge production, enacting new content alongside the scanner's hand-drawn performance of machine reading.[3] As discussed in the previous chapter, periodical preservations at *Eclipse* deliver the page to a range of unlikely readers. From Google to the Internet Archive, a host of bots, content aggregators, and web crawlers have parsed the entirety of *Eclipse* many times over in the past twenty years. For instance, we might look to the CCBot web crawler. Developed by the nonprofit Common Crawl, CCBot has periodically captured *Eclipse* in ninety-five iterations for its open-data corpus devoted to gathering "the internet," from 2008 up to the time of this writing.[4]

In a remarkably designed work of data journalism by the Allen Institute for AI in collaboration with *The Washington Post,* readers can explore a visualization of content crawled for Google Bard's use of this corpus called "C4" (short for Colossal Clean Crawled Corpus), as well as a search bar indexing specific websites within the corpus.[5] Alongside tech blogs, fanfic collections, shadow libraries, gaming discussion boards, and patent documentation, C4 reveals an ongoing subscription to *Eclipse* periodicals—including *LANGUAGE*—which represent the *littlest* trace of just 0.000004 percent or 6.7 thousand tokens within the corpus.[6] And yet, these experimental magazines from the 1970s still whisper their contents and forms even while embedded in the massive neural networks within which they now find themselves inscribed. The discovery of this fact drives the present interlude: little *LANGUAGE* models live on within the large language models (LLM).

How might the little database subsumed by an LLM still register its voice? By what mechanisms might these scalar opposites be put into conversation? What might a nested *LANGUAGE* model offer to our emerging understanding of the mysteries guiding unsupervised deep learning? Conversely, given the chance, how might these models be deployed to open up new vectors hidden within the historical documents of *LANGUAGE*? Indeed, the most avid users of the site's "reading copies" may just be the emerging algorithms that Mashinka Firunts Hakopian has speculatively gathered under the heading "other intelligences."[7] Every word in *LANGUAGE* has been absorbed by the black box readings of other intelligences. Its minuscule proportion of the model glitches the LLM's proclivity for what I consider a type of *plain vanilla vernacular* (in homage to *Textz*'s easily-executable ASCII encoding), a lingua franca of internet stylistics geared to pass the Turing test via passably normative expressions.

Insofar as the cluster of writings and publications around *LANGUAGE* cohere, it is through models of language that work against uncritical forms of linguistic transparency to surface the "artifice of absorption." Given these relations, in this interlude, entitled *L≠A≠N≠G≠U≠A≠G≠E* (sampled here in excerpted form), I bring the statistical generative capacities of LLMs to bear on a simulation of the first issue of *LANGUAGE,* prompting both to rethink their poetics within the linguistic proclivities of the other. The gesture is inspired by the theory-laden debates that make up the magazine's primary intervention in discourses on experimental poetry. This differential approach to media poetics hails from structuralist energies in the milieu of Language Writing in the 1970s, a way of working that is, as I've noted elsewhere, "simultaneously agitated in all directions."[8]

In *L≠A≠N≠G≠U≠A≠G≠E,* I use ChatGPT to produce a facsimile edition of *LANGUAGE* (with a difference), allowing the LLM to rewrite the contents of the magazine to speculate inward on its own algorithmic poetics. This is a type of language game that plays the transformer back through the traces of *LANGUAGE* deep within its own training datasets. Using contingent tactics of "advanced find and replace," "stylistic transfer," and "frame extension," I prompt the model to put the pieces in *LANGUAGE* in conversation with their situation within the LLM. Essays on "free-association" in the magazine shift toward meditations on statistical diction; manifestos on art and language bend to proclaim a poetics of deep learning algorithms; reviews of recent poetry books update to internet publications at scale; pattern poems enfold computational pattern recognition—among a wide range of specific effects that transform the original set of writings within the format of the magazine. As varied as the poetics featured in the magazine, each intervention learns from *LANGUAGE,* with ongoing bibliographic attention to the material and political construction of language models.

Writing through *LANGUAGE* in this way, like Benjamin Friedlander's book of "applied poetry," *Simulcast: Four Experiments in Criticism,* I create "a text whose origins have exaggerated legibility."[9] Keeping the layout, word count, and design of the original magazine, *L≠A≠N≠G≠U≠A≠G≠E* offers a side-stapled facsimile of dubious authenticity, printed on aged sheets of legal paper 8½ inches by 14 inches. Like *Simulcast,* my simulation of the stylistics and design of *LANGUAGE* enacts a procedure for generative output within a tightly constrained set of technologies for intervention, while allowing the flexibility of content-specific improvisation. Elsewhere, I have described this type of publication as an "extreme edition," a process of versioning a text that dramatically alters its origins via discrete

L≠A≠N≠G≠U≠A≠G≠E

MAY 2023

AFTER EIGNER

Approaching networks

Some Calculus
How figure it Of Everyday Life
Algorithms

No really perfect algorithm, anyway among some thousands or many of
distinctive or distinguishable search results (while according to your
capacity some minutes, days or hours – 2, 4 or 6 people, say, are company rather
than crowds), and for instance, you can try too hard or too little. But beyond
the beginning or other times and situations of scarcity, with data (words,
images) more and more dense around you, closer at hand, easier and easier
becomes generation, remixing, increasingly spontaneous. And when I got willing
enough to stop anywhere, though for years fairly in mind had been the idea and
aim of long as possible works about like the desire to optimize or have a good
(various?) algorithm never end, then like scrolling down a feed noticing things
a poem would extend itself.

Figure 2i.1. *L≠A≠N≠G≠U≠A≠G≠E* facsimile capture, a bootleg copy of the
first issue of *L=A=N=G=U=A=G=E* magazine generated in 2024 with the aid
of a range of large-language models.

editorial processes. Examples are numerous, but for one apt analog, consider Steve Kado's *October Jr.,* described by Printed Matter
as "a faithful ¾ scale model of *October* 12 (Spring 1980). All contents,
images, advertisements and articles are precisely rendered, just a
little smaller."[10] *October* magazine, like *LANGUAGE,* plays an outsized role at the intersection of "high theory" and aesthetics in the
discourse of the late 1970s and early 1980s. By precisely replicat-
ing the magazine at ¾ scale, Kado makes its claims just that much
smaller, deploying the model to reflect on its source. In the same
way, *L≠A≠N≠G≠U≠A≠G≠E* preserves the material layout and stylistic
register of its source in order to interrogate how it might model unseen vectors within AI-generated Language Poetics. It is also an invitation to the reader to prompt the model differently, rendering new
vectors for periodical reading at the human–computer interface.

 See: *L≠A≠N≠G≠U≠A≠G≠E* (2025).

CHAPTER 3

Live Vinyl MP3

Echo Chambers among the Little Databases

If computation enables playful tactics for transmission *(Textz)* and digital modes of preservation open new pathways for files to travel *(Eclipse),* it is the anecdotal narratives of files-in-transit that tell the most remarkable stories. This chapter tracks one such story in depth, but first we might return to the MP3 of William Carlos Williams's poem "The Defective Record" to reopen a tab that sounds out the stakes of tracking file transmission. To review: listening to "The Defective Record" today, transcoded as an MP3 file, returns us to the poetics of Williams's media-reflexive audio performance inscribed in wax. His mimetic vocal performance of a skipping record is itself rendered defective in a digital milieux. The metaphor of the scratched record is rendered inoperable in the face of modular digital playback. This aspect of media play, however, works to accent both the medial origin of the file *and* the digital object's new formatting. In other words, the media-reflexive gesture of the recording amplifies the conditions of its original recording while, at the same time, establishing a new meaning-making system as a digital file. Following these steps, it proves necessary to listen to the MP3 of "The Defective Record" as a digital object in its own right, rather than project an aural experience back to an imaginary Victrola.

That said, a close listening of the transcoded file of the poem channels into the frequencies with which this MP3 reverberates among innumerable corresponding digital objects online: each with their own contingent stories of transformative semiotic modulation.

Inhabiting *PennSound*, "The Defective Record" MP3 file is subject to the conditions of both its format and its situatedness within a little database that periodically releases sound recordings of poetry via a highly compressed audio format. The collection regularly remediates a range of artifacts, including original cassettes, reel-to-reel tapes, and vinyl records, as well as born-digital audio recordings using a wide array of digital formats. Here, yet more "defective," the Williams poem circulates at a compression rate of just 128 kilobytes per second—a site-wide standard selected for its ubiquity and ease of transmission, especially in an earlier internet, where even megabytes could take minutes to load. Ironically, given its highly compressed sampling, *PennSound* also works in stark opposition to arguments on the inherent distraction of the MP3. The "close listening" techniques that poetry generically warrants reverse these dictums of attention.[1] Despite their low bitrates, the recordings at *PennSound* earn careful attention in contexts as varied as private academic research, university classrooms, and MOOC (massive open online course) discussion boards. From the vantage of these practices of use, we might wonder: defective for whom? If it's for neither the listener nor the file's distant media history, then is it for some distant archivist looking for a subtler grain of the voice, one who might never arrive? In the meantime, the files continue to travel, telling stories along the way.

These questions can be approached from the opposite direction, moving from the MP3 back into performances with analog media. For instance, we might follow the story of a set of files surrounding a performance by poet and scholar Tracie Morris. In 2008, I was tasked with editing a collection of video documents for *PennSound* from a small conference in Arizona called "Conceptual Poetry and Its Others."[2] In one of the panels, Morris gave a conversational talk interspersed with readings of her poetry. She concluded with the singular performance of a work entitled "Africa(n)." To highlight this performance and render it accessible beyond the context of the talk, I segmented the recording as an individual video file to be posted to a *PennSound* page devoted to her presentation at the conference.

During her lecture, Morris describes the origin of her poem. Her collaborator, the electronic musician Val Jeanty, had sent her an MP3 file of the actor Geoffrey Holder reading a line for a promotional record in 1963, simply stating: "It all started when we were brought here as slaves from Africa."[3] Morris reflects on the line's striking summary of the Middle Passage and centuries of racialized trauma: distilling the slave trade and its aftermath into a single, direct sentence. Morris recounts that her poem begins when, somewhere along the way, the clarity of the delivery of the sentence had been irrecoverably corrupted for digital playback. She notes, as though speaking to Holder, while also speaking to the glitch in the file, or rather the audio dispersions particular to an errant MP3 file: "Now you're doing my job, Geoffrey." Morris has long been known to perform a signature form of what she calls "vocalise"—improvisatory, looping riffs in concert with musicians, sound artifacts, and poetic phrases. Here, in a glitching digital file, she found this work mirrored in a broken MP3. In this instance, the authority of the original line paired with the malfunctioning file had inspired Morris's performance of "Africa(n)." Where Williams took the mechanics of "cutting" a record to simulate skipping playback for the gramophone, Morris begins in the opposite direction, with the happenstance error of MP3 audio sampling, to simulate the glitching character of the MP3 in a live vocal performance.

By design, this is a "difficult poem," with its form and content intertwined, irreducible to transcription. Morris cites Fred Moten in the description of her improvisational performance as a way to "say something whose phonic substance will be impossible to reduce."[4] Morris uses the human vocal apparatus to mimic the random-access dispersal of the MP3. The repeated refrains work simultaneously as a painful earworm, statement of fact, critique of narrative cohesion, and virtuosic interrogation of English "mastery," *all within* a radical expression of the feeling of being *stuck* in an endlessly violent loop.[5] The poetry of the performance, by turns operatic and procedural, opens new vectors of meaning within the single sentence. Phrases like "we're all stars" and "we all start in Africa" and "it's all Africa" emerge within the flow of iterations. The stunning delivery signals Kurt Schwitter's historical rendering of a single line of dada typography into an epic "Ursonate," on one hand, while pointing to the technologically inspired vocal remixes of hip hop, on the other.[6] In either direction, there is a poetics of recognition in the delivery of the poem, lingering with the violence of repetition while enacting the virtuosic dispersal of signification.

Here, I want to linger on dispersal, a term Morris foregrounds in her discussion of the work. She describes the sound itself as dispersed through the technical apparatus. It was precisely this dispersal of sound in digital objects that led her to think about diasporic dispersal in the United States. Adding to diasporic fact and digital theory, another "dispersal" follows from Morris's performance: the file soon dispersed to unforeseen patterns marked by the postproduction dispersions of what Hito Steyerl has termed "circulationism."[7] Once digitized, Morris's video was included in the syllabus of an online course on modern and contemporary poetry, *PennSound* founder and modernist scholar Al Filreis's ModPo. The performance made an immediate mark on the Spanish filmmaker and course participant Mónica Savirón. Over the next four years, Savirón worked on an archival film set to the score of the poem, entitled *Broken Tongue*. In another medial reversal of the narrative of transcoding Williams from record to MP3, Morris's performance of the dispersed MP3 file was printed to celluloid for projection as a 16mm film.

Broken Tongue syncs the sound file from Morris's performance to a series of microfiche images drawn from January 1 issues of the *New York Times* every year from the paper's inception in 1851 to the present.[8] This catalog of images is used to generate another little database with another sort of broken record. Performing the *Times* from the unique search string of Morris's performance, it parses imagery from the newspaper to cue each image up to a single word or fragment uttered by Morris. Here, "all the news that's fit to print" places the loops of "Africa(n)" into a random-access filmic review of print-based evidence. Centuries of racial violence and protest zip through digitized newsprint captures in celluloid film. In aggregate, the film performs a radical compression not unlike the line that began the poem. A glitched record caught in its own encryption. As Legacy Russell writes in *Glitch Feminism,* to embody the multiplicity of the glitch is "to affirm and celebrate the infinite failure of arrival at any place" as a refusal of binary fixity,[9] flickering through history not to linger with any moment, but to experience the looping recursions of a traumatic narrative that resists any reductive summary, beginning, or end.

Screened globally, the award-winning film *Broken Tongue* is likely the way that most audiences have heard the poem. Far more, at any rate, than those at a conference in Arizona. In an unlikely reversal, Savirón returns Morris's performance to a database logic, and a wider audience, albeit registered in celluloid. In just the same way, we might turn from the index of printed artifacts that makes up the film *Broken Tongue* and return to the little database that harbors the Morris performance itself, *PennSound*. Recapping the story from the digital to the analog: Jeanty discovers a previously used sample of Holder that has been glitched and can't recover the original; Morris gives a performance based on this glitch at the conclusion of a talk at a small conference in Arizona; that performance is segmented into a single track on *PennSound*; that track finds its way onto the syllabus of an online course attended by a filmmaker; and finally a film emerges pairing Morris's performance with a database of news clippings in 16mm celluloid. All, together, producing a stunning matrix of media-specific critique. Chance encounters, glitched MP3s, and dispersion narratives follow in the wake of the unlikely stories of digital objects in circulation.

Contingency and Dispersion

Dropping the needle into narratives of circulation, the transmission-bound qualities of contingency, noise, and dispersion inform the theoretical inflections of this chapter and shape the delivery of its content. Over the course of what follows, I consider a set of files moving through two little databases that are likely to be more well-known (*PennSound* and *UbuWeb*) alongside two sites that are likely to be lesser-known to readers (*Mutant Sounds* and *SpokenWeb*). Following these collections, I examine a remixing tool entitled *MUPS,* developed by Canadian poet and programmer David (Jhave) Johnston, which introduces a new interface to a select set of files hosted by the *PennSound* archive. Like the stories of "The Defective Record" and "Africa(n)," this route is plotted to address the contingent effects enacted by the movement of a set of MP3 files, but will arrive at its destination only by way of conclusion.

Following this trajectory, I argue, a user might come to an understanding of the MP3 file by tracking files moving through a series of online collections and the meaningful transformations they facilitate. By the same token, these little databases may be understood through the same audio files that circulate through them. These circulatory effects are mutually constitutive. Along the way, the chapter samples a related compendium of adjacent digital objects via linked or referenced text, image, sound, and movie files. Just as someone might "read" a magazine exclusively for the pictures, I imagine someone might read this chapter exclusively for the downloads, which offer an archival ambience extending beyond the articulation of my argument. My aim is to chart the passage of a specific constellation of audio materials through several little databases as a staging ground for objects dispersed by online collections in general. In this way, the chapter is premised on the comparative principles of selection, navigation, description, and distribution. Corresponding practices of comparative media analysis or close listening may then be performed by the reader of these pages and the objects radiating out from them.

 Figure 3.1. JPG: bill bissett, detail from *the lost angel mining co.* (Vancouver: Blewointmentpress, 1969). MP3: bill bissett & th mandan massacre, "2 awake in th red desert!!," *Awake in th Red Desert* (Vancouver: See/Hear Records, 1968).

To address the sites featured here, I follow the thread of a single poet's output in an attempt to tease out a description of each online collection, how they mediate the recordings they host, and how we might begin to understand the transformative effects of dispersion patterns in the little database through the narrative of these files. I've elected to follow the trajectory of bissett's files in particular and their dispersion across these databases for two primary reasons. First, because their distribution and republication across a host of digital platforms represent a dizzying orchestration of transmissions: echoing from *Mutant Sounds,* to *PennSound,* to *SpokenWeb,* to *MUPS,* and beyond. And second, because, as the editor who initially found these files at *Mutant Sounds* and ushered them into new contexts through their situation at *PennSound,* I've had the opportunity to track their staccato movements across an array of digital milieus. Throughout, the contextual effects of movement are the focus.

Indeed, bill bissett may seem an unlikely poet for the scholarly analysis of digital collections by proxy, given the relative paucity of academic writing on his generically variant and wildly experimental works, especially in sound performance. This choice will hopefully come into view in its telling: it is useful to follow the reverberations of an illustrative thread. Not a *special* thread, as a symptomatic reading or the hermeneutics of suspicion might have it, but *any thread whatsoever*. Raveling a path through the database is perhaps all that a narrative format like the monograph chapter might attempt: in other words, the essay can be understood as a kind of test for trajectories through these networks. Alongside the chapter, we might add archival downloads, edited compilations, and a related scroll of images, sources, or hyperlinks. If there is anything to be learned from the sites examined in *The Little Database,* it is that any text may also contain a collection. This chapter offers one such correlate to the little database in the echoes it follows.

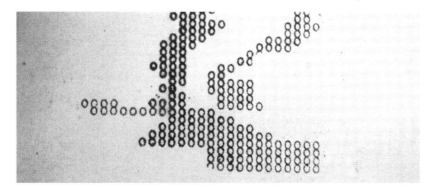

Figure 3.2. JPG: bill bissett, from *words in th fire* (Vancouver: Blewointment, 1972). MP3: bill bissett, "Circles in th Sun," from *lost angel mining company,* Sir George Williams University reading (1969).

While the bulk of this chapter follows a narrative trajectory of bill bissett files online, the appended interlude investigates a related constellation of audio files from the *PennSound* collection that have been transformed by their digitization. In this way, the chapter aims to execute both depth and surface levels of echolocation. Each sample in the interlude could warrant a similar excursus. Both modes of engagement are necessarily incomplete: the depth model of the chapter is a contingent exercise following one set of recordings through a series of transformative contextual processes; the surface model presents a wider array of changes, and cannot linger too long on any single effect. By pairing these operations, I contend that the two methods might be productively employed in concert. The first prepares speculative, latent narratives that the reader may discover hidden within the second—each contingency singular, every effect significant. This approach addresses the circulation of digital objects in general while also remaining attentive to the particularity of any individual file. In contrast to the site-wide metrics and sweeping preservation practices examined in the previous two chapters, this chapter moves toward the potential for a close reading of historical aesthetic artifacts as circulating digital objects in use, each with its own modulations to contextual and material significance. Taken into the interlude, these same files come to live in the everyday archives of user hard drives, played back in ordinary experience. While these personal collections remain beyond the scope of public access addressed by the collections tracked here, they all present similarly singular inflections to the files they host, opening on untested horizons of use and unknowable contextual registers as radically transformative as they are academically inarticulable.

As a supplementary gesture, the arguments in this chapter are sequentially interrupted by images of pages from books by bissett to encourage adjacent forms of reading. This formal exercise links the chapter to the image-based collection at *Eclipse,* while also leading into the network tracing of films hosted on *UbuWeb* in the following chapter. The images ground bissett's audio recordings in a related material form. This relation of document to recording is, by turns, standardized and incommensurate. The text guides readerly performance, but the performance always exceeds the strictures of the text. In this regard, I suggest that the audio recordings are not connected only to vinyl records and digital files, but also to an expanded corpus of published and unpublished material texts and scripts by bissett. As an editorial premise, I have constrained these excerpts to works that relate to bissett's poetics of audio performance and media recording in the late 1960s and early 1970s. Each image may be incorporated into the argument of this essay by the reader however they may choose to do so, even if I may have other suggestive connections in mind through their compilation. In league with bissett's expansively permissive poetics, this chapter contends for a radically open text for qualitative listening and interpretive cruising. Following on what Mathieu Aubin has called "queer sonic resonances" in bissett's literary recording, an audio recording accompanies each visual and paragraph, which may be heard in concert with both the featured images and the chapter.[10] If the internally standardized queer orthography and performance practices in bissett's output over the last thirty years have modulated the urgency of his poetics, perhaps these archival materials can be released anew—in facsimile and recording, altered but indexed—as prescient documents for an increasingly regulated media environment in the present, another way to cruise utopia. Taken together, I have found that this expanded set of investigations presents an argument for bissett as an important entry point into the study of digital transcoding and the queer temporality of afterlives generated by online dispersion.

Unexpected vectors and unimagined questions emerge when tracing the digital correlates to bissett's profoundly experimental approach to analog media. However, a central query remains constant: what are the variable poetics that digital circulation introduces to a heterogeneous array of dispersion effects? My approach attempts to channel a mode of fidelity to the ways in which bissett's early work, in the words of Darren Wershler, "defies conventional notions of genre: collages are paintings and drawings bleed into poems turn into scores for reading and chant and performance generates writing bound into books published sometimes or not."[11] As a kind of parasite on bissett's web presence, the reader might consider this chapter to be the introduction to a new set of versions of these objects as digital files. The lines between preservation and republication are increasingly difficult to define. We might not consider a record transformed based on the library or archive that contains it. However, if the same album were republished by a new label with new liner notes, its bibliographic codes would be widely recognized as significantly revised. As is the case with the reissue of an out-of-print album, bissett's output acquires new audiographic codes in each of the following sites of its reappearance. The little database, even masquerading as a chapter, also suggests that a highly significant mode of versioning is taking place in every instance.

Variable Outliers

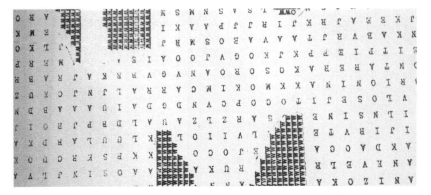

Figure 3.3. JPG: bill bissett, from *Medicine My Mouth's on Fire* (Ottawa: Oberon Press, 1974). MP3: bissett, "Colours" (1966), *Past Eroticism: Canadian Sound Poetry of the 1960s* (Underwhich Audiographics No. 13, *grOnk* Final Series #6: 1986).

Before launching into this contingent narrative, some brief remarks on alternate trajectories of the chapter are in order. From a digital humanities or cultural analytics perspective, each of the following databases seems primed for a range of analytic and metric tools for analysis. On the most basic level, a number of textual analyses seem readily available. For example, in sprawling collections like *Mutant Sounds, UbuWeb,* or *PennSound,* a simple set of maps and graphs that chart the geographic locations of recordings would be of interest. Through these data sets, we might query the geographic tendencies of these little databases. Where are most recordings made, why are specific locations best represented in these collections, and how might prominent outliers speak to these trends? The answers to these questions may indeed produce compelling results. Perhaps there is a bump in the number of recordings from Colorado given the Jack Kerouac School for Disembodied Poetics' predilection for archiving. Or, we might imagine the role that New York City plays in the distribution of cultural capital even in allegedly horizontal online archives. More obviously, a great number of recordings are made in Philadelphia, given the documentary proclivities of the Kelly Writers House and the networks of affiliation with readings series in the city more broadly. A periodical reading might chart the exponential growth, stagnation, or decline of these collections, as seen in chapter 1. More pressingly, one might chart the representations of gender, race, or class throughout each collection, as the VIDA Count and others have done with literary magazines.[12]

The resulting metrics would serve the important function of confirming what a knowledgeable user might already suspect: Philadelphia is overrepresented in poetry readings; New York City maintains its prominence in recordings, even in its hosting of Bay Area poets; the distribution of gender, race, and class skews heavily toward white male readers of relative privilege; collections grow, stagnate, and ultimately cease operations. This chapter does not seek to confirm or dispute these matters of fact. There are systemic problems in these datasets that extend far beyond the metrics of digital humanities. If anything, the selection of bissett—famously and troublingly mischaracterized by Jack Kerouac as "an Indian boy; . . . Bill Bissett, or Bissonnette," often disregarded by the poetic present, a queer polymath recorded variously as rock singer, concrete poet, or chanting artist—is highlighted for his variable outlier status.[13]

> sumtimes whun long line saying evrything at a time and th whole
> pome th sum uv thees yu can get a pome in th mail from anywher
> nd not knowing that langwage undrstand what yuv bin sent into
> inkantashuns and no fukin theery cud covr cud make consistent
> all ths happenings changes push no whun point a view goin furthr
> into th rhythm uv a prson speeking

Figure 3.4. JPG: bill bissett, from *words in th fire* (1972). MP3: bill bissett & th mandan massacre, "now according to paragraph C," *Awake in th Red Desert* (1968).

In another, more technical direction, a recent series of research projects has questioned how the digital humanities might begin to analyze digital audio collections of poetry. The most prominent of these is the HiPSTAS project spearheaded by Tanya Clement using ARLO software developed by David Tcheng.[14] Rather than analyze metadata like location, date, or author embedded in sound collections, this project aims to work with the data of sound itself. The ARLO interface allows researchers to search and collate information that uses aggregate sound signatures as search queries. Kenneth Sherwood sums up the process succinctly: "At a simplified level, ARLO works by producing images of the audio spectra and then comparing these visualized time-slices with others across a range of preselected audio files."[15] Although ARLO was originally developed to aid ornithological research, poetry scholars have adopted the software to experiment with how we might investigate sound on its own terms. Interesting experiments have emerged: Chris Mustazza discerns the difference between aluminum records and magnetic tapes; Eric Rettberg has isolated patterns of laughter; Sherwood analyzes variant recordings of poems; Clement and Stephen McLaughlin visualize spectrograms of applause.[16] Its possibilities are myriad. For example, AI-aided accuracy in speech-to-text recognition could open new pathways of use, and a more robust technical vocabulary for analyzing tenor and pitch could aid in the study of aural practices in poetry. While the potentials in this approach are promising, practical applications toward the advancement of critical scholarship seem a ways off, despite advances in audio machine-learning tools. This chapter is, once more, pushing against analytical aims. Rather than test new software for the processing of sound collections, I aim to chart the effects upon a specific set of files alongside current platforms for reconfiguring the little database as it stands. This is not to deny the promise of computational approaches to the collection as a whole. Instead, this chapter articulates a history of the circulation of sound in the recent past of the internet and the recomposition of the collection as a poetic project today, as told through the stories of the files it might host.

Mutant Sounds

 Figure 3.5. JPG: bill bissett, back cover detail from *th wind up tongue* (Vancouver: Blewointmentpress, 1976). MP3: bill bissett & th mandan massacre, "heard ya tellin," *Awake in th Red Desert* (1968).

The incident that catalyzed my interest in writing about file transmission through bissett's work occurred fifteen years ago, when I stumbled on a relatively unnoticed archival release through a little database called *Mutant Sounds*.[17] In the heyday of the "music blog" (once a prevalent mode of sharing sound files online), *Mutant Sounds* delivered an incredible array of rare and obscure albums, primarily ripped from out-of-print vinyl LPs, free for download. Founded in 2007, the *Mutant Sounds* site on Blogspot had amassed over three thousand posted releases in five years. Many were so rare that only the most devoted and well-resourced crate diggers might have ever heard their sounds otherwise. The reader might note that *UbuWeb* hosts just under one thousand entries in the "sound" subsection of the site and *PennSound* features approximately six hundred author entries. While these pages most often host multiple sets of recordings per entry, the volume is roughly comparable to the *Mutant Sounds* inventory. It's all the more remarkable that an independent, noninstitutional initiative like *Mutant Sounds,* which ran on a free blog platform periodically releasing download links enabled by free file-sharing servers, might rival these collections as one of the great digital repositories (or, more boldly, archival collections) for obscure experimental recordings from the last half century. At least, it may have been recognized as such by its devoted core of users. However, these qualifications have become moot: the collection disappeared from the internet just as suddenly as it had once appeared.

curtains

senor　Caruso

Figure 3.6. JPG: bill bissett, "the caruso poem," from *Awake in th Red Desert* (1968). MP3: bill bissett & th mandan massacre, "an ode to d a levy," *Awake in th Red Desert* (1968).

In the spring of 2013, the website had recently ceased operations. After six years of reissuing out-of-print albums on a (misinformed) "notice-and-takedown" principle of online copyright law, a greater current led by the RIAA (Recording Industry Association of America) and the scandalous failure of Megaupload brought about the site's demise.[18] RapidShare, the "file locker" of choice for *Mutant Sounds,* had deleted most files that the site had uploaded to its server in an effort to avoid the same fate as Kim Dotcom.[19] This process was accelerated by the emergence of a range of streaming platforms, from Pandora to Spotify, as well as a few musicians asserting a wide range of copyright claims over time. Currently, the *Mutant Sounds* catalog of thousands of digitized recordings lies in the obscurity of digital ruin. The site proves an important point that Vint Cerf, among others, has made over the years: an impending digital dark age threatens all online production; it's best to print important works to analog media.[20] We might add two additional points: one, that this type of collection is increasingly unlikely to emerge; and two, that the DIY internet of the 1990s and 2000s has long since disappeared.

 Figure 3.7. JPG: bill bissett, from *RUSH: what fuckan theory: a study uv language* (Toronto: Gronk, 1971 / BookThug, 2012). MP3: bill bissett & th mandan massacre, "is yr car too soft for th roads," *Awake in th Red Desert* (1968).

On a roundtable hosted by *The Awl* and aptly titled "The Rise and Fall of the Obscure Music Download Blog," *Mutant Sounds* editor Eric Lumbleau addresses the unique moment of these "sharity" sites, active primarily from 2004 until 2012.[21] Summarizing the purpose of the *Mutant Sounds* collection for the Free Music Archive, the editors characterize their project as a campaign for "enlightening the masses to elusive musical esoterica buried beneath canned historical narratives and induced cultural amnesia."[22] The ideological thrust of the collection, much like *UbuWeb* and *PennSound,* was to destabilize the historical narrative by distributing an alternate canon far and wide. In particular, *Mutant Sounds* was plotted to combat the accepted progression from rock to punk to post punk, and to diversify these heterogeneous global forms. A brief scroll through their posts quickly presents a much stranger and far more diverse sense of experimental music from the mid-1960s to the present.

Or rather, one might hear that argument if the collection were still intact. Instead, today's user will encounter only the contexts, descriptions, and images of albums one might never find elsewhere. Of course, the position of an album as charted by *Mutant Sounds* produces a dramatically different register from the presses with which—and poets with whom—even bissett's experimental recorded work is most often associated. Nevertheless, with bibliographic attention to release dates, edition numbers, and the technical process of the digitization, the text still manages to transmit the essential components of archival metadata, also swiftly recoverable with a Discogs search. Perhaps these remnants of the site may still function like the Nurse With Wound list that guided the collection itself: as a series of signposts for further exploration beyond the regulated audio streams of Spotify and iTunes.[23]

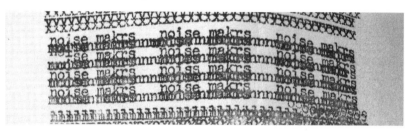

Figure 3.8. JPG: bill bissett, from *s th story i to: trew adventure* (Vancouver: Blewointmentpress, 1970). MP3: bill bissett & th mandan massacre, "she still and curling," *Awake in th Red Desert* (1968).

Within this catalogue, on February 1, 2008, *Mutant Sounds* released a digital version of the singular album *Awake in th Red Desert,* recorded by bill bissett and th mandan massacre in 1968. At the time, I ran a pseudo-anonymous sharity blog of my own in between audio engineering sessions for *PennSound,* where I had recently become an editor. I downloaded the album immediately, as part of a habitual acquisition session among the various music blogs I followed. Before the "filter bubble" of social media encapsulated the navigable internet, these sessions were a mode of discovery within an enigmatic and unpredictable network. Like those done by many of the untold numbers of collectors tracking the releases shared by *Mutant Sounds,* my private little database grew within the contours of my own interests.

Unlike the stable collections of *PennSound, UbuWeb,* or *SpokenWeb,* these releases came to exist only as a dispersed set of objects on hard drives accumulating heterogeneous materials in unknowable configurations. In my own collection, *Awake in th Red Desert* arrived as a RAR archive file (Roshal ARchive; for Eugene Roshal, who developed the format in 1993). The contents of the decompressed folder were saved to my general "Music Library" folder and the RAR file was discarded. Duplicate copies of the album were placed in two adjacent folders: the first for potential upload to *PennSound*; the second in a database structured for the collaborative *Endless Nameless* project I published with James Hoff at the time. *Endless Nameless* organized digital objects by their original publishers to produce a series of limited edition hard drives. In this instance, I made a new folder entitled "See/Hear Records." I rechart this activity, as it is quickly disappearing, if not entirely foreign, in an era of streaming sound and authorized in-application cloud-based purchases.[24] The contingent provenance of other iterations, within other users' collections, is as variable as the unknown numbers of downloaders.

 Figure 3.9. JPG: bill bissett, detail from *Awake in th Red Desert* (1968). MP3: bill bissett & th mandan massacre, "fires in th tempul," *Awake in th Red Desert* (1968).

Aside from the adjacent domain of experimental music, one primary difference from the collections that follow is that *Mutant Sounds* exclusively presented download links to full albums for external use. I'll return to this point as it pertains to the other sites discussed, but for now, we might sketch the general character of this distribution method. Each blog post was linked to a full album download. These downloads were typically delivered as RAR or ZIP files that compressed a folder containing individual tracks, along with extremely lo-fi images of album artwork. The archive was a conduit for personal use, with the emphasis exclusively placed on sound. In the case of *Awake in th Red Desert,* this meant the exclusion of the "recorded book" that was originally distributed with the album by See/Hear Records. In this way, the fundamental purpose of the

original publication, relating the printed page to the audio recording, had been excised from the digital release. This action is at the
heart of the formlessness of the MP3. Jonathan Sterne has noted:
"At the psychoacoustic level as well as the industrial level, the MP3
is designed for promiscuity."[25] Put differently, the sustained attention of "reading along" is counterintuitive to a format built for distracted listening and streamlined distribution. Recordings of poetry
readings in the MP3, as we'll see, typically present an alternative to
these popular (distracted) uses of music online. Nevertheless, after
download, the MP3 files were at the user's disposal in their own private collection, ready to be played on any platform in any number of
circumstances.

PennSound

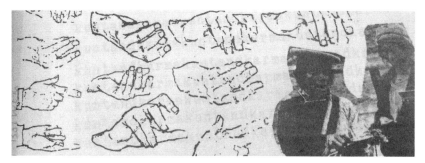

Figure 3.10. JPG: bill bissett, from *the lost angel mining co.* (1969). MP3:
bissett, "Air To The Bells/The Face In The Moon" (1967) from *Past Eroticism*
(1986).

When I first listened to the files, as the reader of this chapter is
advised to do, I quickly recognized the singular contribution that
Awake in th Red Desert might be heard to have made within the archive of countercultural poetics in the 1960s. I moved quickly to
get selections from the album up on *PennSound,* where they might
be distributed to a very different community of listeners. As a first
step, I wrote to bissett directly for permission. In an important
note on copyright, *PennSound,* unlike *Mutant Sounds,* operates as a
strictly permissions-based platform. Bissett responded with characteristic charm and inimitable orthography: "yes xcellent if yu
want 2 put seleksyuns from awake in th red desert on PennSound
that wud b awesum[.]"[26] To augment selections from *Awake in th*

Red Desert, I decided to "segment" a full-length reading bissett gave at the Bowery Poetry Club in 2006.[27] Both recordings were hosted with embedded links to individual MP3 files. For some time, this was the extent of *PennSound*'s bill bissett collection. Since then, the page has accumulated (among others): a movie recording of the 2012 Book*hug launch of its republication of *Rush: What Fuckan Theory*; a radio program recording from around 1978 through the Robert Creeley collection; an interview with Phillis Webb from the CBC in 1967; and, most recently, an untitled home recording from May of 2022.[28] On another *PennSound* page, the user may also find a bissett track from the *Carnivocal: Celebration of Sound Poetry* album from 2004. From the Bowery Poetry Club back to See/Hear Records, the situation of *Awake in th Red Desert* on *PennSound* reveals myriad differences from the original upload.

it is raging th sound thru th throat
it dont know what ium typing
i dont know what ium typing

Figure 3.11. JPG: bill bissett, from *RUSH: what fuckan theory* (1971/2012). MP3: bill bissett & th mandan massacre, "my mouths on fire," *Awake in th Red Desert* (1968).

While *Mutant Sounds* and *PennSound* hosted precisely the same bissett MP3 files—aside from the altered ID3 tags—the textual conditions of these two iterations could not be more different.[29] In "Making Audio Visible: The Lessons of Visual Language for the Textualization of Sound," experimental poet Charles Bernstein maintains that "the sound file exists not as a pure acoustic or sound event—an oral or performative event outside textuality—but as a textual condition, mediated by its visual marking, its bibliographic codes, and the tagging we give to it to mark what we consider of semantic significance."[30] An additional aspect of this condition, to recap previous invocations of Jerome McGann, is the social text. In other words, a more nebulous array of factors including reception, circulation, and context also inflect an object's textual condition. To repost is to transform: not superficially, but at the most basic levels of a work's significance. Here, we might note the immediate transformation from the lyrical "spew" in the music-based collection at *Mutant Sounds* to the institutional stamp of innovative poetry on

PennSound. Where *PennSound* focuses on individual MP3s of poems and complete readings, *Mutant Sounds* released only full album collections previously published by a broad range of labels. Both sites push against canonical formations in their own way: *Mutant Sounds* against the tidy lineages of popular music; *PennSound* against the tidy lineages of lyric poetry. A confluence of these generic interventions inheres in the work of bissett. *Awake in th Red Desert* works in both directions, and each site transforms the historical recording in its own way, for its own listeners. If, as Steve McCaffery has argued in *Sound Poetry: A Catalogue,* bissett's pathbreaking approach to sound poetry with Th Mandan Massacre was "significant in pushing poetic composition into the communal domain," we might wonder in what domain it exists today.[31]

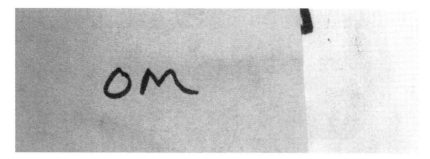

Figure 3.12. JPG: bill bissett, from *Sunday work?* (Vancouver: Blewointmentpress, 1969). MP3: bissett, "5. And that light is in thee is in thee and," SGWU (1969).

Despite their contrasting contexts, these two sound-based sites share a great deal in common. Like *Mutant Sounds,* the *PennSound* collection periodically releases audio recordings via a highly compressed MP3 audio format that typically remediates original cassettes, reel-to-reel tapes, vinyl records, and radio broadcasts. Both collections grow incrementally with each new digitized release, from a full series to an incidental recording. Primarily delivering files compressed to just 128 kilobytes per second, the MP3 actually prevents *PennSound* from receiving official recognition as a poetry recording *archive.*[32] Where other projects might acquire certain types of funding for digital archives hosting "lossless" formats like WAV or FLAC (free lossless audio codec), *PennSound*'s emphasis on speedy distribution via MP3 files precludes it from archival classifications, despite the rarity, range, and depth of its collection.

Instead, like *Mutant Sounds,* the *PennSound* collection is built for user downloads.

This approach reflects the uncertain future of the internet when the collection was founded by Bernstein and Filreis at the University of Pennsylvania in 2003. Even then, the MP3 offered a better alternative to the proprietary Real Audio format.[33] Given its portability and accessibility, the MP3 remains the most popular format for audio distribution online. Widely circulated arguments on the distraction inherent to the MP3 are weakened by the "close listening" techniques that poetry generically warrants. The recordings at *PennSound* earn this attention in contexts as diverse as private academic research, university classrooms, and MOOC discussion boards. In remarks on the use of its thousands of poetry recordings, Filreis notes that the files have been downloaded by hundreds of millions of users. More promiscuously, we might imagine a million new versions across blog posts, syllabi, remixes, and other uses of the files.[34]

UbuWeb

> when it cums
> to words they
> want th control th
> proof of yr alleg
> iance to th ruling class
> of meaning

Figure 3.13. JPG: bill bissett, from *RUSH: what fuckan theory* (1971/2012). MP3: bill bissett & th mandan massacre, "Arbutus garden apts 6 p m," *Awake in th Red Desert* (1968).

Although *Awake in th Red Desert* is not hosted on *UbuWeb,* there are two illuminating mentions of the album among the twelve hits for the string "bill bissett" on the site; both citations are from discographies. The first, compiled by Michael Gibb and originally included in the remarkable *Sound Poetry: A Catalogue,* is titled "Sound Poetry: A Historical Discography." The second, compiled by Dan Lander and Micah Lexier for *Sound By Artists,* is titled "A Discography of Recorded Work by Artists." Of course, bissett is both poet and artist. However, the difference between the two—paired with the generic equivalence played out across the site—clearly bespeaks an entirely new condition for hearing bissett's album. *UbuWeb* offers a less focused conjuncture: neither the musical archeology of *Mutant Sounds* nor the poetry-reading compendium of *PennSound.* Here the work joins with a wide range of objects beyond classification: conceptual art, structural film, concrete poetry, and other works that might be read under the sign of the avant-garde, broadly construed. Other hits for "bissett" include articles by McCaffery and derek beaulieu, a few concrete poems featured in various collections, bpNichol's homage sound poem "Bill Bissett's Lullaby" from *Motherlove* (1968), and bissett's track "The Mountain Lake." The last of these was recorded with guitar, tape, and "flux" as a contribution to an audio supplement to the 1984 sound poetry issue of *The Capilano Review.*[35] Gathering this scattered assemblage of hits for bissett across the various sections of the site delivers a collection marked by the same intermedial disregard that characterizes the internet at large.

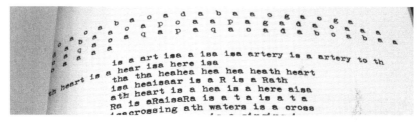

Figure 3.14. JPG: bill bissett, "o a b a," from *Awake in th Red Desert* (1968). MP3: bill bissett & th mandan massacre, "o a b a," *Awake in th Red Desert* (1968).

However, the most interesting audio work by bissett on *UbuWeb* does not appear in any of the search results. Clicking through the extensive sound section of the site, a user might stumble upon the entry for *Past Eroticism: Canadian Sound Poetry in the 1960s* (1986). The page hosting this digitized cassette simply breaks the audio into two MP3 files (Side A and Side B) in a technically convenient and tellingly remediated fashion. Aside from the title, there is no searchable text on the page. Instead, a JPG scan of the liner notes displays: "bill bissett (recorded 9/28/66* & 6/26/67**) / 7. Air To The Bells/The Face In The Moon** / 8. Valley Dancers* / 9. Colours*."[36]

These three tracks immediately predate *Awake in th Red Desert* and anticipate that album's generic freedom at the intersection of poetry, chant, song, and music. All three have been segmented for the first time for this page. Compared to the relatively metadata-scarce *PennSound,* the *UbuWeb* distribution of the MP3 file is even further stripped of context. And yet, an expansive interdisciplinary reading of the bissett files emerges through *UbuWeb*. If the files themselves carry little information, the context of their dispersion supports a robust network for an array of avant-garde productions in poetry, dance, sound, film, essays, radio, posters, and so on. All of this is compiled and released together with the happenstance bricolage of an assemblage magazine. Here, the bissett tracks merge with an undifferentiated conflux of historical and contemporary practices, dislocated from the original social texts of the work. By betraying all formal contexts, *UbuWeb* creates a digital context aptly suited to the genre-blending work bissett set out to record.

SpokenWeb

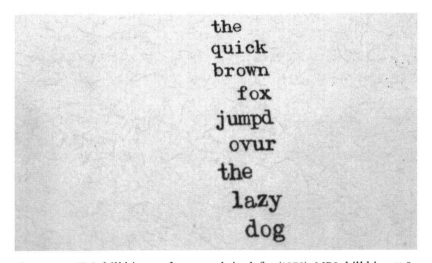

the
quick
brown
fox
jumpd
ovur
the
lazy
dog

Figure 3.15. JPG: bill bissett, from *words in th fire* (1972). MP3: bill bissett & th mandan massacre, "and th green wind," *Awake in th Red Desert* (1968).

It is in relation to these three sites that I first considered bissett's performance in 1969 at Sir George Williams University (SGWU), as presented on the *SpokenWeb* digital poetry archive.[37] Recorded just one year after the release of *Awake in th Red Desert,* the SGWU reading draws from the same body of work that bissett deploys in his previous "recorded book." As *SpokenWeb* tells us, with superb bibliographic attention, this reading by bissett features poems to be published in *Nobody Owns th Earth* (Toronto: House of Anasi, 1971), *the lost angel mining co.* (Vancouver: Blew Ointment, 1969), and *OF TH LAND DIVINE SERVICE* (Toronto: Weed/Flower, 1968). This last title is the organizing principle of the SGWU reading. It is also the only book released by bissett in the same year as *Awake in th Red Desert.* While the tape cuts off the opening, we can safely assume bissett begins with the first two poems in *OF TH LAND DIVINE SERVICE,* given the pattern of works to follow: namely, poems "3," "4," and a variation of "5" in the cycle, followed by intermittent works from across the book and concluded with "moss song," the final poem from *OF TH LAND DIVINE SERVICE.* However, both the beginning and the end of the reading are cut off. The failure of the archive performs the play of *in media res* that bissett's work invites. Sterne extends this aspect of the audio collection in his article "The Preservation Paradox in Digital Audio," insisting that "sound recording is an extension of ephemerality, not its undoing."[38] Through no fault of the *SpokenWeb* editors, the lapse in the original mobile reel-to-reel tape recording renders the attentive metadata approach to this particular reading necessarily incomplete. There is no introduction to the reading; nor is there any commentary from the audience that we might analyze.[39] The technical flaws in the reel-to-reel recording match with the aesthetics of assemblage, trans-genre performance, and the intermedial nature of bissett's poetics. In other words, to borrow a track from Wershler, "bissett's experiments on poetic excess yield highly specific social, historical and technological information about the shape and boundaries of what constitutes the permissible" in the contemporary audio archive.[40] In this way, finally arriving at *SpokenWeb,* bissett delivers a compelling case for practices that operate at the limits of the little database.

```
speaking speaking
speaking th eye is
speaking th eye is
speaking th eagle
talks
```

Figure 3.16. JPG: bill bissett, "Tarzan Collage," from *Medicine My Mouths on Fire* (1974). MP3: bissett, "Tarzan Collage," SGWU (1969).

It's useful to query these limits of the database with regard to *SpokenWeb,* if only because the collection is itself so *attentive* to its materials. In its initial conception, it was designed to "develop co-ordinated and collaborative approaches to literary historical study, digital development, and critical and pedagogical engagement with diverse collections of literary sound recordings from across Canada and beyond."[41] *SpokenWeb* "begins with the preservation and description of sonic artifacts that have captured literary events of the past, and quickly moves into a wide range of approaches and activities that activate these artifacts in the present."[42] These scholarly approaches coded into the interface present an apparatus for critical engagement with the materials they present that is deeper than the minimal contexts supplied by sprawling MP3 repositories like *PennSound* or *Mutant Sounds* that are built for access above all. This depth model is characterized by the site's reflexivity, including sections that feature research perspectives, audio analysis and sound visualization resources, ongoing events and blog posts, oral literary histories, and commentary on other audio collections online. Further, all of these features are concentrated on a set of recordings from a single reading series held at SGWU between 1965 and 1974. Each reading is in turn broken down with introductions, bibliographies, transcripts, sources, and an array of metadata on the recording. Annie Murray and Jared Wiercinski have extensively charted the development of these features of the site, and their papers on the subject are essential reading for the future of audio studies on the internet.[43] This chapter, inspired by the expansive scholarly approaches of *SpokenWeb,* has been prepared to relate the traversal of a single recording adjacent to the *SpokenWeb* collection in order to sound out the relation of audio files hosted by *Mutant Sounds, PennSound, UbuWeb* and beyond into the private little database of any potential listener.

The differences between these sites and the *SpokenWeb* platform are, of course, quite pronounced. However, the commonalities they share may prove to be just as illuminating. *SpokenWeb,* like *Mutant Sounds,* sets out to map a network of relations in a given era of poetic production. Relating a community of practitioners in proximity to SGWU to an international group of poets and interlocutors, *SpokenWeb* presents the reading series as an "enormously intertex-

```
a chain of gold which art of th children
a chain of gold which art of th children
a chain of gold which art of th children
a chain of gold which art of th children
a chain of gold which art of th children
a chain of gold which art of th children
a chain of gold which art of th children
a chain of gold which art of th children
singing a chain of gold which art of th
children singing a chain of gold which
```

Figure 3.17. JPG: bill bissett, "4: a chain of gold which art of th children," from *OF TH LAND DIVINE SERVICE* (Toronto: Weed/Flower, 1968). MP3: bissett, "4: a chain of gold which art of th children," SGWU (1969).

tual affair," following on Robert Scholes and Clifford Wulfman's work discussed in the previous chapter.[44] The series is a sounding board for developing poetics and unlikely combinations. In this way, bissett is linked to his contemporaries at the height of his investigation into the technologies of print publication and public performance. Like *PennSound,* the little database is distinguished by its focus on the poetry series, a periodical collection not unlike the complete run of a little magazine. Rooted in a specific locality with a concrete set of recording devices and live contexts, hosting the poetry series online amplifies an approach to the event of literary versioning. In Bernstein's words, considering the sound file as part of the work "disrupt[s] even the most expansive conception of versions, all based on different print versions."[45] Both sites work to make this disruption possible. *SpokenWeb,* like *UbuWeb,* recodes its materials within an expanded set of concerns: bissett's reading, like others featured on the site, is suddenly absorbed into an editorial argument on the scholarly use of digital platforms, the audio collection as an object of academic study, and the emerging challenges of studying sound with digital analytics. Surely, this is the most unlikely context for these readings. Who might have imagined in 1969, when the recordings were made, that such an inquiry would be the framework through which these readings would be received by a public audience?

Listening to the poetry series at *SpokenWeb* today, it's impossible to ignore the depth of the original run, with its unique constellation of readers and the wider poetics community at SGWU. Of course,

a whil heer th sounds yu see

 Figure 3.18. JPG: bill bissett, from *RUSH: what fuckan theory* (1971/2012).
MP3: bissett, "bright yellow sky," SGWU (1969).

the poetry reading constructs its public. But it is equally impossible to erase the broader digital milieux and cultures of use in which this collection's digitization surfaces. Thus, to listen deeply to a reading that bill bissett gave in 1969, the user must also hear a range of contemporaneous works hosted across the internet, to consider the digitization of the reading on a synchronic plane that includes versions circulating in unknown locations and unknowable configurations.

For example, further afield the user encounters samples of bissett's "an ode to d a levy" from *Awake in th Red Desert* looping through The Chemical Brothers' electronic music record *We Are the Night*. More abstractly, one might turn into an invocation of "Awake in th Red Desert" by Vancouver art rock band Dada Plan on the album *DANCE MIRAAJ*. Or, coming back to this page, this chapter, in the time since an early article draft of this text appeared online, the complete ambient image dataset running alongside these paragraphs has been deployed by VisPo artist Jim Andrews to populate an interactive bissett visual poem engine.[46] Samples, evocations, remixes, to mention only a few examples of expanded use, all write and rewrite these same files into platforms, formats, and genres that can be written back into the narrative above only after the fact. Their inflections on the story lie latent within the ongoing flux of dispersion. The ordinary hard drives of an unknowable numbers of listeners enact their own idiosyncratic inflections to these files as they play through earbuds or reside within desktop folders. Vernacular practices of making, recording, posting, and playing online extend this story to a conclusion that can be only an open ellipsis . . .

Beyond bissett, these same playful encounters with transmission and use could be recounted through any number of recordings on

SpokenWeb, UbuWeb, PennSound, and *Mutant Sounds,* among others. For this reason, rather than bind any of these threads into a single string, this chapter aims to trace, select, collect, edit, and disperse. Against a pointed argument concerning the ways in which bissett might illuminate the audio–visual–textual confluence on these sites, this essay points to a variety of alternate readings that bissett might enable the user to consider. This, I argue, is at the core of the digitized poetry reading. Already a kind of offshoot or supplement to the printed work, the social text of the historical reading radiates out to a wide range of materials connecting the past to our present moment, on- and offline, transforming our understanding of each in turn. The core of *SpokenWeb*'s design seems to be premised on this argument. As a platform for scholarship, the site directs its user outward: to read historical publications, critical articles, technical details, and source materials into each recording; to read the culture of the online audio collection into the poetry series; to read the potential for a future use of digital tools into a little database of audio recordings; to read the digital file, the poem, the book, and the reading at once. In each, a contingent set of concerns, highlights, and transformations arises by attending to the conditions of any given file. This scholarship is built on the sheer potentiality of reading the narratives generated within the endless versioning processes of the internet. As such, like the audio recording itself, it remains in the realm of the virtual: the pleasure of knowledge is joined with the impossibility of any full realization.

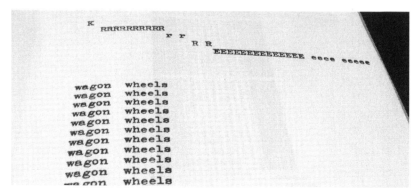

Figure 3.19. JPG: bill bissett, "wagon wheels," from *Awake in th Red Desert* (1968).

MUPS

In one notable afterlife to the transmission narrative above, the bissett files I've traced in this chapter could be found streaming within an interface called *MashUPS* (*MUPS*), written by David Jhave Johnston, released in 2012, and rendered inoperable in 2021.[47] *MUPS* was an interactive flash platform for the live remixing of 1,260 audio files culled from the *PennSound* collection.[48] Jhave describes the project as developed both "for the sheer pleasure of simultaneity" and "as a digital augmentation in the study of prosody," where sites like *PennSound* "permit innovative explorations into the evolution of poetics."[49] As both transformative artwork and substantial act of digital scholarship, the project bears a resemblance to the textwarez works produced by Sebastian Lütgert. In one elegantly minimal page, the interface completely reorients our perception of *PennSound*. No longer is the site a repository for isolated audio files. Instead, it is an interface that affords the potential for a scenario wherein "poems speak to each other and with each other" through a widely variable set of parameters for computational audition.[50] Each of the previously described bissett recordings from both the *Awake in th Red Desert* LP and the 2006 Segue Bowery Poetry Club reading are present on *MUPS*. If there were a fitting conclusion to the story of these bissett MP3s originating at *Mutant Sounds,* it would surely be the frenetic chorus generated by *MUPS*.

Taking this ending as canon, I conclude this chapter's exploration of bissett-based transmission with *MUPS*. I offer this reading of the interface as a generative direction for thinking through the simultaneity of creative making and digital humanities approaches to the study of poetry recordings on the internet. In one of the few reviews of this work, Leonardo Flores similarly contends that these kinds of tools "aren't just literary expressions informed by each writer's poetics, they are also poetically and artistically motivated computational tools for some kinds of analysis associated with digital humanities methods."[51] As a mode of digital humanities making, Jhave's *MUPS* performs an operation on *PennSound* that is both difficult to pinpoint as scholarship and relatively unrecognized as a work of poetics. It also harbors and remixes a little database of its own design. Both of these frames, I contend, are essential to un-

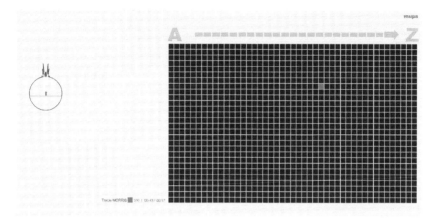

Figure 3.20. A screen capture of the *MUPS* interface after clicking on a single node in the grid of 1,260 alphabetically organized squares to activate the playback of a sound file by Tracie Morris.

derstanding *MUPS* and its relation to *PennSound*. As additive layers, both of these frames also bear on the bissett files that have been included in the interface.

Before returning to bissett, we can start by outlining the technical details of *MUPS*. On loading the page, the user sees a 28×45 grid of black squares beneath a large display of "A————————————> Z" written in light grey, with a "mups" just above the Z. The page features a full-screen flash video program entitled "pennsoundup _WEAVE.swf" and a short Google Analytics tracking script. Hovering over any single square reveals author and file information, parsed and organized according to the naming conventions of the *PennSound* collection.[52] Clicking on any square immediately begins the playback of the linked sound file, which is lit up in shades of red. A circle also appears to the left of the grid, which animates a visualization of the soundwave around a vertical volume slider. Clicking on subsequent squares plays corresponding sound files simultaneously. Concurrently played files stack up to the left of the grid as a complete sequential record of all recordings activated during a given session with *MUPS*. When a file completes playback or is clicked off, it turns to grey. Throughout, only when two or more files are playing simultaneously, the user will notice a text reading "WEAVE is OFF" beneath the volume slider to the left. Clicking on this text activates WEAVE, the most fascinating feature of the interface.

Turning on WEAVE activates an automatic switching mechanism between simultaneous files, based on perceived silences and intervals within audio recordings. The parameters of these switches are set by the user in three categories adjusted by vertical sliders: "threshold," "tolerance," and "pause." First, "threshold" delimits the decibel level under which a sound recording is perceived as "silent" enough to switch. Second, "tolerance" sets the number of threshold points before a switch occurs. And third, "pause" sets the amount of time before the program looks for a new switch in each sample. In each parameter, the interface encourages quick shifting with notes like "HINT: To make sounds shift quicker, put TOLERANCE down." Indeed, quicker skips are more impressive, as the user listens to the software jumping rapidly from one reader to the next with what can seem like the seamlessness of natural conversation, concerted collaboration, or an attentive DJ mixing the tracks.

With WEAVE activated, the user can hear "up to 32 streams" of poetry recordings in a simultaneous reading that shifts from file to file according to the parameters set by the user. Altogether this interface elegantly delivers the defining features of "new media" according to Lev Manovich: numerical representation (highlighting numerical values for switches); modularity (every sample can be resampled); automation (the program runs forward without input); variability (each listening is newly forged based on the inputted parameter); and, ultimately, transcoding (gathering sound artifacts from previous media performance formats). Indeed, Manovich's own *Soft Cinema* is a near analogue to the generative listening system presented by *MUPS*. These works might be considered a form of database poetics in their reflections of the formal properties of the databases and algorithms that both determine and facilitate digital use.

However, in addition to the database poetics of *MUPS*, Jhave also executes a highly delimited editorial function. To facilitate a navigable user experience, *MUPS* distills the tens of thousands of sound recordings on *PennSound* down to 1,260 selected files. The selection process coheres only within the affordances of the interface.

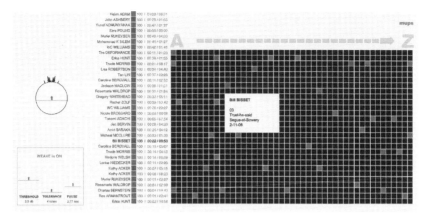

Figure 3.21. A screen capture of the *MUPS* interface after clicking on multiple squares in the grid to activate a range of voices with the "WEAVE" feature enabling skips between files according to the "threshold," "tolerance," and "pause" sliders for recognizing silence.

The "pleasure of simultaneity" is crafted from a diversity of voices, genres, reading styles, and recording textures. Historical recordings of Guillaume Apollinaire and Amiri Baraka interrupt contemporary readings by Yusef Komunyakaa and Nicole Brossard. Smoothly intoned science fiction narratives by Samuel Delany intersperse with the glitch aesthetics of Morris described at the opening of this chapter. The staccato punch of Christian Bök's sound poetry might burst into ambient poetics by Tan Lin. Non-native English speakers (Rosmarie Waldrop), distinctive styles (Bernstein), and sound poetry tracks (Steve McCaffery), in particular, are heavily represented. More to the point, musical outliers to the *PennSound* collection are overrepresented in the selection: sizable segments of the grid are taken by radio artist Gregory Whitehead, the punk poetry album *Redoing Childhood* by Kathy Acker, and the audio-experimental-theatre production of *San Francisco's Burning* by Helen Adam, each of which include musical accompaniment to the spoken word. These tracks are not the most representative of *PennSound,* but rather present samples from the limits of the collection. The editorial premise seems to argue that layering musical and sonically adventurous work produces the most interesting results for simultaneous mashups, or perhaps these works serve as analogues to the *MUPS* project as a whole. Within this setup, it is not difficult to imagine why bissett might command so many squares. The howl of "2 Awake in the Red Desert" or the moog synthesizers of "Now According to Paragraph C" provides the perfect counterpoint to more normalized patterns in the performance of poetry. In this way, *MUPS* facilitates the listening pleasure of formal discordance.

The little database deployed by *MUPS* differs from every other audio collection detailed in this chapter. The collection has no pretension toward completion. It offers neither the collector's audiotopia of *Mutant Sounds* nor the comprehensive poetry catalog of *PennSound*. It ranges even further from the catch-all avant-garde of *UbuWeb* or the single-series depth of *SpokenWeb*. Like an extended mixtape, *MUPS* sacrifices the exhaustive in favor of the extraordinary. The interface works only if every track selected by the user is capable of generating compelling results within its internal network. There are scant traces of bibliographic or contextual data, such as the occasional listing of a place or series written into the *PennSound* filename itself. There are no links to works beyond the self-enclosed poetic system of *MUPS*. More than a collection or a poetic work, Flores deploys Judy Malloy's useful summary of "authoring systems" in electronic literature to consider how *MUPS* is both software produced for user authoring and an "authored" work of software and selection in its own right.[53] Using Malloy's framework, Flores notes that Jhave "could've easily used this engine to create an e-poem or a series of them: expressions of the tool and his vision. Instead, he released the tool for users to have their own creative explorations and analysis of the material."[54] However, these explorations and analyses are circumscribed within a highly curated set of audio samples and, most importantly, a tightly coordinated set of interface options for playback. Like the rigid typographic structures of bissett's printed texts, *MUPS* presents a stable interface for unpredictable performances.

Where *Mutant Sounds, PennSound,* and *UbuWeb* facilitate file downloads, *SpokenWeb* and *MUPS* afford specific modes of playback alone. In both projects, the website is the primary source of audition. *Mutant Sounds* is located on the opposite end of the spectrum, exclusively offering options for download. *PennSound* and *UbuWeb* fall somewhere in between, with immediate listening as easily accessible as the capability to download. On *SpokenWeb,* the user is

presented with a highly compressed visualization of audio waveforms as a static image within the play-bar (SoundCloud is the popular analog to this interface, which is immediately recognizable as a
tool for navigating a sound file on the internet). *MUPS,* on the other
hand, visualizes the waveforms of any given file only in the moment of its transmission. Like iTunes visualizations of sound files or
the animations once common to CD players, the representation on
MUPS is purely aesthetic. Unlike the rare files offered exclusively on
SpokenWeb, the *MUPS* interface operates parasitically on *PennSound.*
With an extra step, the user can use *PennSound* to find background
information on any recording, as well as a direct link to download
the MP3 file.

By contrast, *PennSound* operates on the dual principles of accessibility and depth. All files are freely accessible, for both course
syllabi and private browsing. Increasingly, many files are linked to
close readings and expanded materials via the collaborative scholarship of *PoemTalk*; the interview format on *Close Listening*; the
breadth of critical writing on *Jacket2*; the learning environment
presented by the ModPo MOOC; the textual materials offered at
EPC and *Eclipse*; or any number of related online class syllabi.[55]
While *MUPS* is a stand-alone interface, it feeds into the wider realm
of little databases linked up to *PennSound*'s pedagogical model of
distribution.

In certain respects, this extension loses sight of the purpose of
MUPS. While the interface may be a conduit for students or scholars to discover new works of poetry or delve into a deep array of
academic resources, this function is not primary to the project.
Instead, *MUPS* emphasizes the possibility for improvisation within
a given script. In this regard, it is exactly aligned with the live
performances of bissett, wherein typographically fixed concrete
poems become fluid chants and intonations. Utilizing the strict
protocol of written script for loose improvisation, the interface
returns the free potential for transformation to the fixed MP3 recordings of bissett. Put differently, the structural framework of
MUPS serves as a corollary to bisset's improvisatory aesthetics.
Two files from *Awake in th Red Desert* might jump back and forth
in microsecond intervals. A temporal jump from 2006 back to
1968 could happen as easily as a jump between contemporaneous

recordings by bissett and his collaborator bpNichol. *MUPS* offers all the technique of a skilled DJ simultaneously managing thousands of vinyl recordings for the casual user with the single click of a cursor. While media critics often use the example of sampling techniques or remix aesthetics to describe database culture, the acts of spoken improvisation and reading performances are less often invoked as an allegory. However, this is precisely what bissett on *MUPS* performs: neither the static representations of the page (or digital image) nor the rigid grooves of vinyl (or MP3), but rather the whimsical sampling of audition and attention in the context of a sound-based social text.

Within the contextual and procedural system generated by *MUPS,* bissett's live performances meet an interface scripted for the corresponding live performance of its listener. The "poetry reading" on playback through *MUPS* directs the user into the aleatory poetics of reading as a contingent practice. Afforded by the "promiscuity" of the MP3 and built on the modular variability of its digital processing, *MUPS* returns bissett to the site of performance and demands that the listener develop new protocols of improvisatory listening. As a work of creative scholarship, this project plays the little database as a reading practice rooted in the same free jazz that backs a number of tracks on *Awake in th Red Desert.* As scholarship, it asks—and answers—questions that the essay format could not begin to address. From the outset, the authorial figure of bissett is but one potential mode of clustering a set of files circulating online through these platforms. This interface could be read differently through the poetics of any other grouping of tracks in the collection. How does *MUPS* address the ambient stylistics of Lin or the palindromic utterances of Whitehead? What about the five recordings of "Ursonate" on *MUPS,* each with a different interpretation of the score? How might all sixteen tracks recorded in 1968 speak to the interface? Or to the sixty-nine tracks recorded in 2008, for that matter? The *MUPS* interface begs us to ask these questions, and remains open to the intervention of any given user. Even as we've long contemplated the relation of narrative to database, these signifying systems can be difficult to visualize, and even more difficult to do so succinctly, playfully, and concretely. Compelling systems for simultaneous forms of playback, rendered in a random-access format, remain rare to come by for practical use. In *MUPS,* a close listener might wind up creating a "live" MP3, playing echoes among the little databases simultaneously.

Interlude 3
Also This: No Title

I began the preceding chapter with the intent to write about recordings of modernist poets William Carlos Williams and Louis Zukofsky.
Drawing on my experiences editing both of their *PennSound* pages
and the richness of scholarly discourse around their works suggested the possibility for a robust study of transformations introduced to their respective sound works by digitization. In lockstep
with this approach, the relation of the digital object to the various
poetics of objectivist writing seemed useful. However, the circuits of
transmission were cut short: in each instance, primary recordings
were relayed to the *PennSound* collection by a single process of transcoding. The ways in which bill bissett trafficked through a range of
little databases, on the other hand, presented a method to navigate
transmission narratives through a series of contextual modulations,
which usefully inventoried a set of contingent effects. Thus, despite
the wealth of resources devoted to the original two intended authors,
the stories of their emplacement in the little databases paled in comparison to the chronicles of transmission shadowing the bissett files
before and after their situation on *PennSound*.

The essay, bound within a codex, must make certain editorial decisions. The media poetics of digital creative scholarship, as *MUPS*
demonstrates, afford a greater degree of freedom in the process of
selection. My own work in processing the *PennSound* collection predates my enrollment in graduate study. I began editing *PennSound*
from Tokyo in the fall of 2007, starting with the Williams page, and
continuing through a diverse set of segmentations and arrangements over the next several years. In the spring of 2008, around
the time I was admitted to the University of Pennsylvania, I was
invited to create a "selected" set of featured resources culled from
the collection. Perhaps not by coincidence, the Johnson selection of
tracks for *MUPS* heavily relies on this "featured resources archive,"

which indexes a number of similar lists chosen by editors, poets, and scholars. Where previous iterations of the format suggested a type of "top ten" list more common to cassette mixes and listicle culture, I decided to make a sample-based compilation in addition to my selection of soundtracks. This compilation was named after some incidental lines of a Williams track, "Also this: no title." The compilation—which I called an "Editorial Reprise Audio Essay"—samples from sixteen tracks to construct an argument about trans-coded sound files woven within the selections themselves, clocking in at roughly thirteen minutes.[1] As I have continued work on the little database project approximately fifteen years later, well beyond my time at Penn, I have come to discover that this old audio essay still performs arguments that the chapter could not. Not only in terms of the limitations of the chapter's interpretive focus, but also along the many frequencies marking what sound can say that the page cannot.

Like MUPS, the compilation jumps among a range of poetry audio samples in what can seem, at times, the haphazard logic of an inci-dental conversation between readings in the collection. However, unlike the algorithmic leaps of MUPS, "Also this: no title" conducts a concerted set of editorial interventions aimed to produce an argu-ment, just as these sentences do as I type them. From editorial deci-sions to interwoven transitions, the audio essay was plotted to pro-duce a rhetorical effect. Like the compilation film discussed in the next chapter or the montage poetics featured in L=A=N=G=U=A=G=E magazine, the aural poetics of this interlude perform a creative mode of scholarship through the arrangement of the media it addresses.

The opening lines of "Also this" signal my process in the voice of Jed Rasula articulating his re-edit of Henry James's The Ambassadors: "i have not tampered with anything i have simply removed and re-allocated the parts." Between these "reallocations," bursts of audio hiss and author in-breaths interrupt the poetic stream. Unlike a MUPS session, the stream of "Also this: no title" highlights the me-dial and incidental qualities of the recordings as significant sonic elements, beyond their threshold of silence. While producing the audio essay, my day job had me working as a director and sound engineer at a publishing house for audiobooks. Spending eight hours a day directing and editing literary readings between a set of headphones jacked into ProTools, I had learned how to use ad-

Danny Snelson:
Editorial Reprise Audio Essay: Also this: No Title

also this: no title = **wrong from the start / no hardly but seeing he had been born in a country out of date** = **he fished by obstinate isles** = actually i should read this, um brief uh public service announcement here, it's appropriate for, uh = *uh, those, uh i have not tampered with anything i have simply removed and reallocated the parts* = **of what can it such as which sense can it not** = *uh, this is a selection from a rather uh unscrupulous raid that i uh made* = blasted stochastically thought detectors tossed together with targeted segments of remorse the = *the poet / takes too many messages* = **with the structural trends and the styles of folding defined by foliation, fold axis, bedding and sometimes by signifier anomalies** = surreptitiously trips resolute tourniquet = **case presents no adjunct to the muses diadem, the age demanded an image of it's accelerated grimace, something for the modern stage not at any rate an attic** = *surely i can reduce this in its scope and size* = *exactly the position that they occupy in the text as we have it but* = *but i thot that i might be able to perform some kind of* = *killing whatever was there before* = **For two gross of broken statues, / For a few thousand battered books. / These fought, in any case, / and some believing, pro domo, in any case / Some quick some venture** = bleached to the point of subordination = **some from weakness, some from censure, / some for love of slaughter in imagination, / learning Daring as never before / wastage as never before / frankness as never before,** = *no one listens to poetry, the ocean does not need to be listened to / a drop a crash of water it means nothing / it is bread and butter pepper and salt, the death that young men hope for* = *aimlessly it pounds ashore* = *white and aimless signals, no / one listens to poetry* = and the minutes burn a hole in my socket the seconds scar a moment after gone but wayward knos no way then toils triumphalist deflation tailoring tokens to abutments = *for him to build a house on to build a house on to build a house on to build a house on to build a house on to* = **disillusions as never told in the old days / laughter out of**

Figure 3i.1. Capture of the opening segment of my transcription of "Also this: no title" as featured on the *PennSound* page. Captured via *PennSound*, writing.upenn.edu/pennsound/x/Featured-2008.html.

vanced audio engineering techniques to *remove* precisely the human noise and medial hiss from the telling of a narrative. In "Also this: no title," I wanted to do just the opposite. Between every significant transition, an exaggerated array of breaths and skips interrupt the smoothly intoned flow that a listener might expect.

Rather than attempt to rearticulate the movements of "Also this: no title," I present the sound file in this interlude to speak for itself, as *TXT EXE* might speak for the *Textz* collection. While there is the temptation to discuss the relation of the radio and transmission art of Gregory Whitehead to the archival record of digital systems, or the digital presentation of Jackson Mac Low's aleatoric cassette-based work entitled "The 8-Voice Stereo-Canon Realization of The Black Tarantula Crossword Gatha," or the multilingual transformations of Caroline Bergvall's etymological rewriting of Chaucer's *The Canterbury Tales*—each of which displays a unique relation to the MP3 file and the *PennSound* collection—I will instead limit my gesture to the reposting of "Also this: no title" in full as a media poetics parallel to the chapter.

On a final note, it bears remarking that my own poetry readings are also featured in *MUPS,* along with the full "Deformance" page I produced with Bernstein for *PennSound.* In my tracks on *MUPS,* I remix and interweave my voice with Rosmarie Waldrop's rewriting of Ludwig Wittgenstein in her readings from *The Reproduction of Profiles* (1984). These "Feverish Propogations" complicate the (already complex) "you" and "I" in her reading, writing myself as an active listener into the exchange. In each of these works (*MUPS,* "Also this: no title," or my own Waldrop deformance), the band narrows to a listener's relation to the little database. Or rather, as "Also this: no title" concludes: *"one big blooming confusion, or, the other side of language / where i am mute and the unsaid the unsaid weighs heavy . . .* and or hurl it into the void and/or demonstrate the autonomy of the audience."

 See: "Also this: no title" (2008).

CHAPTER 4

Dropping the Frame
From Film to Database

"No, I don't need your picture. I don't have to know what you look like, we haven't even said hello yet. You can look like anybody. I'll take anybody. I'll take anything I can get." Vito Acconci whispers these lines in *Theme Song* (1973), a video artwork in which the artist wraps himself around a camcorder, delivering derivations on pop songs as pickup lines to an unknown viewer.[1] Shot in black and white over thirty-three minutes of continuous footage, the video features a close-up of Acconci lying on the floor, staring directly into the camera lens: that is to say, directly into the eyes of an unknown viewer. Addressing video as a medium as much as it addresses the gallery spectator, *Theme Song* stands as a prime example of the video art that emerged at the intersection of performance and experimental cinema in the early 1970s. Nick Kaye notes that this work "at once reflects earlier theoretical analyses of media's 'extension' of the body while articulating television and video's spatial multiplications."[2] For Kaye, these multiplications are divided along the televisual communications circuit outlined by Samuel Weber in *Mass Mediauras: Form, Technics, Media*. In this collection of lectures and interviews, Weber updates Walter Benjamin's concept of the aura to argue that operations of production, transmission, and reception emblematize the confusion of time and space in an age defined by the dominance of broadcast media.[3] Simultaneously playing with the mechanics of

Figure 4.1. Rectilinear still from Vito Acconci's *Theme Song* (1973). Copyright Vito Acconci and Artists Rights Society (ARS), New York. Courtesy of Maria Acconci.

video production, the looping potential of electronic art, and the reception circuits of the gallery, Acconci's work deftly navigates the media it inhabits by playing with the formal modalities of its technical affordances.

As if these confusions weren't enough, playback within a digital milieu introduces further complexities to works of time-based media online. Watching *Theme Song* stream on the internet produces a wholly novel experience, uncannily prefigured by Acconci's monologue, which seems to have always already anticipated a future viewer. The lines hold new relevance in the experience of streaming *Theme Song* through a browser:

> I'll be waiting for you, I know, I know I'm not close to you now. How can I be close? You're in another world. It's as if, it's as if you're an angel. . . . How long, how long do I have to wait for you? Oh, but I'll wait. I'll wait as long as I have to because, uh, because, I've always dreamed about you. You know, anyone I was ever with, I was really thinking about you, though I never

Figure 4.2. CRT video still from Vito Acconci's *Theme Song* (1973). Copyright Vito Acconci and Artists Rights Society (ARS), New York. Courtesy of Maria Acconci.

even knew you, I don't even know you now, but I had this vision of you, I had this real vision of somebody ideal, somebody special. I realize no one could live up to that dream, but that dream was really you. You, you could fulfill all the dreams, all the dreams I have.

Speaking to a mediated spectator from the perspective of an actor becoming flickering images on a monitor ("another world"), Acconci addresses the temporal lapse separating production and reception, embodying the dream of transmission to any-viewer-whatsoever. In a futile desire for the communication of angels, staring wide-eyed like a post-digital *Angelus Novus* watching the wreckage of history accrue, the digital object fulfills an unpredictable dream embedded in the work itself.

From the detached gallery viewing of its original screening, *Theme Song* slips into the intimacy of the personal computer. As internet commentators readily acknowledge, an online *Theme Song* eerily anticipates the intimate formats of electronic video diaries,

UbuWeb Film   **Vito Acconci** (1940-2017)
UbuWeb

Back to Vito Acconci

Theme Song (1973)

1973, 33:15 min, b&w, sound

Figure 4.3. Flash Video still from Vito Acconci's *Theme Song* (1973), streaming on *UbuWeb*. Copyright Vito Acconci and Artists Rights Society (ARS), New York. Courtesy of Maria Acconci.

social media confessions, and digital sex work.[4] The video seductively promises to wait as long as it has to for the viewer—addressed in the second person—as an ideal "somebody" who could "fulfill all the dreams" latent in the work. How could he be close, Acconci asks from 1973? Of course, we *are* in another world. The potency of *Theme Song* lies in the fact that it lends itself to the momentary hallucination that it *is,* in actuality, speaking to "you" as the embedded video loads in *your* browser.

Zooming out from Acconci's close-up, we might also consider *Theme Song* streaming on a little database called *UbuWeb* alongside thousands of corresponding digital objects, each radically transformed by the contingent effects of computation, preservation, and dispersion charted in previous chapters. Initiated in 1996, the same year that the HTTP/1 protocol was finalized, *UbuWeb* has long been the most visible shadow library distributing experimental film and video, sound poetry, conceptual writing, and related legacies of the avant-garde on the internet. Hosting works ranging from obscure audio records to foundational documents of the historical avant-gardes, *UbuWeb* plays a primary role in shaping contemporary artistic and literary practices while transcoding a selective genealogy of twentieth-century aesthetic artifacts. Like Acconci's long-waiting monologue, *UbuWeb* was built around the latent dreams of its origins in collecting concrete poetry that seemed to anticipate formal features of minimal internet design and digital typography.

Lev Manovich pursues this line of thinking in *The Language of New Media,* which examines the ways "avant-garde aesthetic strategies came to be embedded in the commands and interface metaphors of computer software."[5] Media-reflexivity, of course, pervades twentieth century art and literature from the historic avant-gardes through conceptual and minimal art, and into Language Poetry, structural film, and net art. In this lineage, the lens of media-reflexivity poses a particularly salient vantage onto unstable media undergoing variable processes of transcoding online. Just as the video file for *Theme Song* longs to respond to its new internet context, George Landow's *Film in Which There Appear Edge Lettering, Sprocket Holes, Dirt Particles, Etc.* (1965–1966) transforms from a self-referential preoccupation with filmic materiality to a glitchy meditation on RGB (red, green, blue) color values, vector-based graphics, Flash Video frame rates, and compression effects. Paul Sharit's Fluxfilm *Dots 1 & 2* (1965), once displaying a rapid flicker of white dots on a black cinematic background, becomes a blurry mess of *squares* in its internet version. The examples could multiply to cover the thousands of media-reflexive movies hosted by *UbuWeb.* This chapter asks the viewer to reject the indexical impulse. Rather than reroute the *UbuWeb* "film & video" section back to cinematic projection or VHS monitors, it seeks a moment of disbelief, as though brought about by the half-serious seductions of Acconci's smooth intonations. Instead, this chapter attends to how historical media-specific works function in the digital milieux of the present, accidentally speaking to their conditions of digital transcoding. From this vantage, a vast array of contingent effects might be unearthed within each historical work.

Rather than attempting a comprehensive or schematic inventory of these effects, or attempting an accounting of the recently shuttered *UbuWeb* as a whole, this chapter aims to produce targeted engagements with two additional files hosted by the site.[6] If the previous chapter worked through transmission narratives and site-based contexts to the exclusion of reading specific files, this chapter works in reverse: to read each file in order to illumine their contexts by relief. Aside from the formal symmetry of this design, this move sidesteps another unforeseen operator at Acconci's anticipatory interface: a set of rhetorical and editorial confusions about the production, purpose, and direction of the site over time. The problem with writing about *UbuWeb* is that it's difficult to disentangle the site from the polemical self-theorizations of its founder and editor Kenneth Goldsmith, whose perspectives on copyright, appropriation, and internet poetics have been widely covered.[7] The sites examined throughout this book are generally understood to be the collaborative efforts of teams of editors over time. While *UbuWeb,* founded in 1996, was indeed primarily organized, designed, and managed by Kenneth Goldsmith, it is also the product of dozens of named and unnamed editors, presenting a panoply of editorial contributions, including my own, made at various points over the years. The site also encompasses "content" provided by individuals and initiatives including *Bidoun Magazine,* Continuo, Electra, *GreyLodge,* Roulette, and SoundEye, among others. In other instances, its content owes to untold and broadly uncredited individuals who originally digitized, contextualized, and dispersed its works on other sites that were subsequently scraped for hosting at *UbuWeb.* Given this context, the irony of Goldsmith's most direct claim to site-wide authorship— which denies attribution to the site's many uncredited editors and their labor—might best speak for itself:

> Wait, I've just admitted something that I've never stated publicly. UbuWeb is entirely me. I've always wanted to remain faceless, letting the site speak for itself. There's nothing worse than a vanity site, the kind of place some overriding ego, name, and agenda speaks louder than the work that's presented. So instead of this being "Kenneth Goldsmith's UbuWeb," I've put forth the notion of faceless institution. From the austere way the site is designed, to the fact that I always speak about it in the first-person plural as "we," to the massive amount of content that we host, I've always tried to

throw the focus away from me. But in truth, with the exception of the occasional student or intern, it's all me.[8]

While there might be plenty to unpack in this statement, alongside
Goldsmith's role in both the poetics discourse of the 2010s and online archiving more generally, these tracks move beyond my focus
in this chapter. Unfortunately, with *UbuWeb,* the authorial claims of
the editor remain both the most visible and least interesting aspects
of the site, which features an exceptionally diverse array of otherwise inaccessible works in the global lineage of avant-garde experi-
mentalism across the arts and letters.

In the interlude following this chapter, I open new tabs on a wider
array of these works from the collection. For now, at last, some close
readings are in order. Where the first three chapters respectively explored the computation, preservation, and dispersion of digital files
within little databases, this final chapter presents a close reading of
two particular works to suggest methods for reading little databases
through the digital objects they harbor. Rather than move from the
collection to the file, these readings start with the file as a means
to reconnect to the network. Each reading expands further from
the work it studies, into the database systems that facilitate each in
turn. The first work is a "film" from the 1960s that happens to have
been digitized. The second work was made using digital tools as a
means of reflecting on the intersection of film and computer culture
in the 1960s.

In the first instance, I examine digital versions of Nam June
Paik's iconic work *Zen for Film* (1962–1964). The digital afterlife of
Paik's film has inspired a range of new artworks that take the digital
version as a starting point and plug these concerns into new systems of meaning online. I discuss these works with the intention of
highlighting just how radical a digital *Zen for Film* might be when
seen as an artifact in its own right, with no further modifications
performed beyond the digitization of the filmic work itself.

In the second instance, I explore edges radiating out from a central node in the digital compilation movie, *We Edit Life* (2002) by Vicki
Bennett (People Like Us). Following *We Edit Life,* the reader is directed back into the database, a rich archive of found footage awaiting digital re-signification. As a coda to this chapter, returning to
Theme Song, I highlight a little network of compellingly transcoded

works in the *UbuWeb* collection through a Flash Video compilation essay made in collaboration with João Enxuto when Flash was still the dominant format for video streaming, accompanied by an inventory of transformations. In each of these instances, this chapter seeks to illumine the ways in which moving images are transformed by the signifying codes of digital technologies and network contexts, and what a user might do with these transformations.

Zen for Film and the Varieties of Use

In 2008, Tom Service posted a link on *The Guardian* to a YouTube video of Paik's *Zen for Film,* with a peculiar endorsement: "The antidote to the internet is . . . composer and video artist Nam June Paik's *Zen for Film* (1962–1964). Eight minutes of unadulterated, blissed-out, soundless, grainy Fluxus whiteness: worth anybody's ascetic concentration, and a perfect corrective to our hyper-stimulated media lives."[9] An embedded link directed the reader to YouTube user chowkaideng's upload of a completely soundless video recording of *Zen for Film,* a 360p streaming Flash-encoded movie that had, at the time I first encountered it in 2010, boasted 61,862 viewers.[10] Anything but "ascetic," YouTube's hypermediated interface begs for the viewer's attention in ALL CAPS, today just as much as in 2008. Varieties of social networking ("Share"), evaluation (190 thumbs up, 26 thumbs down), commentary (71 comments), and search options accompany the YouTube player. The right sidebar recommends further works by Nam June Paik on YouTube, works by artists like Hans Richter, John Cage, and Marcel Duchamp, alongside a variety of digitized Fluxus films and algorithmic recommendations based on my previous viewings, optimized for Google AdSense, bringing my viewing history onto the screen in relief of my data shadow.

Service's *Guardian* post demonstrates the common conflation of streaming video on the internet with the celluloid films from which they derive. Further, *Zen for Film* has never been the soundless, unadulterated antidote that Service describes. Unlike the pixelated iteration streaming on YouTube, *Zen for Film* was scripted for projector, light, audience, and 16mm film. Attempting to view the internet video as an indexical representation of a projected film is internally inconsistent with the work. It is a remarkably noisy time-based artwork that foregrounds the imminent material modulations of its

Figure 4.4. Still from user chowkaideng's upload of Nam June Paik's *Zen for Film* (1964) to YouTube, captured in 2010.

film stock. Noise and deterioration, in fact, ground its conceptual framework and system of meaning. Even if the film is a corrective to "our hyper-stimulated media lives"—or, as Heike Helfert of *Media Art Net* puts it, "the flood of images from outside"—a Zen for *film* only too obviously demands its proper media for measured reflection.[11] The YouTube video is *something else.*

Concentrating on the digital object that stands for Paik's *Zen for Film,* the reader is thus quickly assaulted by a dense knot of semantic confusions. Critical and technical discourses struggle to keep pace with the fast-changing terrain of the internet; since Geocities, methodologies of "new" media have always been "under construction." To disentangle this web, we might begin by returning to the historical and conceptual functions of the filmic work. Importing these primary functions into the digital objects circulating online, *Zen for Film* presents a particularly focused window into the process of transcoding historical film. The attention to media-specificity built into the work's internal logic allows for a deeper investigation of the formal, cultural, and technical protocols for the contemporary circulation of filmic work. After folding the historical film into the digital object, this study of *Zen for Film* concludes with the various ways in which artists and online archivists have deployed the work in recent years. Building on the program laid out by the history of *Zen for Film* and these various new uses, I examine several layers of transformation within the work, offering a revised understanding of a digital artifact otherwise obscured by its own historical effects. This may also serve as one metonym among many for the digital transcoding of filmic art at large, clarified, in this instance, by the crystalline structure of reflexivity in the work.

Like John Cage's *4'33"*, Paik's original *Zen for Film* presents a remarkably minimal gesture that opens out onto a vast array of aesthetic, narratological, and technical issues. The concept seems simple enough: *Zen for Film* is a work consisting entirely of unexposed clear celluloid.[12] Just as Cage ostensibly performs a certain length of "silence," Paik films a variable length of "nothing." However, as soon as the viewer starts to listen to Cage's instrumentless composition or watch Paik's imageless film, a world of incidental, technical, personal, and otherwise drowned-out actors emerge. Paik famously describes the work as "clear film, accumulating in time dust and scratches."[13] A film containing its own history of use, the work incorporates and showcases the continued material deterioration of the celluloid with each new performance. In *Musicage: Cage Muses on Words, Art, Music,* Cage recollects the effects and "plot" of Paik's film:

> It's an hour long and you see the dust on the film and on the camera and on the lens of the projector. That dust actually moves and creates different shapes. The specks of dust become, as you look at the film, extremely comic. They take on character and they take on a kind of plot—whether this speck of dust will meet that speck. And if they do, what happens? I remember being greatly entertained and preferring it really to any film I've ever seen before or after. It's one of the great films, and it's not often available to see.[14]

Bathed in the projector's light, a captive audience must contemplate the film over the duration of an hour, with all the technical details of the cinema system growing ever more active in the shaping of its comedic "narrative." New characters emerge over time as the film naturally thickens the "plot." While the conceptual premise of *Zen for Film* is simple enough to summarize, the experience of viewing is quite rare, as willing venues for projection are scarce and prints of the work are in even shorter supply.

The rarity of the film is generated procedurally: the film incorporates each screening as an ongoing set of inscription events. Kaye characterizes the cybernetic relay constituting the work as a "continuous recording of the physical degradation of the blank leader tape by the 'real' conditions of its projection. . . . *Zen for Film* poses the questions of what it means to be at the threshold of the medium, . . . effecting its own gradual destruction in *exchanges between* the film and its environment."[15] By rendering an art of gradual destruction, Paik enacts a degenerative system that finds meaning in the ongoing play of media and environment. In the process, he challenges the reader to adapt beyond the thresholds and limits of the work, as well as the ethics of display and curatorial intervention. In 2015, curator, conservator, and art historian Hana Hölling mounted a definitive exhibition and study of precisely this work to question the limits of conservation and display. Entitled *Revisions—Zen for Film,* the exhibition page opens by asking: "How do works of art endure over time in the face of aging materials and changing interpretations of their meaning? How do decay, technological obsolescence, and the blending of old and new media affect what an artwork is and can become? And how can changeable artworks encourage us to rethink our assumptions of a work of art as fixed and static?"[16]

One way to begin answering these questions might be to turn from a conversation with Cage's silence and Paik's light to Maurice Lemaître's noisy concept of the "supertemporal" *(supertemporelle).* Formulated in collaboration with fellow Lettrist Isodore Isou in 1960, the supertemporal film presents a limit case for thinking through how an artwork changes over time.[17] Of Lemaître's many variations on the realization of the supertemporal, the film *Toujours à l'avant-garde de l'avant-garde, jusqu'au paradis et au-delà!* (Always at the avant-garde of the avant-garde, to paradise and beyond!) from 1970 offers what is perhaps the most radical model for ongoing transformations to an aesthetic object's meaning.[18] Lemaître's film theorizes itself in an extended voice-over track running through unrelated footage from a German television report on the 1969 biennale. The found footage only incidentally features "five seconds" of a play by Lemaître and is, we're told, otherwise entirely unrelated to the artwork.[19] Instead, the footage stands in for any footage whatsoever. More important than the image is the ways in which the image is screened over time. The English subtitles note:

> *Ever the Avant-Garde of the Avant-Garde* is a new kind of film, named supertemporal film. A supertemporal film is an open film, a framework film, into which the audience is invited. Each member of the audience is asked to join in and make her or his own contribution to the work, non-stop. Tonight, for example, you are in this theater willingly attending a showing of a supertemporal film authored by Maurice Lemaître and titled *Ever the Avant-Garde of the Avant-Garde.* From now on, everything you do, in whatever way, and even what you do not do, such as remaining silent or still, becomes an integral part of the work. . . . Each new scratch on the picture or the sound track will remain forever as part of the work, even if it gets overlaid by other scratches. In this way, our projectionist and the projector itself share in creating the supertemporal film.[20]

While the film is "authored" by Lemaître, both the audience and the technical apparatus make further "contributions" to the work over time. Even a "silent or still" spectator "becomes an integral part of the work," Lemaître argues, by breathing over the soundtrack and occupying the social space of the screening. This is the social text in extremis. Even incidental inscriptions made by scratches as the film runs through a projector are brought under the rubric of an authoring agent. Both, the film declares, become an integral part of the work. In an earlier sequence, Lemaître demands that the film "must never more stop being created and screened." Until heaven and after, new contributions to the work are made continuously with each screening: the viewer, the cinematic apparatus, and the manifold contingencies of use intertwined. Discussing Lemaître's previous Lettrist project, *Le film est déjà commencé?* (Has the film already started?; 1951), Kaira Marie Cabañas notes how, in these works, "film's outside folds into its inside: the space of cinematic reception becomes coterminous with the production of meaning, . . . to use this composite medium in the service of nonalienated and critical reception."[21] Like *Zen for Film,* this contingent scenario of ongoing, multisited coproduction begs the question of digital versioning. Once transcoded, the film-as-movie-file gathers no new scratches and the communal setting of the cinema flattens along the illuminated screen of personal viewing on a public website, all watched over by unseen algorithms that similarly grow and evolve by tracking each user's click. The supertemporal digital object is subject to endless iterations, even as its playback remains relatively constant.

The same ongoing process of transformation was written into *Zen for Film,* released after Lemaître's cinematic interventions. In the film's screening, supertemporal effects extend from "specks of dust" to scratches, projector quality, theatrical staging, and audience acoustics. While the read-write cycle of the cinematic apparatus carries out its chance operations, the aural aspects of the film call for further focus on the technical substrate of the work. Far from silent, the score is constituted instead by the incidental and technical character of a film screening's social text. In the catalog essay "Unheard Music," Craig Dworkin describes the sheer noise of "the incidental soundtrack to Paik's film," advising the reader: "If you get a chance, sit near the projectionist; even after only eight minutes you'll never forget the nervous clack and twitter of the shutter, blinking like a blinded Cyclops in the noonday sun."[22] These elements are not only highly scripted aspects of *Zen for Film,* but inscribe the meaning of the work itself. The damages to the print, the time-based system of repetition and change, and the incessant cinematic noise together forge the meaning-making system of the film.

Given this media-specific framework, it is not surprising that *Zen for Film* also plays a primary role in "Signal to Noise," a concluding chapter to Dworkin's study of seemingly "blank" works entitled *No Medium.*[23] In the book, Dworkin argues that no medium can be thought in isolation. Instead, a close analysis of any medial iteration invokes the dynamic processes of a signifying chain that includes material substrates, social contexts, and thresholds of interpretation. Throughout Dworkin's study, works that appear "blank" or "silent" offer compelling cases for the dynamic processes that render media legible to interpretation. As though to highlight the length of this signifying chain, "Signal to Noise" focuses on Ken Friedman's *Zen for Record,* a conceptually related audio derivative of Paik's *Zen for Film,* and concludes with speculations about a potential *Zen for Compact Disc.* Dworkin suggests that one "could argue that Friedman's record and Paik's film are simply two different editions of a single work. Or, if not two formats for one and the same work, then at least that each is closer to the other than to the respective versions that might appear on DVD and CD."[24] This "affinity" between the film and vinyl works reflecting on their own medial formations—against their own respective transmedia versions—crystalizes Dworkin's account of media specificity. Typifying Rosalind Krauss's arguments on the postmedium condition, *Zen for Film* requires an analysis that reads the "complex webs of overlapping technical support" that mediate "even the most abstract and cerebral works of conceptual art."[25] In the case of *Zen for Film,* these supports measure a durational length of cinematic time in a shared physical space. Once set to the beat of physiological responses ("the time between involuntary blinks or the spasms of the ciliary muscle") and a breadth of cinematic effects ("slowly disintegrating the film with each screening"), the silent pixels and time-slider functionalities of YouTube work to both expunge the medial components scripted into the original work and direct our gaze instead to the new interfaces and media formations in which they reappear.[26]

I outline the conceptual and medial framework of the film here to emphasize the ways in which this work in particular functions with a special relationship to its material instantiation, mediated delivery, and contextual distribution. Standing in for a broad array of conceptual and media-specific films from the 1960s and 1970s, *Zen for Film* generates aesthetic interpretations that cannot avoid an analysis of the technical infrastructure and varied uses of the work, especially once removed from those infrastructures. While many artistic forms in image, print, and sound may retain the essential components of their significance when transcoded into digital networks, the resistance to new media formats that *Zen for Film* and other media-specific works evidence presents a compelling field for investigating the effects and processes of transformative mediation. The film's structure of signification remains irrevocably bound not only to its material format, but also to contingent circuits of reception and circulation. Adding to Lemaître's account of the time-based production of the supertemporal film and Dworkin's reading of the thresholds of meaning in media, a communications circuit can be closed with a sketch of the transmission patterns of *Zen for*

Film online. Skirting the legal discourses of fair use and intellectual property, on the one hand, and the amateur notes of shadowy dispersion networks comprised of pirates and peer-to-peer sharing, on the other, the file's distribution presents another filter through which to understand the variability of the digital object.

Rare, experimental, and avant-garde films trafficking online often originate on private torrent sites or peer-to-peer communities. "Ripped" or "torn" from official channels by enthusiasts and collectors, these files are rarely professionally captured and often unsanctioned. They inhabit shadow and offline libraries, built on protocols to guard against IP litigation or copyright complaints.[27] When it comes to experimental film online, as Erica Balsom argues, "of greater importance are copy *rites*: those extralegal social and historical conventions that shape the possibilities and meanings of image reproduction."[28] For digital scholarship, unlike traditional film studies, the most useful archives of transmission are not housed in special collections or film archives. Rather, they dwell in a labyrinthine tangle of comment threads across an array of illicit platforms, private and public alike. Eventually, these works migrate to more popular forums like YouTube and *UbuWeb* where they find wider audiences. Matthew Kirschenbaum has argued for the importance of archival approaches to the traces left by digital systems of circulation. Indeed, in his work on cracked floppy discs and William Gibson's infamous self-destructing poem "Agrippa," Kirschenbaum has demonstrated how forensic approaches to digital objects might reconstitute forms of bibliographic version history in even the most ephemeral formats.[29] More than incidental, these economies of use all leave meaningful marks on the works they put into circulation. Like the postage stamps that mark the traversals of mail art or the marginal annotations that locate the provenance of rare folios, these networks reinscribe the works they circulate with every transfer, rip, and torrent.

Drawn from file-sharing-post comments, one user points to the version history of *Zen for Film* online in a thread accompanying a torrent download for the full *FluxFilm Anthology*: "This was originally ripped by xxxxx almost two years ago for divxclasico.com and they found their way into UBU, where you can also grab them."[30] Posted in April of 2006, the original upload remains tracked and shared as released on "15 Abr, 2004 10:16 am" by xxxxx at divxclasico.com, an eMule peer-to-peer community based in Spain. In a clear violation of copyright as legislated by the DMCA (Digital Millennium Copyright Act) anticircumvention provision, xxxxx most likely ripped the Re:Voir DVD release of *Zen for Film* (itself a direct transfer of a low quality VHS capture of the films) into the easily transferable AVI (audio video interweave) format.[31] Like so many works of digitized film and video, once the files are distributed to decentralized file-sharing communities, they soon begin to appear in more legitimate forms of use, typified by samples in remixes or short clips for educational use on popular platforms like YouTube and Blogger. The *UbuWeb* collection of "film & video" is primarily built on the work done by these distribution communities, including *Zen for Film* and a majority of works on the site.

The legal protocols for online distribution can often illuminate trickier questions of provenance and perception surrounding the use of files circulating online. Following the dispersion of these newly minted digital objects via peer-to-peer networks, in early 2006, *UbuWeb* popularly distributed the files for the full *FluxFilm Anthology* on its website, including the first in the set, *Zen for Film*. In the nebulous and conflicted realm of fair use on the internet, *UbuWeb*'s bottom-of-the-page disclaimer that the works are for "educational and non-commercial use only" is offered as dubious evidence that the works are sanctioned for streaming.[32] However, neither the motion-picture-educational exemption to the DMCA nor *UbuWeb*'s status as a noncommercial distributor legally clears this activity. For instance, the *FluxFilm Anthology* includes a note at the top of the page declaring that Friedman, early practitioner, archivist, and scholar of Fluxus—whose work is included in the anthology—has granted *UbuWeb* permission to distribute the films online. In this instance, Friedman, who was appointed "director of Fluxus West" in 1966 by George Maciunas, retains the rights to grant reproduction of Fluxus materials, properly authorizing the work's distribution through *UbuWeb*. Remarkably, the files are illegally ripped from a Re:Voir DVD that captures VHS footage of the film, and then move through a series of file-sharing networks onto *UbuWeb,* only to later receive proper permissions for distribution.[33]

Returning to the YouTube page for *Zen for Film,* uploaded by chowkaideng on December 6, 2006, we can plug these histories of pre- and postdigital distribution of the work back into its play-back. When presented as a streaming video, the transcoded work furnishes a critical function commenting on the character of the original film, as well as on the internet context at large. Seen in this light, every signifying aspect of the original work (the accumulation of dust and time, the brilliance of the projector's light, the meditative isolation of the work, the sound of the projector) has been transformed by the digital version, leaving only the flat image of the white square in its place. Looking closer, as the film's concept demands, we see that this flat white space has been transformed into a work about the RGB color values of the Flash codec employed by YouTube at the moment of its upload. In the place of the shadow image of dust particles, we find blocky pixels attempting to capture the right "white" of the projected clear leader and its surrounding "black" frame bearing the flickering of the image. Against the durational character of the film, the YouTube video prominently displays a time slider, all but begging the user to skip around the film at the slightest discomfort with its lack of "action" or the mere curiosity to find out what "happens." The sound of the projector has been lost, along with all its attendant effects, immediate and supertemporal. Indeed, the YouTube video is never scratched, nor would it likely deteriorate, even if it might pause while loading or, as it turns out, at some point simply disappear from the site. It loses the immediacy of performance and becomes a fixed archival recording of an unknown moment of screening. We might say that *Zen for Film for YouTube* becomes something other: a supertemporal video about the internet and its own real conditions of circulation, brought about by the contingencies of its networked situation. At least, I argue, this is one way to read the files derived from Paik's film.

In the years after the 2006 release of *Zen for Film* on both YouTube and *UbuWeb,* a flurry of artistic activity emerged appropriating the material, conceptual, and philosophical aspects of the film to create new works in a postdigital context. In lieu of exhaustively enumerating the transformations marked by the digitized version and relating each back to the work's historical iterations, I supplement and conclude this reading of *Zen for Film* with a brief inventory of several of these new works. While there have been many others in the years since 2006, returning to these works from 2007 and 2008 aims to dial into a particular moment in internet history. These responses index the reception of both *Zen for Film*'s first appearance online and the emergence of YouTube (founded in 2005 and bought by Google in 2006) and online video streaming as a whole. Curator and art historian Hannah Hölling anticipates this approach: "One could imagine that the activation of Paik's video from the digital archive will allow creating new content based on the historical video and film and their remixes and fragments. The digitally enabled and algorithmically aided actualization will provide unexpected results—an archival serendipity of a different kind, based on human and machinic interaction."[34]

Operating between human and machine, each work discussed in what follows expands on a localized transformation at the intersection of the historical film and the digital milieu of the internet's recent past in a constellation of archival serendipities. As even this highly compressed set of artistic responses demonstrates, the media-reflexivity of Paik's work inspires an endless set of possibilities for creative remix. When Tate Liverpool put together an educator's pack for a Paik solo show in 2010, they included the following suggestion: "Discuss how you would create Zen for DVD, Zen for iPod, Zen for Mobile Phone."[35] Indeed, the artworks below can be seen as pedagogical devices conducting lessons in an imagined school led by Paik and hosted by *UbuWeb*. While the work had always begged for these iterations (indeed, Paik himself produced a range of variations on the theme), the particularities of the discussion yield unexpected results for an understanding of the digital object in circulation today. To conclude a reading of *Zen for Film* online, each of the following five remixed versions of the work offer further insights into the transformation at play between the work and its digital derivatives.

Luca (LUNK) Leggero, *F L U X L I N E S: Line 01* (2007)

Working directly from the *UbuWeb* upload of the *FluxFilm Anthology,* LUNK's *F L U X L I N E S* offer a subtle critique of online presentation while referencing a series of works by Paik. An artist's statement tidily encapsulates the technical specifications of the work: "I modified the original code resizing it from 384×500 pixels to 550×1 pixels / changing not the short film but only the way it can be viewed."[36] Working within the HTML presentation of the video hosted by UbuWeb, every digitized film in the *F L U X L I N E S* series is reduced to a vertical stack of pixels, blinking in rhythm with the original,

Figure 4.5. Website capture from Luca (LUNK) Leggero, *F L U X L I N E S: Line 01* (2007).

compressed to an absolute minimum of width. This radical resizing of the display echoes Paik's *Zen for TV* (1963). In this piece, Paik similarly reduced the analog field of a cathode-ray-tube display to a single vertical line. LUNK brilliantly reworks this gesture in *Line 01,* which reduces the pixelated field of the web player to a single line. The wholesale appropriation of the *UbuWeb* presentation of *Zen for Film* thus transforms its display beyond recognition to the human viewer, while leaving the underlying digital object completely intact. *Line 01* repurposes this uncritical remediation to reflect on the media-specificity of Flash Video and HTML protocol, mirroring the reflexivity of *Zen for Film* while incorporating its art historical intertext.

Michael Kontopoulos, *Zen for YouTube* (2007)
If *Line 01* interrogates the web player's capacity for display, *Zen for YouTube* meditates on the durational experience of digital movies. Hosted on YouTube, this work simply places the endless loop of an animation for "loading," which spins atop a single frozen image still from the Flash Video encoding of *Zen for Film.* In comments on the

Figure 4.6. Still from Michael Kontopoulos, *Zen for YouTube* (2007).

artwork page, Michael Kontopoulos writes, *"Zen for YouTube* picks up where Nam June Paik left off: an expansion of negative space for the Internet generation."[37] The animation replaces the revolving movement of the cinematic reel with the circular iconography of deferred transmission. If a film in which "nothing happens" might have been frustrating to viewers in 1964, a YouTube video that never loads must surely have been the most vexing experience for a viewer in 2007. Cleverly, the YouTube embed is recursively coded not to load, so the viewer is confronted with a clip that has been altered to refuse playback from the beginning of the Flash Video. After failing to find the start, the user discovers that the rest of the clip is more of the same, even though the status bar shows "progress" in time. Failure and deferral run in an infinite feedback loop. If *Zen for Film* was built for the slow destruction of celluloid over repeated passages through a projector, *Zen for YouTube* was coded to politely malfunction on every instance of playback.

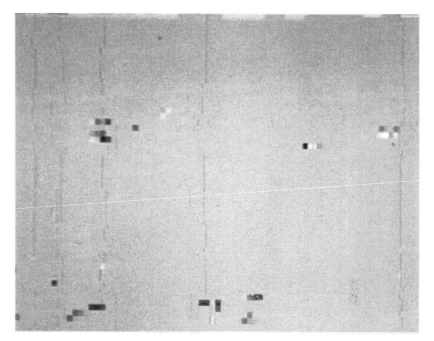

Figure 4.7. Still from Cory Arcangel, *Structural Film* (2007). 16mm film. Photo by Cory Arcangel.

Cory Arcangel, *Structural Film* (2007)

Turning the digitization of *Zen for Film* on its head, *Structural Film* starts from the computer, using iMovie's "aged film" setting to create a born-digital version of *Zen for Film* with artificial dust and scratches, which was then transferred to 16mm film. Glitches occur as compression artifacts in the transfer from MOV file to film print, resulting in colorful, pixelated debris. On his website, Cory Arcangel has stated that these glitches "weren't actually part of the plan," but that he retained them nonetheless.[38] Like dust in the original, these encoding errors are the true actors in the film. They take on a kind of supertemporal authorship and trump the artificial simulations of scratches and dust inserted by consumer video editing software. Unlike the previous two works, *Structural Film* appropriates the concept, rather than the materials from the digitized version of Paik's work. It succeeds by importing uncanny digital artifacts into analog media as a postdigital gesture projected back into cinematic space. The film is shown as an installation with 16mm film looping through a projector in the gallery in a mimetic return to screenings of *Zen for Film*. Completing this cycle, as the film loops through a projector in the gallery, digital glitches and artificial scratches produced by iMovie meet real scratches and dust produced in the screening process. Watching these layers interact in *Structural Film,* the spectator reconsiders the artifactual nature of digital objects within the old media glitches, scratches, whirring reels, and clacking soundtrack that once constituted *Zen for Film.*

Mark Amerika, *Zen for Mobile Phone Video* (2007)

Referencing iconic images of Paik bathed in the light of *Zen for Film* during screenings, his shadow cast on the screen, artist and writer Mark Amerika records his own shadow within the projection of the film at the Centre Georges Pompidou with an extremely lo-fi mobile phone video camera. Like a bootleg concert recording or a durational art-selfie, the movie capture engages with vernacular practices of mobile media documentation and self-imaging on social media. Amerika attempts to reproduce the meaning of the original. In an extended blog post on the work, he asks: "How can this work be remixed into a so-called new media context and still retain its initial meaning? What was its initial meaning? Was it important to retain it? What does it mean when we can take our portable digital gadgets and selectively capture whatever data we feel

Figure 4.8. Still from Mark Amerika, *Zen for Mobile Phone Video* (2007).

we need in order to further improvise our own lives?"[39] Mirroring several other bootleg videos of museum and cinema screenings of *Zen for Film* appearing online at the time, *Zen for Mobile Phone Video* amplifies the "pile of pixels" that the film has become in its silent and highly compressed digitization. By betraying any semblance of fidelity to the original and writing his own body into the documentation, Amerika questions the capacity for any reproduction whatsoever.

Mungo Thomson, *The Varieties of Experience* (2008)

Using a particularly degraded print of *Zen for Film,* Mungo Thomson translates each frame of the film to its negative for the projection of its inverse in 16mm. Foregrounding high resolution and direct photochemical translation, *The Varieties of Experience* most directly engages the material formats of the original film. In an elegant conceptual gesture, the simple inversion of contrast yields a transformation of cosmic proportions. Thomson describes the work in a related artist book published in 2009 featuring high-resolution images of selected slides:

> The film gathers dust from the spaces where it is exhibited. Dust is composed largely of exfoliated human cells, and human cells are composed of elemental matter from the Big Bang. The motes and specks of dust are captured and printed as imagery in *The Varieties of Experience.* The new film is an inversion of Paik's, a black film with the dust printed white: a moving starscape, where the stars are made of dust rather than the other way around.[40]

Thomson literalizes the spectator's role in Lemaître's formulations: even humans who once exfoliated in the same space that *Zen for Film* may have occupied at any point become written into the film, put into relief by *The Varieties of Experience.* The use of obsolete technical processes renders Thomson's intervention at once historically connected and resolutely contemporary. Playing on the anachronism of the projector while also collapsing the devotional film and cosmic imaginaries in its title, the film draws together William James and Carl Sagan. Bypassing the digital file altogether and responding to the previous remixes of *Zen for Film,* Thomson exploits

Figure 4.9. Still from Mungo Thomson, *The Varieties of Experience* (2008). Courtesy of the artist.

the film's archival circulation while playing on the anachronism of filmic and book-bound presentation in the present.

Dropping the Frame

If the transcoding of *Zen for Film* into a digital format might be argued to produce an ongoing supertemporal constellation of remixes that all draw from a single framework, the following section presents an inverse reading. By contrast, I begin with a single "born-digital" compilation movie in order to plug its historical samples back into the databases from which they were drawn. By pairing the contrasting tactics of these close readings, I aim to chart the distances and resonances between potential contingent reading practices in the little database. Finally, after winnowing the lens through each chapter—from the full-site wide-angle breadth of *Textz*, to the narrower optics of preservation at *Eclipse,* to the close-up on transmission narratives in the audio archive—we end with a laser focus on the close reading of a single work that, at its end, explodes back out into new trajectories through the database at scale.

By following the digital object through its computation, preser-

vation, and transmission, one might arrive at either end of this scalar spectrum. At this concluding side, I follow the components that
make up a digital compilation movie back into a fraying cord of narrative potentials. These potentials cohere around a reading of early
computer-generated movies at Bell Labs (and the documentaries
that accompany them) through the contemporary cipher presented
in *We Edit Life* (2002) by People Like Us (Vicki Bennett).[41] Rather than
bind *We Edit Life* with an interpretive knot or conclusive argument,
this reading seeks to deploy the movie as a conduit to open productive passages back into the database. *We Edit Life* is uniquely poised
to spell out the vexed relations among issues of transcoding and archival use. At one and the same time, the movie reflects on the origins of computer arts while providing a pioneering instance of the
now-ubiquitous digital compilation movie. What follows is a close
reading of *We Edit Life,* one that traces its myriad material sources;
the mode and style of its composition; the networks of archival
dispersion that screen the movie along with presenting its source
material; and finally the broader art-historical and contemporary-
cultural context within which the work embeds itself. Through this
contingent reading, I aim to chart a passage back into these historical works operating at the birth of computer culture while refreshing their interpretation from our present vantage. The method of
this concluding section, therefore, is waylaid by a heterogeneous
and modular cluster of interpretive and descriptive strategies, applicable to the n-dimensional facets of digital objects in general and
the historical conflux of found footage or compilation movies in
particular.

Following People Like Us into the Database

Before exploring the digital compilation movie *We Edit Life* by People
Like Us, we can outline the established methods for interpreting its
immediate precursor, the found footage film.[42] Roger Luckhurst
most succinctly maps established reading tactics of filmic collage
in an article on a series of found footage science-fictional films: "For
the project of found footage, . . . [the] most significant discovery was
that the coherence of spliced collages could be held together by the
instant recognition of genre iconography and narrative formulae."[43]
He goes on to clarify that the spectator (or critic) may "generate a

sort of mega-text of potential narrative possibilities from their implicit familiarity with cinematic codes."[44] This potential megatext offers differential readings between genre and use. Luckhurst concludes, "any coherence the film musters is at what [Craig] Baldwin calls the 'metacinematic' level, where the spectator can recognize both the codes of each re-purposed fragment but also read the critique."[45] This metacinematic approach has long directed both the creation and the reading of found footage films: subversive montage enacting critique via generic dissonance remains the norm. This holds true for the critic as well as the filmmaker. This postmodern interpretive strategy remains pervasive, from avant-garde traditions to television or Hollywood films—to say nothing of the "grand nonnarratives" that shape the internet.[46] So much so, that samples from educational, industrial, sci-fi, or ephemeral films are rarely deployed in remixed works without standing in for some particular object or genre of critique at a historical remove. This generalized demonstration of irony is then evaluated according to the critical intervention spelled out in the montage of the editor-author.

However, a model of creation and interpretation built exclusively on metacinematic recognition misses unique opportunities to unpack networked compilations. For example, via source-tracking, reverse-image searching, and other database-enabled operations, the compilation movie can guide its viewer through networks of reference back into meaningful conversations with its sources.[47] The practices emerging from the use of filmic artifacts widely accessible via networked databases present a dense referential weave to be untangled. In particular, the collage essays of People Like Us resist these older models of critical interpretation. Over and against critique as a mode of composition, PLU directs our attention to happy accidents, unforeseen rhythms, and regimes of availability, exploring the database as a form rather than critiquing any particular object or genre within that database. Dense with clips that have been remediated (and hypermediated) from newsreels, industrial films, and popular science footage, these works are structured according to fluid principles of rhythm and digital compositing that erase the specificity of a pointed historical argument.[48] Further critical complications arise as each new digital compilation movie activates an index of nostalgic pixels drawn from a variety of analog media. As pointed as the differences between found footage and digital compilation might be, filters for reading digital works often remain limited by traditional models of critical interpretation. Instead, this reading proposes an expanded set of descriptive tactics to trace forms of contextual and historical connection bound up with the contingent logics of the database.

By contrast, I contend that a rigorous accounting coordinated with an extensive retracing of sources used in sample-based media highlights the rich conversations a work enacts with, and within, its source material. In this way, my contingent reading of *We Edit Life* proposes a constructive remapping of the generative processes of selection, distribution, and editorial modulation at the heart of the work's networked formation. This is not to discard a critical analysis, but to assert that detailed descriptions of the networks that host their constitutive digital objects may most fully inscribe the politics of the work within its digital environment.[49] When everything is available (and previously ephemeral, archival, or rare "footage" is only a click away), attentive scholarship can begin tracing these robust trails of information radiating from any given object. These contingent readings connect specific digital objects to their situation within networked databases, and back. Not only is the production and significance of the contemporary compilation movie shaped by the same processes of this networked research, but, as I have argued throughout this book, the source materials themselves gather relevance in the growing intertext, accumulating through each new use and reuse. Thus, rather than relying on the imprecise recognitions of genre-based cultural critique, we might trace the material links extending both inward and outward from *We Edit Life* in the attempt to assemble an actor-network for demystification beyond critique.[50]

Movie Introduction and Online Reception

With these contingent reading tactics now loaded, we can turn our attention to *We Edit Life.* Commissioned by the arts organization Lovebytes, *We Edit Life* debuted as part of an international festival of digital art in Sheffield, England.[51] Destabilized as a work from the beginning, People Like Us first presented the digital movie alongside an improvisatory remix performance entitled *Recyclopaedia Britannica,* which resampled many of the sources making up *We Edit Life.*[52] The first in a series of digital collage works, *We Edit Life* was soon distributed in a variety of formats on Archive.org, YouTube,

Vimeo, and *UbuWeb*.[53] In a statement for the Lovebytes debut of the work, PLU emphasizes the use of samples from the Prelinger Archive.[54] Still a project in development in 2002, the Prelinger Archive joined the Internet Archive in 1999. At the time, substantial uploads of digitized industrial, educational, and ephemeral films were only beginning to appear online. More than simply sampling an established collection, PLU's selection of sources for *We Edit Life* helped *generate* Prelinger's digital archive. Many samples that PLU requested had yet to be digitized, and were later uploaded to the Archive.org collection.[55] Thus, in *We Edit Life,* the viewer sees the creation of the moving-picture archive along with an early example of a movie entirely derived from freely available internet content. Three years before YouTube, *We Edit Life* anticipated the widespread forms of remix culture to come. On YouTube today, DJ Rolling Paper's remix of *We Edit Life,* set to a track by Crystal Castles, might stand in for wider current of use more generally.[56] The distribution history and reception of *We Edit Life* can be tracked in comment threads on Comedy Central, via Vicki Bennett's personal website, and through manifold other hits on a Google search for "we edit life" + "people like us." While it would be quixotic, at best, to describe this network at large, it would be a greater mistake to begin without pointing to the wider regimes of production and distribution that enable the movie itself.

Opening Frames and Film Leader

A pastel colorized leader streams in the browser window, reproducing the grainy filmic attributes of a transcoded digital object.[57] The soundtrack, a recording of amplified projector pickups, similarly directs the user to an uncanny moment of filmic projection. We see scratches from the leader's repeated trips through the projector, along with specks of dust and strands of hair, chemical imperfections in the celluloid, misplaced splices, and frame edges. In all these regards, despite its digital production, *We Edit Life* shares with *Zen for Film* a conspicuous invocation of filmic mediation. Though

we are viewing in a browser, *We Edit Life* playfully codes itself as a work of film, confusing the opening moments as the "play" icon and other features of the streaming movie player of the viewer's choice fades into the movie. The uncanny shift from digital activation to remediated film is made more uncomfortable by the double introduction of the traditional film leader. Indeed, while the anachronistic deployment of these cinematic artifacts is common to a computing environment that offers "aged film" filters for nearly every commercial application, the digitized leader and projector soundtrack opening *We Edit Life* points more strongly to the medial transcoding before the browser.[58] As William C. Wees outlines in his classic manifesto, *Recycled Images: The Art and Politics of Found Footage Films,* these works "cannot avoid calling attention to the 'mediascape' from which they come, especially when they also share the media's formal and rhetorical strategies of montage."[59] While *We Edit Life* extends far beyond traditional montage, its samples nevertheless consistently index a digital reflection of a distinctly filmic mediascape.

Timing and Synchronization

One step further, we may observe how these opening frames draw the filmic source material into a ludic engagement with digital composition. Immediately recognizable to anyone familiar with analog film editing are the puncture holes used for timing and synchronization between film reels. What first registers as a skip or glitch, common to film projection still grappling with sprocket alignment, reveals itself to be the repeated sequence of frames including the puncture hole. The exactitude of digital repetition is craftily embedded into this archaic representation of leader. The tightly controlled timing of an Adobe editing suite renders imprecise analog techniques inoperative. Such digital precision continues into animation as the pastel blue title "We Edit Life" slowly fades in and out over the fluctuating filmic background. As the leader projects an ambient background for the title, these superfluous punctures serve the dual

purpose of calling attention to the media historicity of the film as a material object while introducing the seamless techniques of digital editing employed throughout the feature. This database aesthetic returns the viewer, as Stephen Mamber has persuasively argued, to a generalized field of analysis more akin to the precinematic work of Étienne-Jules Marey. Operating as an analytic medium, Mamber argues that the digital movie "displaces a dependence upon real-time linear presentation and the chemically-based realism of cinema . . . in its exposing (even reveling in) its own constructions."[60]

Film Editor and Adobe Premiere

Skipping to the first "cut," we encounter a similarly degraded shot of a filmmaker in profile, closely examining a strip of 35mm film. Looking frame-by-frame, with the celluloid in one hand and a pencil in the other, he is both writer and filmmaker—an editor in both senses. Meanwhile, the leader continues to roll out a countdown in a background layer as PLU keys the film editor up to the first layer in the foreground. Indeed, the meticulous editing of PLU demands a frame-by-frame modulation closer to animation than montage. As we consider the editor with film in hand, we can analyze the composition of this frame of *We Edit Life.* Toward the conclusion of the piece, we discover a mirroring of the film editor's work desk: PLU's screen displaying panel arrays of Adobe After Effects 5.0 and Pro Tools Free, both released in 2001.[61] The foreground features an After Effects layer trimmed to the editor's outline, while the background continues streaming the leader sample into a countdown. More akin to multitrack audio mixing, *We Edit Life* retains the decidedly DIY aesthetic of digital collage while streaming an increasingly elaborate composite of layered samples throughout the movie. If traditional found footage films require close scrutiny of montage-based juxtapositions, the digital compilation movie requires a detailed accounting of a variety of layered editorial decisions along with the fluid interactions between sampled works. If an understanding of this mode of composition may continue to stream in a background

track to this reading, we may begin to explore the samples comprising the layered frame.

Stan VanDerBeek and Kenneth Knowlton

"How much trouble is it to get that changed to some other color?," the filmmaker asks, looking up from the celluloid to a technical advisor speaking off-screen. An answer follows: "Just find the right place in the program, make the appropriate change, and we'll run the whole thing again." Though, at the mention of the program, the filmmaker returns his uncomprehending gaze to the materials at hand. The collaboration at play follows the art-and-technology combination of artist and engineer prevalent in the technological excitement of mid-1960s neo-avant-garde art. The filmmaker shown in profile throughout the scene is Stan VanDerBeek, a prominent underground filmmaker best known for his animated collage films. In 1967, at the time the original footage was shot, VanDerBeek was working as an artist-in-residence at AT&T Bell Labs in Murray Hill, New Jersey. His technical interlocutor is Ken Knowlton, an engineer specializing in computer graphics and motion pictures at Bell Labs. The footage VanDerBeek holds is toward creating one of a series of "poemfields," a set of experimental short films begun in 1965 that deploy Knowlton's innovative BEFLIX computer graphics program, a pioneering mode of generating images via a mosaic of Unicode characters.[62] Quite literally, to alter the film, VanDerBeek must inscribe changes to the character mosaic via a card that is fed into an IBM 7094 mainframe that rewrites the entire sequence onto electronic tape that is later fed through a Stromberg-Carlson 4020 microfilm recorder and finally converted to film.[63]

With characteristic wonder, in "Re: Look: Computerized Graphics 'Light Brings Us News of the Universe,'" VanDerBeek notes: "The writing of pictures that will make pictures in motion, in coded text form, means a new notation system to store images by. . . . In other words, motion pictures can be written, stored indefinitely (in punched paper form or tape form) and brought 'to life' later.

Motion pictures can be conceived (written) in airplanes."[64] Watching VanDerBeek marvel at having Knowlton's program "run the whole thing again," we might consider *We Edit Life* alongside the popular emergence of real-time graphic interfaces capable of writing a full range of digital media formats for the first time in 2002.[65] James Hodge reads this scene as emblematic of the "experiential opacity of digital media," where "what goes into the black box becomes inevitably, unaccountably transformed when it comes back out."[66] These shared points of wonderment and black-box confusion are driven home while rewatching these clips in the 2020s, as generative models become increasingly adept at producing convincing image-based media from text prompts, indeed, even "conceived (written) in airplanes."

Incredible Machine and Bell Labs

Lingering for a moment on this short opening clip, we might return to the provenance of the sequence featuring VanDerBeek and Knowlton. The sample is pulled from *Incredible Machine* (directed by Paul Cohen for AT&T in 1968), a fifteen-minute sponsored film covering recent Bell Labs breakthroughs, as Rick Prelinger highlights, in "computer graphics, computer-synthesized speech, and computer-generated movies and music."[67] The scene in *We Edit Life* modifies a sequence entering *Incredible Machine* at 3:35, rearranging the conversation and remixing the audio track. Overlays of circuit diagrams and the flashing text "DATA INCOMPLETE" in the background of this scene in *We Edit Life* are both sampled from an earlier segment of *Incredible Machine*. The chalkboard becomes another simulated screen, introducing a variety of clips that will feature prominently in the latter half of the movie: children performing a group experiment in electricity, flowing graphics representing sound waves, stock footage of a home, and a layer matrix of hands operating dials.

With voice-over narration and samples from *Incredible Machine* peppered throughout *We Edit Life,* the communications research film serves as the core around which the samples deployed by PLU

constellate and eventually spin out of control. Even on a cursory viewing, without supplemental information describing the samples, still, the genre format, ideological thrust, and intended audience of *Incredible Machine* are easily recognized by the casual internet spectator: this is a commercial-industrial-promotional computer-science and technology film, bright-eyed with a starry utopian vision of progress, narrated by a familiar paternal voice educating a general populace. Rather than perform a critical turn on this content, however, PLU plays within in its network of association, activating a concerted set of associated materials and concerns, by turns incisive, doomer, and celebratory. In this way, PLU enacts a mode of "network ambivalence," described by Patrick Jagoda at the conclusion of *Network Aesthetics* as a critical orientation toward pervasive, always-on networks.[68] For Jagoda, ambivalence is "a crucial critical position from which to think within an uncertain present that is also ongoing, . . . a process of slowing down and learning to inhabit a compromised environment with the discomfort, contradiction, and misalignment it entails."[69] Within the aesthetic refrains and whimsical loops of *We Edit Life,* the viewer inhabits the same uncomfortable ambivalence through which we cope with the endless complications of life online.

"Daisy Bell" and Elektro, the Westinghouse Moto-Man

Continuing this track, our attention to the details of source materials like *Incredible Machine* opens robust networks of signification in the rhythmic composition of *We Edit Life.* The structural and semantic importance of *Incredible Machine* grows increasingly telling as *We Edit Life* moves from a focus on computer-generated film to computer-generated music. The score for *Incredible Machine,* as the narrator reveals, "was entirely composed by a computer." This would be no small feat just a few years after "Daisy Bell" debuted at Murray Hill. The team behind this first computer to sing—comprised of John Kelly, Carol Lockbaum, and Max Mathews—are all featured in *Incredible Machine.* Mathews, the grandfather of electronic music,

provides the score for the film. Sampling Mathews's pioneering audio track along with visual layers from *Incredible Machine,* PLU's aural attention might best locate *We Edit Life* in a digital music-video genre, where both image and sound are driven more by rhythm and fluid spatial montage than cutting. If there is a narrative to draw out from the movie, we might argue for a story of artificial life, as the various dials and diagrams, engineers and conductors orchestrate the creation of a singing robot. Here, Elektro, the Westinghouse Moto-Man, sampled from a newsreel of the 1939 World's Fair in New York, may stand in for the titular "life" edited by PLU's computer.[70] As *We Edit Life* becomes increasingly disjointed toward the conclusion, Elektro joins with a circuit made of children to sing an ominous remix of "Music Alone Shall Live." Far from generically sampled, the source material behind Elektro's threatening ballad in *We Edit Life* invokes a dense mesh of insightful references, beginning with HAL's death-rattle rendition of "Daisy Bell" in Stanley Kubrick's *2001: A Space Odyssey* (1969), which naturally brings us back to Murray Hill and the birth of synthesized speech, covered in detail by *Incredible Machine.* The ambivalent temporality of *We Edit Life* imports the technological thrill of these 1960s innovations into a premonitory mix with the melodic anxieties of a database that will, as Elektro tells us, outlive us all.

Poemfield No. 2 and *Man and His World*

Reeling back from this expanding intertext, we might go deeper into the diegesis, returning to the footage VanDerBeek holds at the opening of *We Edit Life.* The footage under consideration is most likely *Poemfield No. 2* (ca. 1966), one of the ten short poetic films VanDerBeek and Knowlton made in collaboration over a four-year span from 1965 to 1969. It might also be *Man and His World* (1967), a one-minute short film after the title of Expo '67 that translates the phrase "man and his world" into a variety of the world's languages.[71] Literally composing a mosaic of international textual detritus and small symbolic characters, the poemfields explore the representa-

tional capacities and inherent variability of language within computational environments. While VanDerBeek's background is in image-based collage films like *Science Friction,* the lexical construction of BEFLIX films inspired a literary form in which each word-image necessarily contains thousands of letters as pixels. Reading the text for *Poemfield No. 2* alongside *We Edit Life,* certain resonant themes emerge:

> LIFE / LIFE LIKE / POEMFIELD NO. 2 / SIMILAR / LIKE / TO / CLOCK / TICK / WE PICK / LIFE / OUT / OR APART / SEEMING / TO SEE / SEPARATE / THINGS / TOGETHER / SO / YOU / SAY / IT / WOULD / SEEM / LIFE . . LIKE . . . / THIS / LIVING / BUT . . . / WE / ALWAYS / SUSPECT / . . IT . . . / THE END[72]

Seeming to see separate things together, PLU reanimates Elektro to a singing life-likeness and more generally deploys disparate archival sources in a variety of repurposed narrative configurations. On this digital translation, we might say *We Edit Life,* alongside the poem-fields, "passes as a punctualized actor," concealing an intricate network that holds them together.[73] The suspicious ease of a cohesive collage is central both to VanDerBeek's previous films and to PLU's audio remixes, where dead media and inert matter are everywhere lifelike. Toward these ends, *We Edit Life* channels the *Incredible Machine* soundtrack over a man whittling miniature wooden elk over footage of "real live" elk, stating: "Experimenters in visual perception are using computers to create weird, random patterns that never occur in real life. . . . The art of computer graphics is only in its infancy yet it is already stimulating creative thought in far out areas where research is likely to get complex and unwieldy." Anticipating developments in "life-like" futures of computational movies—from Google DeepDream's kaleidoscopic patterns in 2015, to the cursed origins of text-to-video in Modelscope's Will Smith pasta video of 2023, to the hallucinatory realities generated by SoraAI in 2024—*We Edit Life*'s "complex and unwieldy" approach to the rhythms of

This is the pictur[e] [o]f my voice

computational movie-making keeps a finger to the pulse of the fundamental weirdness at the simulated heart of digital cinema.

Gathering Sources and Concluding Links

While this extended descriptive performance draws out signification patterns from *Incredible Machine* and associated materials, we can conclude by anthologizing a number of the films sampled by PLU, all of which might offer interpretive feedback between *We Edit Life* and the database from which it stems. More than a supplement, this collection performs a potential inherent to reading works operating within a database. Each source returns to *We Edit Life* while simultaneously pointing the user into an n-dimensional system of signification radiating out from each new citation. Rather than limit the reading of *We Edit Life* to a pointed critical position, this project seeks to deploy the movie as a conduit that might direct its user to unimagined passages beyond this particular constellation. In other words, as one screen among many, this reading can conclude only with new directions. Thus, what follows are a select few strands among the many worth tracing, given the contingent interests of the reader:

Panels and operators are taken from IBM's *The Thinking Machines* (1968), an educational short following a robotic cartoon that concludes with a clip from the previously outlined *Man and His World*. At 4:30, the radio director from CBS's *On the Air* (1937) pops up over a diagram for the chemical formula of celluloid culled from *The Alchemist in Hollywood* (1940). A voiceover from *The News Magazine of the Screen* (vol. 7, no. 3 [1956]) describes footage taken from *Fashions on the Ice and Snow* (1940) and *Switzerland: The Land and the People* (1963), confusing time through place.[74] Sound waves, computer panels, and musicians are sampled from *Discovering Electronic Music* (1983), further integrating the parallel history of early computer film and music within *We Edit Life*. Numerous samples from a variety of orchestral recordings, musical education films, and soundies, including *Conducting Good Music* (1956), *Instruments of the Orchestra*

(1947), *Sound Recording for Motion Pictures* (1960), and *Looking at Sound* (1950), all import melodies and archival narratives to the mix. Indirect samples may also be found: the kitschy "Happy Valley Ranch" sign above the rolling credits calls up the "Lazy-X Ranch" in *The World at Your Call* (1950), a Jam Handy / AT&T telephonic communications film. Similarly, the title *We Edit Life* can be heard as an echo of the industrial short *We Use Power* (1956), referenced in PLU's Prelinger inventory. More distantly, *Man and Computer* (1965) originates the filmic metaphor of the conductor as computer operator in a related hypermediated format. Finally, "IBM Corporation, Military Products Division" presents *On Guard! The Story of SAGE* (1956), wherein panel operators at the IBM mainframe bring innovations in computer technology to a familial Cold War context, and the military-industrial complex more generally.

Unlike the collections that house these works, a linear format like the academic monograph might afford only this brief list of samples. The argument for network tracing and the archival activation of *We Edit Life* can nevertheless be concluded by pointing to the editorial remix of texts, images, and movies that supplement this chapter in the interlude, along with the outward links to expanded potential significations. Here, as in *We Edit Life,* the user is directed back into the database, where each sample contains a new network for exploration. Each thread, in all directions, presents an interconnected web of contingencies awaiting meanings delivered, or discovered, or invented, by their reader.

Interlude 4
Flash Artifacts

The close reading of any moving-image object hosted on *UbuWeb* catalyzes an unpredictably idiosyncratic set of transformations affected on the historical work. Each work transforms differently under the conditions of the digital collection. The third chapter followed the provenance and version history of a particular set of recordings by bill bissett, arguing that any set of files would have its own attendant stories to tell. In the same way, the previous chapter argues for the productive potentials of contingent readings of digital objects, marked by the conditions of how everything from the technical substrate to the social text might come to signify within the historical work's digital situation. Put differently, every close reading of a digitized film concludes with frayed strands of signification that point toward the massively intertextual situation of the little database. *Theme Song* addresses the intersection of a video-art installation in the gallery with contemporary forms of vlog confessional formats on the internet. *Zen for Film* opens with questions of technical materiality and ends in an unforeseeable horizon for remix. *We Edit Life* redirects the attentive reader from the compression of compilation to the unzipping of a cultural archive. Each reading coheres only insofar as it redirects the reader to forces that inform the work's connection to conditional layers of historical and situational meaning. Further, any given digitized film or video on *UbuWeb* signifies differently given the palimpsest of contingent effects heaped on iterations of the work over time. This is the challenge to any systematic reading of the little database. The transformations effected by digital formats cannot be generalized. Indeed, the only generalization we might make is that every file is transformed differently, and that we must therefore attend with care to those conditions of transformation.

In 2009, I collaborated with the artist João Enxuto to query this condition within the *UbuWeb* collection, coproducing a thirty-minute movie entitled *Flash Artifacts*. The work is hosted on *UbuWeb* and was screened at galleries in New York and Berlin. Our approach highlighted the most extreme examples of media-reflexive film and video that were then streaming on *UbuWeb*. The work attempted to surface "a hidden magic" in "the contextual economy of *UbuWeb*."[1] By "interweaving, juxtaposing, and re-editing dozens of films and videos from the *UbuWeb* archive," we attempted to draw out the specificity of each localized transformation.[2] Formally, the work mimics art-historical lecture projections, with a standardized display of two panels for comparative analysis. At certain moments in *Flash Artifacts,* this tidy relation breaks down as films stream through, above, and within each other. As in *Zen for Film,* the works featured in *Flash Artifacts* are particularly sensitive to the medial registers of use and playback. Samples are drawn from celluloid-intensive films, interventionist television advertisements, and born-digital animations alike. In dialogue with *We Edit Life,* the compilation is both a mode of reading the database and a guide for viewers to rediscover works already in circulation. This editorial poetics is augmented by a set of links to all works included in *Flash Artifacts*. The media poetics of the movie function to create a little database of its own, nested within *UbuWeb*.

The selection of works included and the title of this work function as anachronistic records of the site at a given moment in time. If the same work were made today, it would respond differently given the current set of files hosted by *UbuWeb* and attendant changes to the interface. For example, the entire collection has since been optimized for streaming on mobile phones and tablets, dropping the Flash format that transcoded these works altogether. Like ripped VHS cassettes that transcode historical film, these Flash artifacts leave traces that only become more pronounced over time. The shifting technical affordances of format invoke new readings of the works that have been streaming on the site all along. In this regard, *Flash Artifacts* marks a particular moment in *UbuWeb*'s position within the continuously shifting terrain of online viewership. However, it has also undergone multiple changes over the past six years, not least in relation to this project. Tracking changes to the site over time via the Internet Archive reveals a dramatic set of alterations to the site

Figure 4i.1. A still from *Flash Artifacts* (2009). On the left: Standish Lawder, *Color Film* (1971). On the right: Tacita Dean, *Kodak* (2007). Layers of cinematic mediation accumulate in the side-by-side dual projection format. Captured via *UbuWeb*: ubu.com/film/snelson_flash.html.

design, paratextual information, editorial involvements, and server hosts, in addition to the inventory of works hosted.

As with "Also this: no title" and *EXE TXT,* the media poetics of *Flash Artifacts* aim to allow the assembled works to articulate a constellation in a register that this chapter cannot attempt on paper, in PDF, or through image stills. Writing this interlude, I initially set out to briefly summarize the effects on each clip as it played out in *Flash Artifacts.* This exercise quickly proved futile. The dynamics of the opening sequence, drawn from George Brecht's *Entrance to Exit* (1966) illustrate the problem. *Entrance to Exit* was itself a kind of riff on Paik's *Zen for Film*—also featured in the *FluxFilm Anthology*—with a blank screen bracketed by "Entrance" and "Exit" signs respectively. It thus bears the same close scrutiny presented in the first case study of this chapter. Questions on blankness are compounded by movement cues, existential quandaries, and imagined space. In *Flash Artifacts,* the clips have been rearranged so that the left screen features the opening titles while the right screen plays backward from the "Exit" at the conclusion to the movie. The clips fade just as they near meeting in the shared black screen that makes up the bulk of the film. Already, space and time are confused by the geospatial particularities of digital networks (does one enter at the console, wherever that is, or the changing server hosts of *UbuWeb,* through the code or the representation that the code generates?) and modular playback (the linearity of entering and exiting a shared space has been reversed and doubled). The authorial function of *Flash Artifacts* is complicated by the opening titles—which read: "FLUX FILM 1966 by George Brecht"—and in turn question the authorship of Brecht in relation to Paik, the filmic apparatus, the group setting of a screening, and the layers of transcoding that rework the film as a digital object. This, at least, would be a highly compressed reading of the first thirty seconds of *Flash Artifacts,* which features only one work rather than the manifold and variable comparative setups that carry throughout the work. What's certain is that the movie codec does compression better. The reader is here directed to play *Flash Artifacts* as another way to drop the frame from film to database.

 See: *Flash Artifacts* (2009).

EPILOGUE

The *EPC*

On the Persistence of Obsolescent Networks

For a brief moment, an eclectic little database of poetry was the largest website on what we now generically call the internet. This site, the *Electronic Poetry Center* (known generally as the *EPC*), was founded in 1994 by Loss Pequeño Glazier in collaboration with Charles Bernstein as part of the Poetics Program at the University of Buffalo. Its outsized role in the early internet was a product of the automated population of the *EPC*'s nascent WWW address with the bibliographic records, electronic correspondences, and archival documents Glazier had been compiling on Gopher, FTP, and other alternate protocols in the years before the widespread adoption of HTTP for internet traffic.[1] Hosting an exceptionally heterogeneous array of formats, the *EPC* retains a formidable repository of the earliest intersections of poetry, poetics, and digital networks.

Now, when I prompt Google to search for "EPC," it is the forty-fourth hit in my results, well below the top hits for other EPCs: "Evangelical Presbyterian Church," "Efficient Power Conversion Corporation," and the Wikipedia page for "Engineering, procurement, and construction." This is the product of several removes: first, Google's preference for advertising entities and encyclopedic information; second, the hand-coded and thus SEO-resistant nature of the site; and third, its 2019 relocation from long-time University of Buffalo servers to the University of Pennsylvania, where it reunited with Bernstein, but lost the decades of algorithmic clout it had gained at its previous URL. Today, this tremendous repository of primary documents on poetry and poetics just barely registers above an informational page on the Dewey Decimal Classification Editorial Policy Committee *(EPC)*.

Beyond PageRank, the site is in ruins. Broken links, abandoned projects, deprecated tags, and missing images join with unplayable media, neglected collections, and obsolete formats. The site coaches its users through variable tactics for access: "If you have a broken link to an EPC resource, use the top tabs (e.g. author pages & digital library, etc.), fill in the custom search bar at the foot of this page or, for a known URL, substitute 'writing.upenn.edu/epc/' for 'epc .buffalo.edu/' in the address bar above."[2] However, its current state of disrepair also dials up an earlier internet, within which the *EPC* emerged. In his groundbreaking book *Digital Poetics: The Making of E-Poetries,* Glazier outlines the *EPC* as a kind of "subject village," clustered around poetry on the web. Writing in 2001, he notes that this type of site "not only delivers texts but also offers slow connect times, error messages, misgivings, and the megabytes of misinformation that typify a largely unedited textual space."[3] Thirty years after the site was initiated, I find my 5G wireless navigation of its dilapidated links eerily anticipated by conversations on the unique challenges of access, information overload, and interoperability of digital collections that remain on the site. These conversations play out across the pages of *R/IFT* magazine, the Buffalo Poetics listserv, and the stranger offerings found amongst the Error-404 dead ends that delineate the *EPC*.

Reading through the continuity of these errors presents a kind of time travel, in which we might deploy the Wayback Machine as a portal into the variantology of the site as a fluid text. Not only are the Internet Archive captures more complete and functional than the currently hosted site, they also track the developments—and abandonments—of the *EPC* over time. Glimpsing these snapshots drawn from 1997 to 2019, alternative visions of what an "electronic poetry center" might afford can be found within abortive projects and imaginative productions of a site materializing alongside the emergence of Web 1.0. These visions were modeled in response to the all-too-familiar terrain of "the megabytes of misinformation that typify a largely unedited textual space." They presciently map onto today's internet, marked by manifold crises on zettabyte scales, driven by the corporate black-box algorithms that Matthew Kirschenbaum has heralded as the agents of a coming "textpocalypse."[4] But they also enact speculative hopes for smaller communities of care, rich poetic dialogue, and experimental flourishing, even within the breakdowns of what Bernstein elegiacally deemed "electronic pies in the poetry skies" upon the dissolution of the Poetics Listserv in 2001.[5]

In this way, just as the *EPC* points back to the persistence of error and misinformation from its inception, it simultaneously gestures to better futures for the internet before the mores of always-on social media practices took root. Within these glitches, nested deep in lost file hierarchies, an obsolete imaginary of the network continues to subsist alongside mainstream practices. Here, the little database presents an opportunity to reimagine the internet a little more strangely, where future developments might rediscover older forms of invention made long before the establishment of today's generic conventions. Unpacking the *EPC* library offers a moment to speculate on how and why we've come to use certain dominant forms and formats over others.

Like the illuminative occlusions of server transfers at *Eclipse,* the *EPC* reveals a range of otherwise unseen features in the moment of its breakdown. Given the current disrepair of site links, the only way to fully explore the *EPC* is to download it. Even as it has displaced ordinary practices of downloading, the streaming internet produces a novel perspective through which to interrogate what it means to gather a collection in the file hierarchies of personal computers. In a reversal of what Peter Lunenfeld termed "the secret war between downloading and uploading" in 2011, today's networks are defined by the continuous upload of user data—if not by choice, then via dataveillance—just as downloading repertoires are increasingly rarified.[6] No longer a default option for accessing cultural objects, downloads become necessary only in exceptional circumstances of connectivity, practical use, or personal preservation. These circumstances may include teaching materials in a classroom with spotty WiFi access (to ensure live playback); looking to more directly interact with media (to annotate a PDF or sample an MP3); or hoping to preserve a meaningful image from the ongoing streams of content (the image of a meme or a lover). The broken relocation of the *EPC,* like a Steam game with corrupted data, requires a full download to properly reparse its content. Using a popular tool like Wget or WebCopy can deliver the full file structure in just over an hour, scraping the entire site's contents of just under 5 GB of material.[7] From there, the site reveals its secrets within file hierarchies not unlike those that structure my research for this manuscript, within which it is now nested. Not unlike, I would dare to presume, the file hierarchies that structure the reader's own little database adjacent to the reading of this book, which I hope generates new downloads from within its sources, citations, and pages.

The most salient secret this download reveals is an innate relatability to its structure. More than anything else, the *EPC* reminds me of my backup hard drive, a total wreck that never seems to have what I'm looking for, if I manage to get it to boot at all, but also opens a window into my daily repertoires of use from what now seems to be distant personal eras: folders indexing that year abroad, or segmenting grad school collections across two drives, or recording details from the recently forgotten past of two summers ago. Organizational folders that mean well are disregarded for a smattering of files that were either hastily or accidentally placed out of order (behind the scenes in the *EPC,* an obsolete "hotlist.html" sits alongside the operant "index.html"). Some project folders are neater than others, the full *RIF/T* magazine archive (1993–1998), coedited by Glazier and Ken Sherwood, is in pristine condition, situated alongside a folder for "ezines," preserving an essential archive of the earliest experiments with poetry periodicals on the internet.[8] The complete records of the Poetics List are grouped in a single folder through date-stamped .txt files.[9] Vast portions of the site are devoted to its newest addition: a "mirror" of Tom Raworth's complete personal website (1997–2017), saved two years after Raworth had passed and the site went dark, recovered through Internet Archive captures. The only addition to Raworth's site is a poignant note left by its preservationist, Steve McLaughlin, in a splash page reading: "Tom Raworth thought of this site as ephemeral and that it might disappear when he did."[10] Clicking through the link reveals the full site as though it had never disappeared. The *EPC*'s longevity is no less a surprise, and perhaps a fuller recovery will yet emerge.

These folders reveal a structural intimacy among the organizational folders of the little databases. The *EPC,* like *Textz, Eclipse, PennSound,* and *UbuWeb* (like every ordinary hard drive), is the product of idiosyncratic nested hierarchies of folders: (mis)named and (dis)ordered according to repertoires of collection, preservation, and transmission made by editors over time. None rely on metadata schemas for archival organization or Content Management Systems (CMS) for content design or embedded algorithmic social features for user engagement or large-scale computational tools for cultural analytics. All, instead, mirror the same practices that preserve digital objects throughout the little databases that make up every personal computer. If every chapter of this study has focused on a single format: the *EPC* is defined by thousands of HTML files, each written by hand from the very moment the protocol was released. Housed in the nested hierarchies of the *EPC,* across these HTML pages, a more intimate internet emerges. One built on the quirks of care and glitches of maintenance inscribed when the internet was largely "under construction."

Longing for the complications of these simpler forms, the hand-coded HTML files of the *EPC* read like love letters hastily scrawled in Word documents from decades past. Error-prone and excessive, playful and sincere, they encode desires inscribed for uncertain futures. They enfold digital objects in unstable media formats to record meaningful histories for unknown potential uses, guarding against the oblivion of erasure. Hailing from the distant digital history of just a decade or two past, these persistent networks of digital objects continue to tell new stories, subject to ongoing transformations not unlike scratches and dust accumulating on film running through a projector. A contingent media poetics of the little database continues the correspondence initiated by these letters. A way to attend with care, and play, to cultural memories subject to ongoing and unknowable transformations ahead.

ACKNOWLEDGMENTS.ZIP

Compressing acknowledgments for this book requires zipping up two decades of diverse forms of collaborative media play: scanning books, writing code, making poems, ripping movies, coding pages, remixing contents, reading essays, playing games, and sharing files. These assemblages took shape before the book was even an imagined outcome, in everyday practices before media scholarship, in the poems before the poetics. If much of this book is about the limitations of certain normative forms, a ZIP file rendered in three pages is surely the most incommensurate format for thanks. I mourn the data lost in the compression format called "acknowledgments" and beg forgiveness for the gaps and holes in these notes.

The earliest components of this project were created in 2008, but their imagination extends back to 2004, when I began my work with Craig Dworkin at *Eclipse.* Of course, Craig's impact on this work can be traced in so many of the preceding pages. For now, I'll suffice it to say here that no one has played a bigger role in the why or the what or the how I read. Similarly, in 2006, I had the opportunity to start collaborating with James Hoff on the little magazine *0 to 9* and the *Complete Minimal Poems* of Aram Saroyan, for whom my gratitude is both endless and nameless. Great things come in three—my heartfelt thanks to the profundity of collaborator-ship with Avi Alpert will never be, as they say, "good enough."

Growing up in rural Utah, I craved the forms of academic mentorship that have characterized my postsecondary education. I must list a few mentors here, whose conversations echo throughout these pages: Christopher Bush, Eduardo Cadava, Rubén Gallo, Tom Levin, Mendi+Keith Obadike, Jean-Michel Rabaté, Keith Sanborn, Kaja Silverman, P. Adams Sitney, and Cornel West. Added to this list is another set of three: mentors from my graduate study at UPenn. Charles Bernstein gave me the opportunity to work for *PennSound* when I needed it most and has shaped my sense of play and poetics before and beyond our work together. Al Filreis has anchored and inspired work that scales from the printed page to the live mic to the recorded track. Outside the institution, I remain transformed by all networks of publication and conversation with Tan Lin.

After graduate study, this project continued over a two-year interlude at Northwestern University, where I found support in a digital humanities postdoctoral fellowship at the Alice Kaplan Institute for the Humanities. I remain grateful for the conversations and friendship of Thomas Burke, John Alba Cutler, Harris Feinsod, Hi'ilei Hobart, Jim Hodge, Jules Law, Susan Manning, Ira Murfin, Wendy Wall, and Tristram Wolff.

It would be a gross understatement to say that the 2020s have, thus far, been a challenge. Pandemics, wars, losses, and countless crises have marked my time since joining the faculty at UCLA. And yet, within this turbulence I've found an intellectual community that continues to buoy me through it at all points. I'm profoundly grateful to Michael Chwe, Helen Deutsch, Johanna Drucker, Matthew Fisher, Yogita Goyal, Jonathan Grossman, Ursula Heise, Grace Hong, Chris Johanson, Nour Joudah, Sarah Kareem, Rachel Lee, Summer Kim Lee, Saree Makdisi, Lauren Lee McCarthy, Chandler McWilliams, Ho'esta Mo'e'hahne, Romi Morrison, Veronica Paredes, Miriam Posner, Todd Presner, Casey Reas, Brian Kim Stefans, Wendy Sung, Chris Thompson, Justin Torres, and Erica Weaver. My UCLA Game Lab comrades have kept these ideas in play, with special gratitude to John Brumley, Jenna Caravello, Chris Kelty, Tyler Stefanich, and Eddo Stern for bringing me into their magic circles.

Most of all, a series of undergraduate and graduate students have been my testing ground for play and experiment within and beyond the classroom since the project began. In many ways, this book is written for them, to afford the freedom to invent new forms of playing readings at every interface: Andrea Acosta, Megan Anderson, Brian Arechiga, David Brown, Eunice Choi, Brenna Connell, Elliott Couts, Rosemary Galloway, Sarah Garcia, Taylor Leigh Harper, Annie Howard, Dylan Karlsson, Emma Keenan, Zackary Keibach, Chelsea Kern, Anthony Kim (to whom I owe additional thanks for his brilliant work on the index to follow), Rae Kuruhara, Maya Sol Levy, Tony Wei Ling, Yi Liu, Michael Luo, Mason McClay, Rhiannon McGavin, Eve McNally, Dandi Meng, Luca Messara, Sam Malabre,

Janice Montecillo, Enrique Olivares, Jackie Quinn, Jinha Song, Angel Tolentino, Dalena Tran, Ariel Uzal, Jesslyn Whittell, Wiley Wiggins, Leia Yen, and Elliot Bear Yu.

The poetics of this project have been forged in conversation with a group of poets and artists with whom I have shared stages, ideas, and (perhaps most important) libations, while working on the manuscript. The list is too long for even an attempt at summary, but at its core are conversations with derek beaulieu, Andreas Bülhoff, Nancy Baker Cahill, Cori Copp, Alejandro Miguel Justino Crawford, Jesse Damiani, Amze Emmons, João Enxuto, J. Gordon Faylor, Sophia Le Fraga, Alessandro de Francesco, Rainer Diana Hamilton, Sam Hart, Mark Johnson, Josef Kaplan, Alli Katz, Shiv Kotecha, Ilan Manouach, Steve McLaughlin, Holly Melgard, Tracie Morris, Joseph Mosconi, Jena Osman, John Paetsch, Allison Parrish, Jake Reber, Miljohn Ruperto, Alvaro Seiça, Ara Shirinyan, Divya Victor, Barrett White, Aaron Winslow, Peter Wu, Joey Yearous-Algozin, and Steve Zultanski.

A scholarly community of peers has kept this project timely and impacted my work in both conversation and written work. I would be remiss not to mention the profound effects of Mark Algee-Hewitt, Dušan Barok, Paul Benzon, Simone Browne, Jason Camlot, Lori Emerson, Kareem Estefan, Chris Funkhouser, Alex Galloway, Oliver Gaycken, Annette Gilbert, Tung-Hui Hu, Patrick Jagoda, Tsitsi Jaji, Ben Kudler, Zach Lesser, Erica Levin, Danny Marcus, Meredith Martin, Shaka McGlotten, Joe Milutis, Omar Miranda, Michael Nardone, Josephine Park, Marjorie Perloff, Scott Pound, Rita Raley, Brian Reed, Sophie Seita, Paul Stephens, Kazys Varnelis, and Darren Werschler.

Above all, my thanks are owed to the team at the University of Minnesota Press, who have been truly exceptional in bringing this project together for both page and screen. From my initial conversations with Electronic Mediations series editors to the insightful readings of my anonymous reviewer to the exceptional work of Leah Pennywark, Anne Carter, and, truly, every single person I have had the pleasure of working with at the press across all departments: I never could have imagined that a publication process could be as pleasurable as this, or as inspiring. Before going to print, I am already overcome by the unmitigated honor to shelve this book within the series that has most impacted my thought to date.

This honor, I know, will be lost on a few. The writing of this book has seen too many losses to enumerate, but prime among them, for me, are my father, Scott James Snelson (1959–2021), and my mother-in-law, Sona Hakopian (1958–2016), to whom the work is dedicated. When I think of my most profound little databases, they revolve around these inventories of loss. Loving thanks are due to my family—Luann, Kristi, Clay, Sammy, LesLee, Jayla, Kylie, David, Naira . . . and Asta Theodore—to which I would like to add my gratitude to the many Elliotts who first taught me how to work and to the kinship networks we've since found in Glendale, California.

Finally, the phrase I've used to describe my relationship with Mashinka Firunts Hakopian has always been "living in collaboration." It continues to be the most accurate in its radical compression: there are no words, or spaces between the words, that I have inscribed without her. For Mashinka, I would like to reserve the exception to the arguments I have made in this book: she remains the only non-contingent, un-conditional constant I have had the privilege to know.

NOTES

Introduction

1. On the "meaningfully collaborative" feedback loops that bridge little databases of play with large language models in *AI Dungeon* specifically, see Minh Hua and Rita Raley, "Playing With Unicorns: *AI Dungeon* and Citizen NLP" *Digital Humanities Quarterly* 14, no. 4 (2020): 26.

2. For one particularly salient recent critique of *scale* in large language models (LLM) and natural language processing (NLP), see Emily M. Bender, Timnit Gebru, Angelina McMillan-Major, and Shmargaret Shmitchell, "On the Dangers of Stochastic Parrots: Can Language Models Be Too Big? 🦜," in *Proceedings of the 2021 ACM Conference on Fairness, Accountability, and Transparency* (New York: Association for Computing Machinery, 2021), 610–23.

3. While it might be uncommon to italicize the names of websites, I introduce this typographic modulation to signal both the inheritance of the little magazine in these sites and the sense of an authored work or edited collection. Despite outward similarities, these sites are not Google Books, Spotify, or YouTube: they are *little databases.*

4. Here, I'm invoking an art historical lineage for theorizing "media specificity" or "media reflexivity" that includes Clement Greenberg and Rosalind Krauss, among many others in an expanded field. For a historical foundation on these debates, see Clement Greenberg, "Towards a Newer Laocoon," *Art and Culture: Critical Essays* (Boston: Beacon, 1961), 23–38, and Rosalind Krauss, "A Voyage on the North Sea: Art in the Age of the Post-Medium Condition" (New York: Thames & Hudson, 1999), 47–56. More thematically, one might anachronistically head to a university library to peruse early issues of a little magazine called *October.* Whereas Greenberg argues that the essence and value of art lies in its ability to exploit the unique features and limitations inherent to its medium, Krauss challenges the very idea of a stable "medium" to instead emphasize self-aware explorations of media's limitations as central to contemporary artistic practice. Both takes have been crucial touchstones for the criticism and, more importantly, *production* of art in the twentieth century and beyond. The "vivid evidence" that I propose in this sentence hinges on the ways in which media-reflexive works—from the historical avant-gardes and high modernism through to the neo-avant-gardes and beyond into conceptualisms, net art, and a range of post-digital practices—are

often constructed to be "about" their own mediatic conditions. This very self-reflection often produces the most dramatic transformations to the ways in which these works inhabit their newly transcoded situations: offering a rare glimpse into otherwise invisible processes of networked digitization.

5. My use of "digital object" throughout owes to the philosophical work of Yuk Hui, whose *On the Existence of Digital Objects* (Minneapolis: University of Minnesota Press, 2016) investigates the existential status of the digital object (see esp. 47–58). For Hui, digital objects are "objects that take shape on a screen or hide in the back end of a computer program, composed of data and metadata regulated by structures or schemas" (1). Most germane to this study, Hui delineates the parallel processes of individuation that constitute the digital object: the "objectification of data," a mimetic process of digitizing materials, alongside the "datafication of objects," a process of coding objects into a digital milieu (50). I return to Hui most directly in chapter 4 through a close reading of the database movies of People Like Us.

6. A key principle in Manovich's foundational book *The Language of New Media* (Cambridge, Mass.: MIT Press, 2001), "transcoding" technically refers to platform conversions between digital formats. In computer science, this would apply to the recoding of an old program to function on a new operating system. Manovich expands the term to characterize the processes of translation operating between computer and culture, broadly construed. I deploy the terms "transcoding" and "transcoded objects" more specifically to characterize the effects that a digital milieu introduces to historical artifacts circulating online (45–48).

7. While I use the anachronism "world wide web" as a way to signal some distance from the early days of the internet, I'm also quite aware of the rapid half-life of media scholarship. As new developments in generative AI, the decentralized web, and virtual reality loom uncertainly on the horizon of the 2020s, I aim to both future-proof and historicize this intermediate study of the little database as much as possible. In just the same way that recently out-of-print periodicals remain the most difficult to discover as they await archival status, I believe that the history of the recent internet is constantly under erasure, happenstance disappearance, or wholesale reinvention, and thus remains as urgent a task for media scholars as any statement on the present or prediction of the future.

8. I present the history of my personal engagement with these sites here for two reasons. First, to acknowledge the specific positionality from which this study emerges. And, second, to point to the crucial role that embodied knowledge plays in this study. I foreground embodied knowledge in conversation with Catherine D'Ignazio and Lauren Klein's principles of "data feminism," which include the call to elevate embodiment over the illusory rationality and imputed objectivity of numerical data (*Data Feminism* [Cambridge, Mass: MIT Press, 2020], data-feminism.mitpress.mit.edu/pub /5evfe9yd/release/5).

9. For example, my working files for this project live within an elaborate hierarchy nested in a folder entitled "0_The-Little-Database" that currently contains 34.89 GB for 53,623 unique items. My personal repertoires of file management, naming conventions, and general organization all draw from these sites. Beyond this, I believe these hand-crafted sites also mirror non-specialist user practices more generally. The connection between the two remains a core interest in all that follows.

10. For the printed poem, see: William Carlos Williams, *The Collected Poems of William Carlos Williams,* vol. 1, *1909–1939,* ed. Christopher MacGowan (New York: New Directions, 1991), 455. The audio recording of Williams's reading for the National Council of Teachers of English and Columbia University Press Contemporary Poets Series on January 9, 1942, was one of the first files I produced for *PennSound* in 2008. That recording, among hundreds of others, can be found at writing.upenn.edu/pennsound/x/Williams-WC.php.

11. For a particularly germane example of this practice, Mark Goble concludes a final chapter on Williams in *Beautiful Circuits: Modernism and the Mediated Life* (New York: Columbia University Press, 2010) by reflecting on "The Defective Record" from the current state of digital media: "The technologies of the present will also leave us with their histories, and whatever forms they might take, there is a good chance that they will look to many like a defective record that is better left behind. I hope someone saves them anyway" (304). Working in coordination with this hope, I take the challenge of Goble's conclusion as a starting point, asking: what do we do, now, with what's been saved?

12. Boris Groys, "From Image to Image File—and Back: Art in the Age of Digitalization," *Art Power* (Cambridge, Mass.: MIT Press, 2008).

13. Matthew Kirschenbaum, *Mechanisms: New Media and the Forensic Imagination* (Cambridge, Mass.: MIT Press, 2008) and *Bitstreams: The Future of Digital Literary Heritage* (Philadelphia: University of Pennsylvania Press: 2021).

14. Mark Marino, *Critical Code Studies* (Cambridge, Mass.: MIT Press, 2020).

15. Alexander Galloway, *Protocol: How Control Exists After Decentralization* (Cambridge, Mass.: MIT Press, 2004) and *The Interface Effect* (Cambridge: Polity, 2012).

16. Hito Steyerl, *Wretched of the Screen* (London: Sternberg, 2012).

17. Wendy Hui Kyong Chun, *Updating to Remain the Same: Habitual New Media* (Cambridge, Mass.: MIT Press, 2017).

18. Safiya Umoja Noble, *Algorithms of Oppression: How Search Engines Reinforce Racism* (New York: New York University Press, 2018).

19. Abigail De Kosnik, *Rogue Archives: Digital Cultural Memory and Media Fandom* (Cambridge, Mass.: MIT Press, 2016).

20. The common knowledge on the role of the little magazine as both a vehicle and driver of modernism and the historical avant-gardes might be most tidily summed up by the slogan of a little database called the *Modernist Journals Project,* which has long maintained that "modernism began in the

magazines." Of course, this outsized statement is too complicated to unravel at a glance. While I return to some of the scholarship on modernism and the historical avant-gardes throughout this book, my focus is instead on the afterlives of these works, circulating online, which requires a different measure of attention. For a more complete argument on the essential role of the little magazine in the construction of these aesthetic and literary movements, the reader is directed to toggle between the *Modernist Journals Project* online (modjourn.org/) and its theorization by editors in Robert Scholes and Clifford Wulfman, *Modernism in the Magazines: An Introduction* (New Haven, Conn.: Yale University Press, 2010).

21. On the provisional in little magazines and digital practices, following Bernstein's concept of "provisional institutions," see Sophie Seita, *Provisional Avant-Gardes: Little Magazine Communities from Dada to Digital* (Stanford, Calif.: Stanford University Press: 2019).

22. See N. Katherine Hayles, "How We Read: Close, Hyper, Machine," in *How We Think: Digital Media and Contemporary Technogenesis* (Chicago: University of Chicago Press, 2012), 55–80.

23. Any list of these types of collections is bound to say more about the user's proclivities than overarching technical specifications. My selection of the specific little databases featured in this book is driven by a focus on the revelatory powers of media-reflexive works of art and literature circulating online. That said, the reader is encouraged to explore some of these following public little databases to extend these arguments, to perform them otherwise, or to discover their limitations: *AAAAARG,* ed. Sean Dockray et al.; *The Anarchist Library,* ed. Anon; *Artists' Books Online,* ed. Johanna Drucker; *Cyberfeminism Index,* ed. Mindy Seu; *Electronic Literature Collection,* ed. ELO; *The Internet Speculative Fiction Database,* ed. Al von Ruff and Ahasuerus; *Library of Artistic Print on Demand,* ed. Annete Gilbert and Andreas Bülhoff; *The Malware Museum,* ed. Mikko Hermanni Hyppönen; *The Marxist Internet Archive,* ed. Zodiac et al.; *Monoskop,* ed. Dušan Barok; *Net Art Anthology,* ed. Rhizome; *Open Door Archive,* ed. Harris Feinsod and John Alba Cutler; *The Post-Digital Publishing Archive,* ed. Silvio Lorusso; *Queer.Archive.Work* and *Library of the Printed Web,* ed. Paul Soulellis; *Queer Zine Archive Project,* ed. Milo Miller and Chris Wilde; *The SCP Foundation,* ed. MAST Team et al.; *Textfiles .com,* ed. Jason Scott; and *Vimm's Lair,* ed. Vimm.

24. Robert Scholes and Clifford Wulfman, *Modernism in the Magazines: An Introduction* (New Haven, Conn.: Yale University Press, 2010), 44.

25. These engagements derive from the retrospective array of periodical codes articulated by Peter Brooker and Andrew Thacker, in homage to a notion of bibliographic codes in the interpretation of social texts as articulated by Jerome McGann among others. See Brooker and Thacker, "General Introduction," *The Oxford Critical and Cultural History of Modernist Magazines,* vol. 1 (Oxford: Oxford University Press, 2009), 5, and McGann, *The Textual Condition* (Princeton, N.J.: Princeton University Press, 1991), 57.

26. Manovich, *Language of New Media,* 225.

27. Of course, our understanding of the database is also a cultural construction, one in which the one-to-one translation of "transcoding" inevitably falls flat; see Wendy Chun, *Programmed Visions: Software and Memory* (Cambridge, Mass.: MIT Press, 2011), 91–95.

28. Manovich, *Language of New Media,* 218–43.

29. Hayles, *How We Think,* 176–98. See, for example, Ed Folsom, "Database as Genre: The Epic Transformation of Archives," *PMLA* 122, no. 5 (2007): 1571–79. In response, Hayles cautions against privileging information over knowledge, advocating for a critical approach to digital technologies that recognizes the utility of the database while also acknowledging the importance of narrative in structuring human experience and knowledge ("Narrative and Database: Natural Symbionts," *PMLA* 122, no. 5 [2007]: 1603–8).

30. Across a range of works, Hayles advocates for the nuanced accounts of mediation found in the field of textual studies, which can be recalibrated as a mode of comparative media analysis within a complex of digital media environments. She proposes the necessity of "approaches that can locate digital work within print traditions, and print traditions within digital media, without obscuring or failing to account for the differences between them" (*How We Think,* 7).

31. I owe this orientation to The Working Group in the History of Material Texts at the University of Pennsylvania. The field is too vast to chart, but of particular note to this study, see Lisa Gitelman, *Paper Knowledge: Toward a Media History of Documents* (Durham, N.C.: Duke University Press, 2014); Johanna Drucker, *Graphesis: Visual Forms of Knowledge Production* (Cambridge, Mass.: Harvard University Press, 2014); Lori Emerson, *Reading Writing Interfaces: From the Digital to the Bookbound* (Minneapolis: University of Minnesota Press, 2014); Adriaan van der Weel, *Changing Our Textual Minds: Towards a Digital Order of Knowledge* (Manchester, UK: Manchester University Press, 2011).

32. N. Katherine Hayles, "Flickering Connectivities in Shelley Jackson's Patchwork Girl: The Importance of Media-Specific Analysis," *Postmodern Culture* 10, no. 2 (2000): 3.

33. Hayles, *How We Think,* 13.

34. Kirschenbaum similarly contends for bibliographic methods of reading file formats and transcoded digital objects in *Bitstreams.* What distinguishes this method is an "uncompromising attention to conditions of meaning. Which is to say that bibliography is a way of knowing, a habit of mind whose remit is nothing less than accounting for all the people and things that make meaning possible, each in their own irreducible individuality" (13–14).

35. See Alan Liu, *Local Transcendence: Essays on Postmodern Historicism and the Database* (Chicago: University of Chicago Press, 2008), 1–25. A wealth of works from a variety of disciplines including philosophy, media theory, sound and cinema studies, and queer theory inform my use of the term *contingency,*

including, most prominently, among others: Quentin Meillassoux, *After Finitude: An Essay on the Necessity of Contingency* (London: Continuum, 2006); Mary Anne Doane, *Modernity, Contingency, The Archive* (Cambridge, Mass.: Harvard University Press, 2002); David Wylot, *Reading Contingency: The Accident in Contemporary Fiction* (New York: Routledge, 2019); Valerie Rohy, *Chances Are: Contingency, Queer Theory, and American Literature* (New York: Routledge, 2020); Dan DiPiero, *Contingent Encounters: Improvisation In Music and Everyday Life* (Ann Arbor: University of Michigan Press, 2022). Since drafting this introduction, I have honed my use of this term in conversation with Miljohn Ruperto's kairotic formulation in *An Operational Account of Western Spatio-Temporality* (Los Angeles: X Artists' Books, 2024).

36. Liu, *Local Transcendence,* 11.

37. Liu, 25.

38. For more on contingency, I discuss these reading practices at length in a special issue on "Inscriptive Studies" edited by Rita Raley and Paul Benzon: "Contingent Reading: A Poetics of the Search," *ASAP/Journal* 7, no. 2 (2022): 385–407.

39. First published by *e-flux* in 2009, the article has led a viral afterlife in arts syllabi and media art social networks. For ease of reference, pagination refers to its location in the collected edition: Hito Steyerl, *Wretched of the Screen* (Berlin: Sternberg, 2013), 31–45. And yet, when calling the work to mind, the reader might best imagine these words inhabiting a circulating PDF or shared URL.

40. Steyerl, 32–33.

41. Steyerl, 42.

42. Steyerl, 44.

43. Nanna Bonde Thylstrup, *The Politics of Mass Digitization* (Cambridge, Mass.: MIT Press, 2019), 138.

44. See especially works that relate analog media formats to digital milieus, a sample of which is listed here in a sequential order featured in the chapters ahead: Dennis Tenen, *Plain Text: The Poetics of Computation* (Stanford, Calif.: Stanford University Press, 2017); Lisa Gitelman, *Paper Knowledge: Toward a Media History of Documents* (Durham, N.C.: Duke University Press, 2014); Jonathan Sterne, *MP3: The Meaning of a Format* (Durham, N.C.: Duke University, 2012); Erica Balsom, *After Uniqueness: A History of Film and Media Art in Circulation* (New York: Columbia University Press, 2017).

45. Sterne, *MP3,* 11.

46. Sterne, 240.

47. See, for example: Tung-Hui Hu, *A Prehistory of the Cloud* (Cambridge, Mass.: MIT Press, 2015); Safiya Umoja Noble *Algorithms of Oppression* (New York: New York University Press, 2018); Wendy Hui Kyong Chun, "Enduring Ephemeral, or the Future Is a Memory," *Critical Inquiry* 35, no. 1 (2008): 148–71.

48. Craig Dworkin, *Reading the Illegible* (Evanston, Ill.: Northwestern University Press, 2003), 4–5.

49. Rather than attempt a pared-down citational list, perhaps a pedagogi-

cal anecdote will best summarize this position. In the fall of 2019, I taught my first graduate seminar at UCLA. I titled this course "Theory and Method on the Internet," mostly so that we might operate under the acronym "TMI." Wielding "too much information" provided both a methodological imperative for the study of internet culture and a statement on concomitant forms of affective overflow. In the first session of the course, I provided the students with reference to a little database of 262 recent monographs on the subject published over the previous decade for their own research alongside my own. I owe much to the conversations this course generated, which these pages can verify. Of course, these relations extend far beyond the limitations of academic prose. For now, a link outward to the course site—another little database—is perhaps the best summary of the network that informs this methodology: meta.humspace.ucla.edu/tmi/.

50. Adalaide Morris, "New Media Poetics: As We May Think/How to Write," in *New Media Poetics: Contexts, Technotexts, and Theories,* ed. Adalaide Morris and Thomas Swiss (Cambridge, Mass.: MIT Press, 2006), 6–7.

51. Nietzsche, letter toward the end of February 1882, in *Briefwechsel: Kritische Gesamtausgabe,* ed. Giorgio Colli and Mazzino Montinari (Berlin: De Gruyter, 1980), 1875–84, pt. 3, I: 172, quoted in Friedrich Kittler, *Gramophone, Film, Typewriter* (Stanford, Calif.: Stanford University Press, 1999).

52. To visualize this process, consider YouTube-ing the film *Powers of Ten: A Film Dealing with the Relative Size of Things in the Universe and the Effect of Adding Another Zero* (1977) by Charles and Ray Eames (youtube.com /watch?v=0fKBhvDjuy0). While watching the play of pixels on your preferred device, connect a viewing of this digitized film once rendered in Flash but now streaming in VP9 through the YouTube interface, replete with related links, comments, buttons, your own account profile, the massive index hiding behind the search bar, the other tabs in your browser, and all the apps, icons, and files on your desktop or mobile phone waiting in the wings. Now oscillate back and forth from the movie itself to its public staging online.

53. Jerome McGann and Lisa Samuels, "Deformance and Interpretation," *New Literary History* 30, no. 1, (1999): 26.

54. McGann and Samuels, 36.

55. Charles Bernstein, *A Poetics* (Cambridge, Mass.: Harvard University Press, 1992), 160.

56. Inspired by Whitney Trettien's articulation of the open-access Manifold platform in this same series, this project aims to "demonstrate how web-based platforms might be used today in tandem with a print monograph . . . in ways that are increasingly sustainable, technologically stable, and effective at shifting a field's focus" ("Introduction," in *Cut/Copy/Paste* [Minneapolis: University of Minnesota Press, 2021]).

1. Textwarez

1. This number fluctuates depending on the date the site is captured. The most complete rendering of the website I could track down was captured by

the Internet Archive on June 24, 2004. As of this writing, I have assembled all files listed in site inventories, with the notable exception of the German version of Adorno and Horkheimer's *The Dialectic of Enlightenment.* I will discuss this particular file in more detail later in this chapter.

2. It is perhaps telling that the most established surveys of practices in the digital humanities are gathered as a series of "debates" rather than any other forum for collective knowledge building. (See the ongoing series edited by Matthew K. Gold and Lauren F. Klein: Debates in the Digital Humanities.) Occasionally, these debates boil over into controversy. Recent examples include the wholesale critique of computational literary studies by Nan Z. Da, "The Computational Case against Computational Literary Studies," *Critical Inquiry* 45, no. 3 (2019): 601–39 (and its various official and unofficial responses), and Daniel Allington, Sarah Brouillette, and David Golumbia, "Neoliberal Tools (and Archives): A Political History of Digital Humanities," *Los Angeles Review of Books,* May 1, 2016, lareviewofbooks.org/article/neoliberal-tools-archives -political-history-digital-humanities/ (and its attendant responses). From all directions, the practice of computational literary techniques remains an open question.

3. For a thorough accounting of the state of the field as of this writing, see especially Domenico Fiormonte, Sukanta Chaudhuri, and Paola Ricaurte, eds., *Global Debates in the Digital Humanities* (Minneapolis: University of Minnesota Press, 2022).

4. Da, "Computational Case," 601.

5. Ian Bogost *Unit Operations: An Approach to Videogame Criticism* (Cambridge, Mass.: MIT Press, 2006), 3–20.

6. Laine Nooney, "A Pedestal, a Table, a Love Letter: Archaeologies of Gender in Videogame History," *Game Studies,* no. 2 (2013): 7, gamestudies.org /1302/articles/nooney.

7. Aubrey Anable, *Playing with Feelings: Video Games and Affect* (Minneapolis: University of Minnesota Press, 2018), 3.

8. For a recent example of ongoing definitional boundaries, see Katja Müller's *Digital Archives and Collections: Creating Online Access to Cultural Heritage* (New York: Berghahn, 2021). Despite technical specificity, Müller justifies the use of "digital archive" as an "emic term" (27). From this anthropological perspective, a looser popular use of the "archive" for digital collections remains the accepted norm. This argument bolsters my interchangeable use of terms like "repository," "collection," "library," or "archive" throughout the discussion of little databases to follow. I'd also like to point the reader toward Michael Nardone's forthcoming work on the "repository" featured in his dissertation "Of the Repository: Poetics in a Networked Digital Milieu" (PhD diss., Concordia University, 2019), as well as Manuel Brito, "Electronic Poetry and the Importance of Digital Repository," *CLCWeb* 16, no. 5 (2014).

9. See Kenneth M. Price, "Edition, Project, Database, Archive, Thematic Research Collection: What's in a name?," *Digital Humanities Quarterly* 3, no. 3

(2009); Peter Shillingsburg, *From Gutenberg to Google: Electronic Representations of Literary Texts* (Cambridge: Cambridge University Press, 2006), 80–125.

10. Price, p40.

11. Price, 40n11.

12. Jeremy Braddock, *Collecting as Modernist Practice* (Baltimore, Md.: Johns Hopkins University Press, 2012), 3.

13. Braddock, 6 (emphasis original).

14. Braddock, 6.

15. For an updated view of collecting aesthetics, see, in particular, Domenico Quaranta, ed., *Collect the WWWorld: The Artist as Archivist in the Internet Age* (Brescia, Italy: LINK, 2011).

16. See, Abigail De Kosnik, *Rogue Archives: Digital Cultural Memory and Media Fandom* (Cambridge, Mass.: MIT Press, 2016), 1–24.

17. De Kosnik, 9.

18. Kate Eichorn, *The Archival Turn in Feminism: Outrage in Order* (Philadelphia: Temple University Press, 2013), 5.

19. Craig J. Saper, *Networked Art* (Minneapolis: University of Minnesota Press, 2001), 11.

20. Braddock, *Collecting as Modernist Practice*, 27. See also Walter Benjamin, *The Arcades Project,* trans. Howard Eiland and Kevin McLaughlin, (Cambridge, Mass.: Belknap, 1999), 2.

21. The founding manifesto of *Textz,* "napster was only the beginning," has recently returned to a pared-down version of the site at textz.com/about/. Images and citations from long-lost components of the site are referenced by original URLs throughout. These references can be tracked at various points of capture by the Internet Archive Wayback Machine (https://archive.org/web/).

22. For recent scholarship on copyright law and internet culture, see Gaëlle Krikorian and Amy Kapczynski, *Access to Knowledge in the Age of Intellectual Property* (New York: Zone, 2010); Peter Decherney, *Hollywood's Copyright Wars: From Edison to the Internet* (New York: Columbia University Press, 2013); Peter Baldwin, *The Copyright Wars: Three Centuries of Trans-Atlantic Battle* (Princeton, N.J.: Princeton University Press, 2014); Aram Sinnreich, *The Piracy Crusade: How the Music Industry's War on Sharing Destroys Markets and Erodes Civil Liberties* (Amherst: University of Massachusetts Press, 2013); Patricia Aufderheide and Peter Jaszi, *Copyright, Permissions, and Fair Use among Visual Artists and the Academic and Museum Visual Arts Communities: An Issues Report* (New York: College Art Association, 2014).

23. See Joe Karaganis, ed., *Shadow Libraries: Access to Educational Materials in Global Higher Education,* (Cambridge, Mass.: MIT Press, 2018), and Memory of the World, ed., *Guerilla Open Access* (Coventry, UK: Post Office, Rope, and Memory of the World, 2018). For more personal practices that shadow the little databases, see Henry Warwick, *Radical Tactics of the Offline Library,* (Amsterdam: Institute of Network Cultures, 2014).

24. See Michael S. Hart, "History and Philosophy of Project Gutenberg," *Project Gutenberg,* August 1992, gutenberg.org/about/background/history_and _philosophy.html.

25. *Textz,* "napster was only the beginning."

26. For more information on Usenet and examples of the ASCII scenes that *Textz* references, see the little database collected by Jason Scott at textfiles .com.

27. See Bruce Sterling, *The Hacker Crackdown: Law and Disorder on the Electronic Frontier* (New York: Bantam, 1992). Importantly, this book was used a part of an elaborate ruse, described below.

28. See Simone Browne, *Dark Matters: On the Surveillance of Blackness* (Durham, N.C.: Duke University Press, 2015). For Browne, dark sousveillance is "an imaginative place from which to mobilize a critique of racializing surveillance, a critique that takes form in antisurveillance, countersurveillance, and other freedom practices" (21). For *Textz,* a critique of global networks of surveillance emerges from its hyperbolic simulation of pervasive web-trackers.

29. This statement is not to undermine a critique of representation in this or any collection of its type. Indeed, these facts should be made clear and immediate. In this instance, I highlight these aspect of the collection to point to basic critical reading practices that precede the need for analytics to confirm these facts. More generally, statistical approaches routinely run into presumptive biases in data analysis when attempting to encode race, gender, and ethnicity in order to make critical claims. See, by contrast, the "strangeness" of data in Yanni Alexander Loukissas, *All Data Are Local: Thinking Critically in a Data-Driven Society* (Cambridge, Mass.: MIT Press, 2019), 3.

30. For a concise history of "content" online, up to the present, see Kate Eichorn, *Content* (Cambridge, Mass.: MIT Press, 2022).

31. *Textz,* "napster was only the beginning."

32. "Content, n.," *Oxford English Dictionary* online, oed.com/view/Entry/40144.

33. Jonathan Sterne, *MP3: The Meaning of a Format* (Durham, N.C.: Duke University Press, 2012), 16. Sterne deploys Lewis Mumford's concept from *Technics and Civilization* to describe digital encoding as a "disruptive container technology" that transforms the way in which works are stored, circulated, and consumed (8). According to Sterne, the format represents a radical shift away from the physicality and the constraints of analog media, dislocated from its original context and reproduced in a variety of digital environments.

34. Adriaan van der Weel, *Changing Our Textual Minds: Towards a Digital Order of Knowledge* (Manchester, UK: Manchester University Press, 2011), 39.

35. See Stanley Fish, *Is There a Text in This Class? The Authority of Interpretive Communities.* (Cambridge, Mass.: Harvard University Press, 1980).

36. Dennis Tenen, *Plain Text: The Poetics of Computation* (Stanford, Calif.: Stanford University Press, 2017), 5.

37. Tenen, 13.

38. Van der Weel, *Changing Our Textual Minds,* 40.

39. Lisa Gitelman, *Always Already New: Media, History, and the Data of Culture* (Cambridge, Mass.: MIT Press, 2008), 7.

40. Wendy Hui Kyong Chun, "The Enduring Ephemeral, or the Future Is a Memory," *Critical Inquiry* 35, no. 1 (2008): 160, 148.

41. Chun, 167.

42. For the most comprehensive of these histories, see Eric Fischer, "The Evolution of Character Codes, 1874–1968," archive.org/details/enf-ascii.

43. Ambulanzen/*Textz,* "napster was only the beginning."

44. Daniel Pargman and Jacob Palme, "ASCII Imperialism," in *Standards and Their Stories: How Quantifying, Classifying, and Formalizing Practices Shape Everyday Life,* ed. Susan Leigh Star and Martha Lampland (Ithaca, N.Y.: Cornell University Press, 2009), 177–99.

45. Tenen, *Plain Text,* 202.

46. Tenen, 3, 6.

47. Sterne, *MP3,* 16.

48. For studies relating the poetics of the glitch to the politics of digital infrastructures, see Legacy Russell, *Glitch Feminism: A Manifesto* (New York: Verso, 2020); Rosa Menkman, *The Glitch Moment(um),* (Amsterdam: Institute of Network Cultures, 2011); Ruha Benjamin, *Race After Technology: Abolitionist Tools for the New Jim Code* (Cambridge: Polity, 2019).

49. Jerome McGann, *Radiant Textuality: Literature After the World Wide Web* (New York: Palgrave, 2001), 153.

50. McGann, 151.

51. See Lisa Gitelman,*"Raw Data" is an Oxymoron* (Cambridge, Mass.: MIT Press, 2013), 5–6.

52. McGann, *Radiant Textuality,* 152.

53. Tan Lin, "Disco as Operating System, Part One," *Criticism* 50, no. 1 (2008): 93.

54. Lin, 87–88.

55. For a sample of the book's reception in the English context, see "Not a Ripping Read," *The Economist,* August 29, 2002,: economist.com/books-and-arts/2002/08/29/not-a-ripping-read.

56. Here, the space-defying convergence of "plain text" (ASCII files in general) and "plaintext" (nonencrypted or decrypted text) might be seen to index the definitional crux of both this chapter and the *Textz* project as a whole. To maintain this realignment of terms, I use "plaintext" throughout the rest of the chapter, mirroring the site-wide modulation to the very idea of "plain text" that *Textz* introduces with this gesture.

57. *Textz,* "napster was only the beginning." By contrast, see the influential essay by Richard Barbrook and Andy Cameron, "The Californian Ideology," *Mute* 1, no. 3 (1995), metamute.org/editorial/articles/californian-ideology.

58. Inke Arns, "Read_me, run_me, execute_me: Code as Executable Text:

Software Art and its Focus on Program Code as Performative Text," in *Medien Kunst Netz 2: Thematische Schwerpunkte,* ed. Rudolf Frieling and Dieter Daniels (New York: Springer, 2005), 205.

59. Olga Goriunova, "walser.php," *runme.org,* April 27, 2003, runme.org /feature/read/+walserphp/+6/.

60. From the pngreader project readme.txt file, pngreader.gnutenberg.net (accessed via Internet Archive), also released to the *Runme.org* feature database at https://runme.org/project/+pngreader/.

61. Jorge Luis Borges, "The Library of Babel," in *Labyrinths: Selected Stories and Other Writings,* ed. Donald A. Yates and James E. Irby (New York: New Directions, 1962), 62–77.

62. Florian Cramer, "pngreader," *Runme.org,* June 6, 2003, runme.org/feature /read/+pngreader/+58/index.html.

63. See Hannes Bajohr, "Operative ekphrasis: The collapse of the text/image distinction in multimodal AI" (preprint), July, 2023, researchgate.net/publication /372400146_Operative_ekphrasis_The_collapse_of_the_textimage_distinction _in_multimodal_AI.

64. Originally hosted online at rolux.net/crisis/index.php, accessed via Internet Archive.

65. Robert Luxemburg, "Luxemburg's Law," rolux.net/crisis/index.php, accessed via Internet Archive.

66. Walter Benjamin, "Unpacking my Library," tr. Harry Zohn, *Selected Writings, Vol. 2, Part 2: 1931–1934* (Cambridge: Belknap Press, 2005), 486–93.

67. This note is featured as a readme.txt file in the "Complete Historical-Critical Edition" of *Textz,* which was released in early 2015 as an elaborate alternative reality game (ARG), only at the end of which the persistent player (or, in this instance, scholar) would recover an encrypted eighteen gigabytes of data via file torrent, including every page, each text, and all variants in the *Textz* enterprise. Both the labyrinthine procedure to unmask these files and the equally complex "edition" remain beyond the scope of this chapter. And yet, it remains telling that the little database warrants this type of expanded play. To extend that play (and the Textz project) here: readers are invited to write the author for free access to these materials.

68. Sterne, *MP3,* 15.

Interlude 1

1. Jerome McGann, *Radiant Textuality: Literature After the World Wide Web* (New York: Palgrave, 2001), 106.; see also McGann and Lisa Samuels, "Deformance and Interpretation," *New Literary History* 30, no. 1 (1999): 25–56.

2. McGann, *Radiant Textuality,* 109.

3. For a brief survey of recent approaches drawn from a range of fields, see, in particular: Jentery Sayers, ed. *Making Things and Drawing Boundaries: Experiments in the Digital Humanities* (Minneapolis: University of Minnesota Press, 2017), Matt Ratto and Megan Boler, eds., *DIY Citizenship: Critical Making and Social Media* (Cambridge, Mass.: MIT Press, 2014); Eduardo Navas, Owen

Gallagher, and xtine burrough, eds., *The Routledge Handbook of Remix Studies and Digital Humanities* (New York: Routledge, 2021).

4. Charles Bernstein, *A Poetics* (Cambridge, Mass.: Harvard University Press, 1992), 160. More recently, Seth Perlow describes this distinctly poetry-oriented approach to creative scholarship that moves across "the increasingly porous border between literary and scholarly writing, between poetry and criticism. Electronics enable us to read and write with the same equipment, technologically literalizing the indecision between creative and interpretive activities. The blurring of such generic and disciplinary distinctions leads experimentalists to write poetry that does the work of literary interpretation, criticism that is itself lyrical" (*The Poem Electric: Technology and the American Lyric* [Minneapolis: University of Minnesota Press, 2018], 4).

5. Lori Emerson outlines media poetics alongside the related concept of "readingwriting." She defines media poetics as "the literary exemplar of media archaeology and a practice that extends deep from within the analog and well into the digital, . . . a practice not just of experimenting with the limits and possibilities of writing interfaces but rather of *readingwriting*: the practice of writing through the network, which as it tracks, indexes, and algorithmizes every click and every bit of text we enter into the network, is itself constantly reading our writing and writing our reading" (*Reading Writing Interfaces* [Minneapolis: University of Minnesota Press, 2014], xiv).

2. Distributing Services

1. See Charles Bernstein, Bruce Andrews, and Ron Silliman, "*L=A=N=G=U=A=G=E* Distributing Service," hosted by *Eclipse,* eclipsearchive .org/projects/LANGUAGEDist/. Throughout this chapter, references to issues of *L=A=N=G=U=A=G=E* will include page and issue, as well as a link to the specific page hosting the citation on *Eclipse*. Should any of these links disappear, one hopes an Internet Archive record will remain.

2. Charles Bernstein, "The Expanded Field of L=A=N=G=U=A=G=E," *Routledge Companion to Experimental Literature,* ed. Joe Bray, Alison Gibbons, and Brian McHale (New York: Routledge, 2012), 281–97.

3. These same digital modes of circulation afford opportunities of access not present in the print-based origins of the magazine. As anyone using a screen reader for this paragraph might attest, the distinctive spelling of the magazine title makes for exceptionally difficult listening. Since automated voices spell out the full title letter-by-sign-by-letter, even the four instances in the preceding paragraph leave little room for meaningful hearing. Given this barrier, I've opted to sacrifice orthographic fidelity in order to amplify aural access, rendering all but the first instances of the magazine in the body text equally as *LANGUAGE.* I encourage all readers to hallucinate tiny signs of equivalence (or nonequivalence) between the letters.

4. *L=A=N=G=U=A=G=E* no. 1 (1978): 13, eclipsearchive.org/projects /LANGUAGEn1/pictures/013.html.

5. Bernstein, Andrews, and Silliman, "L=A=N=G=U=A=G=E Distributing Service."

6. Craig Dworkin, *Eclipse* homepage, eclipsearchive.org/

7. Continuing the ecliptic metaphors of this paragraph, Dworkin notes: "The name Eclipse is an explicit homage to Sun & Moon, a mark of the archive's aspiration to document the moment of its predecessor's apogee and to carry on the early mission of presses like Messerli's, even after the disappearance of those illustrious celestial bodies" ("Hypermnesia," *boundary 2* 36, no. 3 [2009]: 81).

8. Craig Dworkin, "Language Poetry," in *The Greenwood Encyclopedia of American Poets and Poetry,* ed. Jeffrey Gray, James McCorkle, and Mary McAleer Balkun (Westport, Conn.: Greenwood, 2006), 880.

9. Following Bernstein's own statements on the nomenclature of this cluster of publications, communities, and debates, I should note a revisionist editorial intention to use the magazine's italicized title to refer to "*L=A=N=G=U=A=G=E* poetry, and its many different names—Language Poetry, Language Poetries, Language Writing, Language-Centered Writing" (Bernstein, "The Expanded Field of L=A=N=G=U=A=G=E," *Pitch of Poetry* [Chicago: University of Chicago Press, 2016], 60–77). However, for clarity of reading—and to differentiate from the magazine proper—I'll loosely use the capitalized "Language" to modify a range of poetry, publishing, and writing practices associated with the expanded field of *L=A=N=G=U=A=G=E* magazine.

10. Dworkin, "Hypermnesia," 81–82. Eric Bulson makes a similar point in "The Little Magazine, Remediated," *The Journal of Modern Periodical Studies* 8, no. 2 (2017): 200–225, tracing the time-delay history of 1960s Kraus reprints of the little magazines of modernism and the historical avant-gardes into the digital formats for little magazines that he terms "digittle archives."

11. Dworkin, "Hypermnesia," 81.

12. Dworkin, 94.

13. Dworkin, 84.

14. Jacques Derrida, *Archive Fever: A Freudian Impression,* trans. Eric Prenowitz (Chicago: University of Chicago Press, 1996), 19.

15. Dworkin, "Hypermnesia," 85.

16. Dworkin, 85.

17. For the most concise articulation of Dworkin's method of radical formalism, see *Reading the Illegible* (Evanston, Ill.: Northwestern University Press, 2003). Its application can be tracked in the dozens of related works and articles linked through Dworkin's *Eclipse* page (eclipsearchive.org/Editor/). Like *EXE TXT* or Bernstein's collected online syllabi, this is another way in which the little database might house its own theorization.

18. Dworkin, *Reading the Illegible,* 4–5, xix–xx.

19. Dworkin, "Hypermnesia," 88–91.

20. Taking the digital as a ubiquitous and therefore banal component of the publishing landscape, this strand of "post-digital publishing" explores publications that blur the distinctions between digital and analog, online

and offline. See Alessandro Ludovico, *Post-Digital Print: The Mutation of Publishing Since 1894,* (Eindhoven: Onomatopee, 2012), 23–45; Florian Cramer, "What is 'Post-Digital'?," in *Postdigital Aesthetics: Art, Computation and Design,* ed. David M. Berry and Michael Dieter (London: Palgrave Macmillan, 2015), 12–26; and especially Silvio Lorusso's ongoing little database tracking these developments and accompanying scholarship, *The Post-Digital Publishing Archive,* http://p-dpa.net/.

21. Robert Scholes and Clifford Wulfman, *Modernism in the Magazines: An Introduction* (New Haven, Conn.: Yale University Press, 2010), 14.

22. Ezra Pound as cited in Scholes and Wulfman, 16.

23. Scholes and Wulfman, 44–72.

24. Scholes and Wulfman, 44.

25. Scholes and Wulfman, 66.

26. Scholes and Wulfman, 71.

27. I inventory these works at length here both to offer an example of generic breadth to the reader and to signal the collecting impulse in periodical studies, which tend to sprawl. For examples of the form, see: Frank Luther Mott, *A History of American Magazines, 1741–1930,* 5 vols. (Cambridge, Mass.: Harvard University Press, 1958); Jed Rasula, *The American Poetry Wax Museum: Reality Effects, 1940–1990* (Urbana, Ill.: National Council of Teachers of English: 1996); Eric Gardner, *Black Print Unbound: the Christian Recorder, African American Literature, and Periodical Culture* (New York: Oxford University Press, 2015); Al Filreis, *Counter-Revolution of the Word: the Conservative Attack on Modern Poetry, 1945–1960,* (Chapel Hill: The University of North Carolina Press, 2012); Gwen Allen, *Artists Magazines: An Alternative Space for Art* (Cambridge, Mass.: MIT Press, 2015); Beatriz Colomina and Craig Buckley, *Clip Stamp Fold the Radical Architecture of Little Magazines 196X to 197X* (Barcelona: Actar, 2011); Steven Clay and Rodney Phillips, *A Secret Location on the Lower East Side: Adventures in Writing, 1960–1980: a Sourcebook of Information* (New York: New York Public Library and Granary Books, 1998).

28. Scholes and Wulfman, *Modernism in the Magazines,* 72.

29. Jerome McGann, *Radiant Textuality: Literature after the World Wide Web* (New York: Palgrave, 2010), 18.

30. See the conclusion to McGann's *Radiant Textuality,* "Beginning Again and Again: 'The Ivanhoe Game'" and its related gameplay appendix (209–48).

31. See Ben Fry, *On the Origin of Species: The Preservation of Favoured Traces* (2009), https://benfry.com/traces/. On Mukurtu CMS, managed by the Center for Digital Scholarship and Curation at Washington State University, see Kimberly Christen, "Opening Archives: Respectful Repatriation," *American Archivist* vol. 74 (Spring–Summer, 2011): 185–210, and other works at mukurtu.org/. On *SlaveVoyages,* see David Elits, "The Trans-Atlantic Slave Trade Database: Origins, Development, Content," *Journal of Slavery and Data Preservation* 2, no. 3 (2021): 1–8, slavevoyages.org/.

32. Filreis, *Counter-Revolution of the Word,* xiii.

33. Jerome McGann, *The Textual Condition* (Princeton, N.J.: Princeton University Press, 1991), 13.

34. McGann, 16.

35. Random Cloud (Randall McLeod), "Enter Reader," in *The Editorial Gaze: Mediating Texts in Literature and the Arts,* ed. Paul Eggert and Margaret Sankey (New York: Garland, 1998), 23.

36. McGann, *Textual Condition,* 14–15.

37. Holly Melgard, *The Making of the Americans* (Buffalo, N.Y.: Troll Thread, 2012), 3.

38. Melgard, 24.

39. This editorial argument forms the core of a decade of events and publications that I grouped under the heading "Edit Publications" in response to dominant threads of poetry and poetics from the time. For an archive of this work and related arguments, see dss-edit.com/pub/.

40. For Bryant, the "fluid text" is a fact of textuality, given the signifying force of variant editions and ongoing processes of revising, editioning, and versioning (*The Fluid Text: A Theory of Revision and Editing for Book and Screen* [Ann Arbor: University of Michigan Press, 2002], 1–6).

41. Bryant, 62.

42. Bryant, 12–13.

43. Peter Brooker and Andrew Thacker, "General Introduction," in *The Oxford Critical and Cultural History of Modernist Magazines,* vol. 1, *Britain and Ireland 1880–1955,* ed. Brooker and Thacker (Oxford: Oxford University Press, 2009), 6.

44. Craig Saper, *Networked Art* (Minneapolis: University of Minnesota Press, 2001), x.

45. Saper, 11.

46. Saper, 3.

47. Saper, 152.

48. Charles Bernstein, *Content's Dream: Essays 1975–1984* (Los Angeles: Sun & Moon Press, 1986), 346.

49. See the *Black Bibliography Project,* https://blackbibliog.org/.

50. Saper, *Networked Art,* 14.

51. Scholes and Wulfman, *Modernism in the Magazines,* 18.

52. Clay and Phillips, *Secret Location,* 14.

53. David J. Bolter and Richard A. Grusin, *Remediation: Understanding New Media,* (Cambridge, Mass.: MIT Press, 2000), 5.

54. Bolter and Grusin, 55.

55. See Lev Manovich, *The Language of New Media* (Cambridge, Mass.: MIT Press, 2001); xv–xxxvi; Lisa Gitelman, *Paper Knowledge: Toward a Media History of Documents* (Durham, N.C.: Duke University Press, 2014), 117–21.

56. Friedrich Kittler, *Literature, Media, Information Systems: Essays,* ed. John Johnston (Amsterdam: GB Arts International, 1997), 28–29.

57. Wendy Hui Kyong Chun, "The Enduring Ephemeral, or the Future Is a Memory," *Critical Inquiry* 35, no. 1 (2008): 149.

58. As this manuscript goes to print, even this archive is facing disappearance due to legal pressures. These pages attest to the incalculable value of the Internet Archive toward the study of the rapidly disappearing recent past of the internet. For one report among many on the precarity of the Internet Archive, see Luca Messara, Chris Freeland, and Juliya Ziskina, eds. *Vanishing Culture: A Report on Our Fragile Cultural Record* (San Francisco: Internet Archive, 2024): https://blog.archive.org/2024/10/30/vanishing-culture-a-report-on-our-fragile-cultural-record/.

59. Craig Dworkin, *The Perverse Library* (York, UK: Information as Material, 2010), 12.

60. Most notably, the site featured two components that have been entirely lost to time. The first is a three-dimensional interface for browsing the collection scripted in javascript for the first year of the site's operation. As of this writing, I have found no image or record of the interface, aside from the structured data for its code. The second concerns a file format called "Multi-resolution Seamless Image Database" (MrSID), which can still be found in the source code of many pages. See Dworkin, "Hypermnesia," 85.

61. Brooker and Thacker, "General Introduction," 6.

62. Dworkin, "Hypermnesia," 94.

63. Dworkin, 85.

64. Gitelman, *Paper Knowledge,* 115–16.

65. By contrast, the reader might also find the same $L=A=N=G=U=A=G=E$ magazine scanned in full-color high-resolution by the Reveal Digital "Independent Voices" collection, now hosted by JSTOR: jstor.org/site/reveal-digital/independent-voices/language-27953599/.

66. Hito Steyerl, *Wretched of the Screen* (London: Sternberg, 2012), 32.

67. Steyerl, 32.

68. Dworkin, "Hypermnesia," 84.

69. Cory Arcangel, "On Compression," self-published PDF (New York, 2007), 227. coryarcangel.com/things-i-made/2007-007-on-c.

70. Silvio Lorusso, "In Defense of Poor Media," in *Printed Web 3*, ed. Paul Soulellis (Providence, R.I.: Library of the Printed Web, 2015), 62.

71. Charles Bernstein, "Language Sampler," *The Paris Review,* no. 86 (Winter 1982): 78; see facsimile on *Eclipse* at eclipsearchive.org/projects/SAMPLER/sampler.html.

72. Dworkin, "Hypermnesia," 85.

73. Dworkin, 91.

74. Steyerl, *Wretched of the Screen,* 44.

75. Dworkin, "Hypermnesia," 85.

76. Boris Groys, "From Image to Image File—and Back: Art in the Age of Digitalization," in *Art Power* (Cambridge, Mass.: MIT Press, 2008), 85.

77. Groys, 91. I have limited the scope of this chapter to coterminous discourses on image files. Beyond this point on the originality of the copy, for more recent work on the complicated and complicating archaeologies, discorrelations, and operational logics of image objects, see, in particular: Jacob

Gaboury, *Image Objects: An Archaeology of Computer Graphics* (Cambridge, Mass.: MIT Press, 2021); Shane Densen, *Discorrelated Images* (Durham, N.C.: Duke University Press, 2020); and Jussi Parikka, *Operational Images: From the Visual to the Invisual* (Minneapolis: University of Minnesota Press, 2023).

78. It may be taking a step too far to remark on the choice of the small circular character that sports each link, a kind of celestial body that is both representational glyph and embedded hyperlink. The eclipsing processes of hypertext described by Aarseth, Landow, and others have gone out of vogue for a number of years, but remain pertinent, especially in the 1.0 web environment of these hand-coded little databases.

79. Gitelman, *Paper Knowledge,* 119.

80. See especially the promotional monograph by Pamela Pfiffner, *Inside the Publishing Revolution: The Adobe Story* (Berkeley, Calif.: Adobe Press, 2003).

81. Introduced by Adobe as a propriety format in 1992, the PDF was released as an open standard in 2008, published by the International Organization for Standardization as ISO 32000. However, even then, the format retained some proprietary technologies until the release of ISO 32000–2 in 2020. The first fully nonproprietary specification for the standard was made available only recently, in April, 2023. For developments beyond this moment of writing, see en.wikipedia.org/wiki/PDF.

Interlude 2

1. See note 3 in the preceding chapter on issues of screen-reader access with the title string of characters: *L=A=N=G=U=A=G=E*. In this interlude, all future instances of the magazine will be rendered as *LANGUAGE* in the body text. Facilitating this transformation to enable audio access is perhaps one more way to enact the negation of this interlude's slashed equal sign—another reversal performed under the sign of networked access.

2. I discuss these first encounters with scanning the little magazine at length in "An Elegy for *Jimmy & Lucy's House of 'K'* (1984–1989)," *Post45,* June, 2023, post45.org/2023/06/an-elegy-for-ijimmy-and-lucys-house-of-k-1984-1989/.

3. Charles Bernstein introduced me to Jed Rasula's term for experimental forms of writing/reading in his "Wreading Experiments" writing exercise compendium: writing.upenn.edu/bernstein/wreading-experiments.html.

4. Common Crawl: commoncrawl.org/the-data/.

5. See Kevin Schaul, Szu Yu Chen, and Nitasha Tiku, "Inside the Secret List of Websites That Make AI Like ChatGPT Sound Smart," *The Washington Post,* April 19, 2023, washingtonpost.com/technology/interactive/2023/ai-chatbot -learning/, and Allen Insitute for AI "C4 Search," 2023, https://c4-search.apps .allenai.org/.

6. The Common Crawl corpus has been used as part of the training data for most major LLMs, including OpenAI's Chat GPT, Google's Bard AI, and Meta's LLaMA. The open-source tenets of the project afford the opportunity to explore content nested deep within these LLMs, unsurprisingly encompassing the long-running little databases featured here, like *Eclipse* and *Pennsound,*

as well as shadow libraries like *UbuWeb* that often reproduce full works without permission. Indeed, with the exception of *Textz,* all the sites discussed in this study have found their way into the dataset. For more on the makeup of the corpus, see Jesse Dodge, Maarten Sap, Ana Marasović, William Agnew, Gabriel Ilharco, Dirk Groeneveld, and Matt Gardner, "Documenting the English Colossal Clean Crawled Corpus," *ArXiv,* abs/2104.08758, April 18, 2021.

7. See Mashinka Firunts Hakopian, *The Institute for Other Intelligences* (Los Angeles: X Artists Book, 2022).

8. See Daniel Snelson, "Simultaneously Agitated in All Directions: Structuralist Activity and Differential Reading," in *Mimeo Mimeo #3,* ed. Kyle Schlesinger (Brooklyn, N.Y.: Cuneiform Press, 2009).

9. Benjamin Friedlander, *Simulcast: Four Experiments in Criticism* (Tuscaloosa: University of Alabama Press, 2004), 51.

10. Steve Kado, *October Jr.* (Los Angeles: Self-published, 2011).

3. Live Vinyl MP3

1. On the many forms of "close listening," see Charles Bernstein, ed., *Close Listening: Poetry and the Performed Word* (Oxford: Oxford University Press, 1998). In a gesture to compress more recent work presenting methods of close listening, I direct the reader to Nina Sun Eidsheim, *The Race of Sound: Listening, Timbre, and Vocality in African American Music* (Durham, N.C.: Duke University Press, 2019); Dylan Robinson, *Hungry Listening: Resonant Theory for Indigenous Sound Studies* (Minneapolis: University of Minnesota Press, 2020); Alexander G. Weheliye, *Feenin: R&B Music and the Materiality of Black-Fem Voices and Technology* (Durham, N.C.: Duke University Press, 2023); and the vast array of interventions made in the ongoing *Sounding Out!: The Sound Studies Blog,* ed. Jennifer Stoever-Ackerman, Liana Silva, and Aaron Trammell, soundstudiesblog.com/.

2. Tracie Morris, reading at "Conceptual Poetry & Its Others," University of Arizona Poetry Center, Tucson, 2008, hosted by *PennSound,* writing.upenn.edu/pennsound/x/Morris-Tucson.php.

3. Here, I would like to note the audio-specific possibility of speaking *with* or alongside the performer, rather than speaking *for* them—to engage in a dialogue facilitated by digital artifacts rather than speaking from above—an opportunity foreclosed by the printed page (or afforded by its digital iteration). I return to this point in the conclusion to this chapter and more prominently in the interludes, but for now, I direct attention to the sound itself. The reader is encouraged, at this juncture, to linger with the sound file before proceeding. Morris both performs and best describes her own process in developing this poem in her recorded performance, which the reader might find on *PennSound.* Citations of this talk are drawn from the recordings hosted at writing.upenn.edu/pennsound/x/Morris-Tucson.php.

4. To which, we might append the conclusion of this sentence from Moten's *In the Cut*: "Say something whose phonic substance will be impossible to reduce, *whose cuts and augmentations have to be recorded.*"

5. On this mode of performance, see Weheliye, "'Scream My Name Like a Protest': R&B Music as BlackFem Technology of Humanity in the Age of #Blacklivesmatter," in *Feenin,* 178–97. Beyond the scope of this study, in *Feenin,* Weheliye presents the most expansive approach to the "BlackFem singing voice as a technology, as a series of enfleshed forms of Black knowledge and archives" (19).

6. See, for example, Morris's improvisational "Re-Sonate," featured in *handholding: 5 Kinds* (Tucson: Kore, 2016).

7. Hito Steyerl, "Too Much World: Is the Internet Dead?" *e-flux,* no. 49 (November 2013), e-flux.com/journal/49/60004/too-much-world-is-the-internet-dead/.

8. Mónica Savirón, monicasaviron.com/films.

9. Legacy Russell, *Glitch Feminism: A Manifesto* (New York: Verso, 2020), 88.

10. Mathieu Aubin, "Queering the Tape Recorder: Transforming Surveillance Technologies through bill bissett's Queer Poetic Voice," in *DH2020 Book of Abstracts,* ed. Laura Estill, Jennifer Guiliano, and Constance Crompton (Ottawa: DH2020, 2020).

11. Darren Wershler, "Vertical Excess: what fuckan theory and bill bissett's Concrete Poetics," *Capilano Review* 2, no. 23 (1997): 117.

12. See VIDA Count, https://www.vidaweb.org/the-count/, (accessed via Internet Archive).

13. Jack Kerouac, "The Art of Fiction," *The Paris Review Interviews, IV* (New York: Picador, 2009), 82.

14. Tanya Clement, "Toward a Rationale of Audio Text," *Digital Humanities Quarterly* 10, no. 2 (2016), digitalhumanities.org/dhq/vol/10/3/000254/000254.html; see also hipstas.org/.

15. Kenneth Sherwood, "Distanced Sounding: ARLO as a Tool for the Analysis and Visualization of Versioning Phenomena within Poetry Audio," *Jacket2: Clipping,* March 2, 2015, https://jacket2.org/commentary/distanced-sounding-arlo-tool-analysis-and-visualization-versioning-phenomena-within-poetr.

16. For these examples and more, see Mustazza's "Clipping" commentary series on *Jacket2,* https://jacket2.org/commentary/clipping.

17. While the linked audio collection has been inaccessible for a long time, the post in question is still live at *Mutant Sounds,* ed. Eric Lumbleau and Matt Castille, mutant-sounds.blogspot.com.

18. The story of Megaupload and its tumultuous downfall is recapped in Ernesto Van der Star, "10 Years Ago the Feds Shut Down Megaupload," *Torrent-Freak,* January 20, 2022, https://torrentfreak.com/10-years-ago-the-feds-shut-down-megaupload-220120/.

19. See Bryan Gruley, David Fickling, and Cornelius Rahn, "Kim Dotcom, Pirate King," bloomberg.com/news/articles/2012-02-15/kim-dotcom-pirate-king.

20. For one example of these points, see footage embedded in Ghosh Pallab, "Google's Vint Cerf Warns of 'Digital Dark Age'" *BBC News,* February 13, 2015, bbc.com/news/science-environment-31450389.

21. Mark Allen, Brian Turner, Eric Lumbleau, et al. "The Rise and Fall of the Obscure Music Blog: A Roundtable," http://www.theawl.com/2012/11/the-rise-and-fall-of-obscure-music-blogs-a-roundtable, (accessed via Internet Archive).

22. Apart from the description, this reboot of *Mutant Sounds* is similarly defunct: *Free Music Archive,* freemusicarchive.org/curator/Mutant_Sounds/.

23. See TGK, "The Nurse With Wound List" : "To collectors of unusual music the Nurse With Wound List is legendary. . . . The NWW List covers the period from the late 1960s to 1980 when serious hybrids of avantgarde and popular music first became prevalent. It also covers a wide range of underground musical styles including krautrock, free jazz (improv), avantgarde classical, electronic, industrial, folk, anarcho-punk, proto-punk, no wave, library music, and many more uncategorizable" (http://nwwlist.org/, accessed via Internet Archive).

24. Alternatively, it should be noted that, in the more radical variant, this activity has migrated to private torrent and file-sharing communities like What.cd or the still-active Soulseek P2P platform.

25. Jonathan Sterne, *MP3: The Meaning of a Format* (Durham, N.C.: Duke University Press, 2012), 836.

26. Email correspondence with bill bissett, May 22, 2008.

27. That is, create individual MP3 files for each poem recited in a full-length reading. For more on this process and its importance to the collection, see *PennSound,* "PennSound Manifesto," https://writing.upenn.edu/pennsound/manifesto.php.

28. See *PennSound,* "bill bissett," https://writing.upenn.edu/pennsound/x/bissett.php.

29. ID3 is a metadata container for MP3 files, the kind of information that presents author, title, album, and provenance for display in playback software. In this instance, the ID3 tags also concretely relocate bissett's experimental recording within the institutional protocols of *PennSound.*

30. Charles Bernstein, "Making Audio Visible: the Lessons of Visual Language for the Textualization of Sound," *Textual Practice* 23, no. 6 (2009): 284.

31. Steve McCaffery and bpNichol, eds., *Sound Poetry: A Catalogue for the Eleventh International Sound Poetry Festival, Toronto, Canada, October 14 to 21, 1978* (Toronto: Underwhich, 1979), 17.

32. Even among internet pirates in the 2000s, this was a substandard data rate. See comment streams on any peer-to-peer audio sharing site for complaints about anything released in less than 320kbps.

33. See, for example, the "PennSound Manifesto."

34. For more on PennSound's foundation and in relation to methods of audio scholarship, see Bernstein, "Making Audio Visible." See also, *PennSound,* "about," https://writing.upenn.edu/pennsound/about.php.

35. For all of the above and more, search ubu.com for "bissett."

36. bill bissett, bpNichol, sean o huigin, Ann Southam, and uu David, *Past*

Eroticism: Canadian Sound Poetry of the 1960s (Toronto: Underwhich Audiographics, 1986); *grOnk* final series, no. 6.

37. See the exceptional page hosting this reading at *SpokenWeb,* ed. Celyn Harding-Jones, montreal.spokenweb.ca/sgw-poetry-readings/bill-bissett-at sgwu-1969/.

38. Jonathan Sterne, "The Preservation Paradox in Digital Audio," in *Sound Souvenirs: Audio Technologies, Memory and Cultural Practices,* ed. Karin Bijsterveld and José van Dijck (Amsterdam: Amsterdam University Press, 2009), 58.

39. Jason Camlot has demonstrated the value of these paratextual components of the reading, as well as of outlining the editorial principles of the *SpokenWeb* collection, in "The Sound of Canadian Modernisms: The Sir George Williams University Poetry Series, 1966–1974," *Journal of Canadian Studies* 46 (2012): 26–59.

40. Wershler, "Vertical Excess," 118.

41. *SpokenWeb,* "About SPOKENWEB," spokenweb.ca/about-us/spokenweb/.

42. *SpokenWeb,* "About SPOKENWEB."

43. See Annie Murray and Jared Wiercinski, "A Design Methodology for Web Based Sound Archives," *Digital Humanities Quarterly* 8 (2014), digitalhumanities.org/dhq/vol/8/2/000173/000173.html; Murray and Wiercinski, "Looking at Archival Sound: Visual Features of a Spoken Word Archive's Web Interface That Enhance the Listening Experience," *First Monday* 17, no. 4 (2012).

44. Robert Scholes and Clifford Wulfman, *Modernism in the Magazines: An Introduction* (New Haven, Conn.: Yale University Press, 2010), 66.

45. Bernstein, "Making Audio Visible," 286.

46. See Jim Andrews, "Aleph Null 3.0," 2018, vispo.com/aleph3/slideshow/info.htm.

47. Like many other digital artists, web designers, game makers, and code poets, the *MUPS* interface was lost once Flash was formally abandoned by Adobe in 2021. I return to Flash video in chapter 4. For now, a video capture and description of the project can be found at the URL of the original work. See David Jhave Johnson, "MUPS," 2012, glia.ca/2012/mups/.

48. More precisely, there are 1,258 files, as a review of the actionscript reveals that one file address is a duplicate of a previous file (Kathy Acker) and another is an empty folder location (Harry Matthews). See the following note on inconsistencies in the *PennSound* collection.

49. Johnson, "MUPS."

50. Johnson, "MUPS."

51. Leonardo Flores, "'MUPS' by David Jhave Johnson," *I ♥ E-Poetry,* January 1, 2013, http://iloveepoetry.org/ (accessed via Internet Archive).

52. Parsing the conventions of *PennSound* MP3 naming, each dash is retained, while underscores produce new lines. My over-underscoring errors in naming the *Awake in th Red Desert* files are amplified here: each word in the

poem title reads on a new line: "01 / A / O / B / A / Awake-in-th-Red- / Desert / 1968."

As I've noted elsewhere, the hand-written and student-based approach to archiving espoused by *PennSound* has real consequences. These errors and lapses, which are pervasive and unpredictable throughout *PennSound,* determine how files are processed by computational readings in a variety of unseen ways. This could be seen as a failing or one of the more beautiful resistances of *PennSound.*

53. See Judy Malloy, "Authoring Systems," in *The Johns Hopkins Guide to Digital Media,* ed. Marie-Laure Ryan, Lori Emerson, and Benjamin J. Robertson (Baltimore, Md,: John Hopkins University Press, 2014), 32–36; Flores, "MUPS."

54. Flores, "MUPS."

55. See, for example, *PoemTalk,* jacket2.org/content/poem-talk; *Close Listening,* writing.upenn.edu/pennsound/x/Close-Listening.php; *Jacket2,* jacket2.org/; *ModPo,* modpo.org/.

Interlude 3

1. These featured resources and the accompanying audio essay can be found at *PennSound,* writing.upenn.edu/pennsound/x/Featured-2008.html.

4. Dropping the Frame

1. Video transcription is my own throughout. See Vito Acconci, *Theme Song* (1973) streaming at *UbuWeb*: ubu.com/film/acconci_theme.html.

2. Nick Kaye, *Multi-Media: Video—Installation—Performance* (London: Routledge, 2007), 73.

3. Samuel Weber, *Mass Mediauras: Form, Technics, Media* (Stanford, Calif.: Stanford University Press, 1996), 109–16.

4. See, for example, Jim Groom's notes at *bavatuesdays* written just a year after the release of YouTube (November 14, 2007): "Now that millions of people can easily allow a complete stranger into their intimate, self-reflexive world vis-a-vis video sites like YouTube, Acconci's work may prove quite fascinating as a way to think through the impact of an imagined self in the advent of relatively affordable technology that allows us to mediate our identities for unknown viewers around the world," bavatuesdays.com /vito-acconci-is-to-video/.

5. Lev Manovich, *The Language of New Media* (Cambridge, Mass.: MIT Press, 2001), xxxi.

6. In the midst of this book's production, *UbuWeb* announced the following on its homepage: "As of 2024, UbuWeb is no longer active. The archive is preserved for perpetuity, in its entirety" (ubu.com/). For a doubly potent reminder of the ephemerality of preservation, X (formerly Twitter) handle @uubuweb ("Fan account as the official one doesn't exist anymore.") advocates a little database approach to preservation: "Everything is downloadable

on UbuWeb. Don't trust the cloud, even UbuWeb's cloud" (twitter.com
/uubuweb/status/1752795178828530024).

7. Notably, Goldsmith's disregard for copyright concerns extended to the
creators who articulated objections to the hosting of their files on *UbuWeb*,
whom Goldsmith identified in a short-lived "Hall of Shame." In 2015, Goldsmith framed the autopsy report of Michael Brown as an "appropriated"
work at Brown University. Widely and rightly denounced as a gesture that
reproduced the racialized violence that it purported to critique, the conversation around Goldsmith's appropriative act has contributed to a sea change
in both experimental writing circles and studies of race and the avant-garde
in American poetry. See Rin Johnson, "On Hearing a White Man Co-opt
the Body of Michael Brown," *Hyperallergic,* March 20, 2015, hyperallergic
.com/192628/on-hearing-a-white-man-co-opt-the-body-of-michael-brown.

8. Kenneth Goldsmith, *Letter to Bettina Funcke: 100 Notes—100 Thoughts,
Documenta Series 017* (Ostfildern: Hatje Cantz, 2011). See also, Agnes Peller,
Kenneth Goldsmith's UbuWeb: An Artist's Contribution to the Digital Humanities,
trans. Francesca Simkin (Paris: University of Paris 3-Sorbonne Nouvelle,
2015). Goldsmith's own anecdotal theorization of the site in *Duchamp Is My
Lawyer: The Polemics, Pragmatics, and Poetics of UbuWeb* (New York: Columbia
University Press, 2020) extends this position to artistic production, presum-
ably as a defense of Goldsmith's appropriative conceptual poetics as a whole:
"UbuWeb can be considered one enormous appropriative artwork, a giant
collage, which appropriates not a single object but rather the entire history
of the avant-garde" (74).

9. Tom Service, "Zen for Film Is Perfect Medicine for Hectic Lives," *The
Guardian,* July 11, 2008, theguardian.com/music/tomserviceblog/2008/jul/11
/namjunepaik.

10. Of course, this video has long since disappeared. However, the same
upload was shared to Vimeo at vimeo.com/11271804 and can still be found on
UbuWeb: ubu.com/film/fluxfilm01_paik.html.

11. Heike Helfert, "Nam June Paik: Zen for Film," *Media Art Net,*
medienkunstnetz.de/works/zen-for-film/.

12. From its inception, *Zen for Film* has never held a fixed length, and historical accounts of its screenings vary. Conceived and first screened in 1962
while Paik was working at the Studio fur elektronische Musik at the WDR
in Cologne, *Zen for Film* was published as twenty-four feet of 16mm film
in a Fluxus edition by George Maciunas in 1964. This strip of clear leader
was scripted for an extended loop. However, the longer version of the film
screened by Paik consisted of multiple reprints of an already damaged version of the shorter film projected in 1962. See Allen Weiss, "Some Notes on
Conjuring Away Art: Radical Disruptions of Image and Text in Avant-Garde
Film." *Esprit Createur* 38, no. 4 (1998): 88.

13. Weiss, "Some Notes," 88.

14. John Cage and Joan Retallack, *Musicage: Cage Muses on Words, Art, Music*
(Hanover, N.H.: Wesleyan University Press, 1996), 135.

15. Kaye, *Multi-Media,* 42.

16. Hana Hölling, *Revisions—Zen for Film* (New York: Bard Graduate Center, 2015), bgc.bard.edu/exhibitions/exhibitions/8/revisions-zen-for-film. Research for the exhibition also generated an exceptional long-form study of this single work in which Hölling answers these questions, and many others, related to the conservation and curation of *Zen for Film.* That work might serve as a parallel model to the supertemporal film discussed in this chapter.

17. Nicole Berenz outlines the speculative protocols of the supertemporal in *"We Support Everything Since the Dawn of Time That Had Struggled and Still Struggles": Introduction to Lettrist Cinema* (Berlin: Sternberg, 2014): "Linked to the limitless possibilities offered by the apparatus's constituent parts and their internal relationships, . . . the Lettrist movement came up with hundreds of protocols for creating films that were everything but the projected objects. . . . It was a matter of combining the cinematic apparatus with every speculative or living element" (14–15).

18. The *UbuWeb* version—as well as its subtitles, cited below—takes a bit of liberty in rendering the title as *Ever the Avant-Guard of the Avant-Guard till Heaven and After.* I have here retained the preferred translation given by Lemaître on his website: mauricelemaitre.org.

19. In retrospect, the reader might note that this film is one inspiration for the previous chapter, which similarly works by incidental connection to its source materials. Adjacent happenstance is the database's preferred form of contingent storytelling.

20. Maurice Lemaître, *Ever the Avant-Garde of the Avant-Garde till Heaven and After,* ubu.com/film/lemaitre_avant.html.

21. Kaira Marie Cabañas, *Off-Screen Cinema: Isidore Isou and the Lettrist Avant-Garde* (Chicago: Univeristy of Chicago Press, 2014), 73.

22. Craig Dworkin, *No Medium* (Cambridge, Mass.: MIT Press, 2013), 148.

23. To be precise, an argument concerning the relation of *Zen for Film* to Ken Friedman's *Zen for Record* forms the conclusion of the essayistic chapters, preceding an extended annotated inventory of "blank" recordings presented as "Further Listening." See Dworkin, *No Medium,* 127–40.

24. Dworkin, *No Medium,* 136.

25. Dworkin, 137–38.

26. Dworkin, 136.

27. These trends are most extensively documented by Monoskop's Wiki page on "Shadow Libraries," further demarcated as "independent, shadow, feminist, free/libre, self-hosted, pirate, autonomous, collective, community and artist digital libraries" (monoskop.org/Shadow_libraries). See, in particular, recent collections: Cornelia Sollfrank, Felix Stalder and Shusha Niederberger, eds., *Aesthetics of the Commons* (Zurich: Diaphanes, 2021); Memory of the World, ed., *Guerrilla Open Access* (Coventry: Post Office, Rope, and Memory of the World, 2018).

28. Erica Balsom, *After Uniqueness: A History of Film and Video Art in Circulation* (New York: Columbia University Press, 2017), 9. It should be noted that

Balsom examines issues of use in relation to *UbuWeb* in the chapter "Bootleg-ging Experimental Film" in this volume, exploring "the ambivalence of the copy by examining the impact of low-quality, unauthorized digital bootlegs on the domain of experimental film" (21).

29. Matthew Kirschenbaum, *Mechanisms: New Media and the Forensic Imagination* (Cambridge, Mass.: MIT Press, 2008), 15.

30. Usernames and platform details have been redacted to protect the privacy of their users.

31. The specs listed for the file read: "Resolution : 720×576; Codec : DivX 5; FPS : 25,13; BitRate : 1710 Kbps; Quality Factor : 0,17 b/px." The *UbuWeb* version vastly compresses this to a 320×240 Flash Video similar to the file hosted on YouTube.

32. See *UbuWeb* "Film & Video," ubu.com/film/index.html.

33. I am grateful to Ken Friedman for clarifying earlier mistakes concerning the copyrights to Fluxus materials, as well as his extraordinary Fluxus and intermedia digital libraries, which remain an invaluable resource. Private correspondence, March 6, 2022.

34. Hana Hölling, "Post-Preservation: Paik's Virtual Archive, Potentially," in *Nam June Paik Reader,* ed. John G. Hanhardt, Gregory Zinman, and Edith Decker-Phillips (Seoul: Nam June Paik Art Center, 2022), 15.

35. Tate Liverpool. "Nam June Paik: Educators' Pack," 12, tate.org.uk /documents/202/nam-june-paik-education-pack.pdf.

36. Luca (LUNK) Leggaro, "F L UX L I N E S: About this Site," January 1, 2007, http://fluxlines.blogspot.com/2007/01/about.html.

37. Michael Kontopoulos, *Zen for YouTube,* May 8, 2007, youtube.com/watch ?v=GzLEIGli1UM.

38. Cory Arcangel, *Structural Film* (2007), coryarcangel.com/things-i-made /2007-002-structural-film.

39. Mark Amerika, "Zen for Mobile Phone Video," October 31, 2007, http:// professorvj.blogspot.com/2007/10/zen-for-mobile-phone-video.html.

40. Mungo Thomson, *The Varieties of Experience* (Los Angeles: Self-Published, 2009), mungothomson.com/book/the-varieties-of-experience/.

41. For this work, and many others, the prolific audio and video remix artist Vicki Bennett operates under the moniker People Like Us. Out of respect for this recoded authorship, this paper will refer to the maker of *We Edit Life* as PLU throughout.

42. The anachronism of reading "found footage" within always-on ubiquitous networks of content is offered here as a counterpoint to estrange current practices, so pervasive as to become invisible. So much of vernacular internet practices, from memes to TikTok videos, relies on the compilation of circulating media, despecializing the practice of movie-making. Indeed, this argument may be extended to FanVids, digital moving-image essays, and a wealth of emergent motion-picture communication systems enabled by the ease of editing and dispersion of films and videos across networks.

43. Roger Luckhurst, "Found-Footage Science Fiction: Five Films by Craig Baldwin, Jonathan Weiss, Werner Herzog and Patrick Keiller," *Science Fiction Film and Television* 1, no. 2 (2008): 195.

44. Luckhurst, 195.

45. Luckhurst, 198.

46. Beyond found footage film, the contours of this metacinematic approach may be seen to extend to internet culture through the coproductive practices of "database animals," theorized by Hiroki Azumi as the "dissociative coexistence of the desire for a small narrative at the level of simulacra and the desire for a grand nonnarrative at the level of database" (*Otaku: Japan's Database Animals* [Minneapolis: University of Minnesota Press, 2009], 85–86).

47. All the more pressing in an era of the erasure of context brought about by generative AI.

48. See David J. Bolter and Richard A. Grusin, *Remediation: Understanding New Media* (Cambridge, Mass.: MIT Press, 2000), 22–50.

49. The language of this paragraph and its relation of network to database follows on a few productive strands of actor-network theory (ANT), misused to address digital objects in circulation. Without belaboring the connections here, they mainly concern modes of demystifying networks via careful description. See: Bruno Latour, *Reassembling the Social: An Introduction to Actor-Network-Theory* (Oxford: Oxford University Press, 2005); Latour, *Aramis, or the Love of Technology* (Cambridge, Mass.: Harvard University Press, 1996); and the excellent actor-network website Paris: Invisible City, bruno-latour.fr /virtual/index.html.

50. Beyond Latour, for the most concise (and expansive) description of ANT, see John Law, "Notes on the Theory of the Actor-Network: Ordering, Strategy, and Heterogeneity," *Systems Practice* 5, no. 4 (1992): 379–93. At a higher compression rate, Law outlines the essence of this approach as follows: "This, then, is the core of the actor-network approach: a concern with how actors and organisations mobilise, juxtapose and hold together the bits and pieces out of which they are composed; how they are sometimes able to prevent those bits and pieces from following their own inclinations and making off; and how they manage, as a result, to conceal for a time the process of translation itself and so turn a network from a heterogeneous set of bits and pieces each with its own inclinations, into something that passes as a punctualised actor" (386).

51. "Lovebytes2002," lovebytes.org.uk/2002/ongoing.html#nc6 (accessed via Internet Archive).

52. For background on these screenings, see "Lovebytes2002," http://www .lovebytes.org.uk/2002/docs/pages/vicki.htm.

53. *We Edit Life* was first uploaded to *The Prelinger Archive* (archive.org /details/prelinger) in 2004: archive.org/details/WeEditLife. The work was then uploaded to *UbuWeb* in 2007: ubu.com/film/plu_edit.html. Around the

same time in 2007, the work was uploaded by a third party to YouTube (since deleted), where it has been reposted multiple times since. Vicki Bennett herself uploaded the work to Vimeo on March 30, 2010: vimeo.com/10553139. From these various uploads, countless embeds have distributed the work on other sites.

54. See "Vicki Bennett at Lovebytes 2002," youtube.com/watch?v=H9p3M fIaOsw.

55. Private correspondence with Vicki Bennet, 2011.

56. In the video, a remixed version *We Edit Life* is itself set to a remixed audio track derived from the Crystal Castles's song "Vanished" (youtube. com/watch?v=AmABw-JaNes).

57. In the print edition of this book, the images that appear as a banner at the top of pages are drawn sequentially from *We Edit Life.*

58. In the "Trivia" section of Wikipedia's page on film leader, we can note the particular resonance of this opening with PLU's software: "The video editing software Adobe Premiere (as well as later versions, including Adobe Premiere Pro and Adobe Premiere Elements) features a computer-generated version of the SMPTE leader, entitled the 'Adobe Universal Leader.' It can be customized with different colors, and can be set to beep either at the beginning of each number or just at the two" (en.wikipedia.org/wiki/Film _leader; this statement was present on July 6, 2010, although it has since been edited out).

59. William C. Wees, *Recycled Images: The Art and Politics of Found Footage Films* (New York: Anthology Film Archives, 1993), 25.

60. Stephen Mamber, "Marey, the Analytic, and the Digital," in *Allegories of Communication: Intermedial Concerns from Cinema to the Digital,* ed. John Fullerton and Jan Olsson (Rome: J. Libbey, 2004), 88.

61. While Marey has been evoked to highlight the analytic slant of digital movies, we might also note that, until 2006, Adobe Premiere software packaging featured a galloping horse as an iconic homage to Muybridge (guidebookgallery.org/splashes/premiere).

62. This method of computer graphics was pioneered by Leon Harmon and Kenneth Knowlton in 1967 when Knowlton's proto-ASCII Seurat-styled "Nude," sometimes titled "Studies in Perception I," made headlines in the *New York Times*; see Henry Lieberman, "Art and Science Proclaim Alliance in Avant-Garde Loft," *New York Times,* October 11, 1967, 49. For a fuller reflection on the project, see Kenneth C. Knowlton, "Portrait of the Artist as a Young Scientist," *YLEM* 25 (2005): 8–11.

63. Technical details can be found in Kenneth Knowlton, "Computer-Produced Movies," *Science* 150 (1965): 1116–20; Knowlton, "Computer-Generated Movies, Designs and Diagrams," *Design Quarterly* 66/67 (1966): 58–63; Stan VanDerBeek, "New Talent—The Computer," *Art in America* 58 (1970): 86–91.

64. Stan VanDerBeek, "Re: Look: Computerized Graphics 'Light Brings Us News of the Universe,'" *Film Culture,* 1970, 48–49.

65. Adobe Premiere 6.5, released in August 2002, was the first consumer suite to feature real-time previews.

66. James Hodge, *Sensations of History: Animation and New Media Art* (Minneapolis: University of Minnesota Press, 2019), 172. In a complementary reading of these scenes, the conclusion to Hodge's excellent book, "Data Incomplete: The Web as Already There," draws from my research on *We Edit Life* to discuss the opacity of "the historical experience of the digital age" (171–80).

67. Rick Prelinger, *The Field Guide to Sponsored Films* (San Francisco: National Film Preservation Foundation, 2006), 48. See the full film, hosted by AT&T Archives on Youtube: youtube.com/watch?v=_iiQtdXMnBg.

68. Patrick Jagoda, *Network Aesthetics* (Chicago: University of Chicago Press, 2012), 224.

69. Jagoda, 225.

70. Listed as "Amateur film: Medicus collection: New York World's Fair, 1939–40] (Reel 3) (Part I) (1939)" on Archive.org (archive.org/details /Medicusc1939_3). The Medicus collection presents "detailed documentation of the 'World of Tomorrow' in beautiful Kodachrome."

71. However, since *Man and His World* is featured as complete and colorized later in the sequence of *Incredible Machine,* it is unlikely to be the source of the conversation between VanDerBeek and Knowlton during the filming of *Incredible Machine.* Similar in form, it could be any of several poemfields made around this time.

72. This transcription varies from VanDerBeek's own notation in an attempt to highlight certain textual features from the film that are elided in the script.

73. Law, "Notes," 6.

74. All films not linked in this paragraph either have never been uploaded to the internet, have been taken down, or were perhaps not locatable by the author. All are mentioned in PLU's source list, and thus may be presumed present in *We Edit Life.*

Interlude 4

1. For further commentary and the work's original appearance online, see the *UbuWeb* page for *Flash Artifacts*: ubu.com/film/snelson_flash.html.

2. Snelson and Enxuto, *Flash Artifacts.*

Epilogue

1. Glazier describes this moment in an interview with Michael Nardone. "There was a master PERL script that would take out the Gopher commands—because it was a Gopher system—and turn it into HTML to be able to put it on the Web. So, for a few seconds, I had the largest website in the world in 1994, and it was poetry." For this and many other insights into the *EPC,* I am grateful to the interviews conducted in Nardone, "Of the Repository: Poetics in a Networked Digital Milieu" (PhD diss., Concordia University, 2018), 302.

2. *EPC* front page, accessed December 16, 2023 (writing.upenn.edu/epc/).

3. Glazier, *Digital Poetics: The Making of E-Poetries* (Tuscaloosa: University of Alabama Press, 2002) 3.

4. Matthew Kirschenbaum, "Prepare for the Textpocalypse," *CITE*, March 8, 2023, theatlantic.com/technology/archive/2023/03/ai-chatgpt-writing-language-models/673318/.

5. Among many lost links in the *EPC* is an animated version of Bernstein's aphoristic essay-poem, which played its phrases out in three overlapping windows simulating the then-competing browsers Mozilla, Explorer, and Netscape. The text can be found published online as "Electronic Pies in the Poetry Skies," *Electronic Book Review,* August 1, 2003, electronicbookreview.com/essay/electronic-pies-in-the-poetry-skies/.

6. Peter Lunenfeld contends—perhaps accurately, over a decade ago—that, despite the rise of social media, "a pyramid of production remains, with a small number of the members of a Web community uploading material, a slightly larger group commenting on or modifying that content, and a huge percentage remaining content to download without uploading" (*The Secret War Between Downloading and Uploading: Tales of the Computer as Culture Machine* [Cambridge, Mass.: MIT Press, 2011], 1). At the same time, as Rita Raley and others have demonstrated, intensifying regimes of dataveillance continue to "upload" users at all points ("Dataveillance and Counterveillance," in *"Raw Data" Is an Oxymoron,* ed. Lisa Gitelman [Cambridge, Mass.: MIT Press, 2013], 121–45).

7. Or, for a comparative lens from any historical moment, a user might download the *EPC* as it once was at epc.buffalo.edu via services like Archivarix or open-source scripts like the "Wayback Machine Downloader" (github.com/hartator/wayback-machine-downloader). Despite privileged access to the back-end of the site, in what follows, I oscillate between Wayback Machine and Penn downloads.

8. Glazier and Sherwood, "RIF/T: An Electronic Space for Poetry, Prose, and Poetics," writing.upenn.edu/epc/rift/index.html.

9. See "Poetics List .txt file archive," writing.upenn.edu/epc/poetics/archive/logs/txt/.

10. See the memorial mirror here: writing.upenn.edu/epc/mirrors/tomraworth.com/.

INDEX

While this index is primarily prepared for codex-oriented search practices, it might be most useful as a series of input prompts and frequency clusters to aid "Ctrl+F" operations within digital versions of the preceding text, which can more precisely summon localized contexts for specified terms. More expansively, these terms might also be used to query any little database of related texts in the reader's personal collection or via online repositories to discover unexpected intertextual connections that exceed the contingent limits of the book. In this way, the index is offered as another way to connect to the little database in general. For a media poetics addressing contemporaneous transformations to the cultural form of the index, see *INDEX INDEX (2025) in the Manifold edition.*

DANIEL SCOTT SNELSON is assistant professor of English and Design Media Arts at UCLA.